COMES LOVE

Richard Harteis

Poets Choice Publishing

"Comes love, nothing to be done"

Billie Holiday

"….waiting for all this to give way to love itself, to
look into the eyes of another and feel something—
the pleasure of a new lover in the unbroken
night, your wings folded around him, on the other
side of this ragged January, as if a long sleep has
ended."

January O'Neil

Many thanks to technical advisor, Ron Egnor

Printed in the United States of America

Consultant work: www.WilliamMeredithFoundation.org

Bulk discounts available through www.Poets-Choice.com

ISBN-13: 978-0-9909257-5-0

Poets Choice Publishing
337 Kitemaug Road
Uncasville, Ct. 06382

Poets-Choice.com

Poets' Choice

For William and Nancy
who have shown me
what it means to love.

FOREWORD

When he finished playing his jazz set at the gallery on Sunday, I had a word with the local legend of a piano man, Mark Taber. His hands, as they flew over the keys, looked like the hands of Moses except that he wore beaded bracelets and sported rings on every finger. I'd run into this old hippie over many years and enjoyed his jazz versions of the Beatles and the American Songbook. John Lennon's "Imagine" seemed to be his theme song, and he never gave up on the dream over the decades.

"So, are you writing these days," he asked me, with a friendly sort of one-artist-to-another tone.

"Well, I've dusted off something I wrote 15 years ago, and I'm trying to see if it stands up."

"It's good to see what you thought 15 years ago," he said.

And this little encouragement from an older brother has given me the will to move ahead. My real older brother thinks I make too much of myself, and he's probably right. Many writers start out with autobiography – Joyce, Hemingway in the Michigan stories, etc. But they GOT OVER IT. It seems my entire oeuvre has been the story of my life, beginning with a book I wrote in the Peace Corps in which I try to understand why I have fallen in love with my roommate. CHAMELEON has never seen the light of day: "Drinking from they sense and sight, beauty majesty and might, as a lover or a chameleon grows like what it looks upon." Perhaps that one should really keep collecting dust out there in the shed.

Then came MARATHON and a string books filled with confessional poems dealing with the challenges of life with William after his illness. Most lately, WMD: A Memoir picks up the tale as I'm presented with my own diagnosis of a de-mylinating disease that my sweet neurologist refrains from calling Alzheimer's or MS. The MRI change he noted recently are just, "signs of progression, getting older," he tells me. And I'm not about to press him. Is this why my friend David fixed on autobiography for much of his writing career, did he intuit the great grey disappearing act that Alzheimer's has finally forced him into?

Out of the blue, my neurologist offers me the option of medical marijuana to manage blood pressure and control pain. Is he just trying to keep me happy? Like, "Viagra is a recreational drug" – duh.

Oh Brave New World! Is that how Shakespeare had it in the Tempest? Gay Marriage now legal in all 50 states, the browning of America, Hillary and Bernie Sanders dukeing it out to win the progressive follow on to Obama's extraordinary 8 years as the first black president.

Just how dated or interesting this account may be I do not know. I first gave up on COMES LOVE when my mentor, Betty Lussier put the kibosh on the book. I always loved Betty because she loved William more than she loved me – though she did, I think, love me too. She always stuck up for him no matter what and felt this book didn't give him his due. Many people would have felt the Nicky affair was disloyal, and writing about it would be like shooting myself in the foot. But for twenty five years I hung in there as William's full-time care giver after his stroke, and I was not always Mother Teresa. Walk a mile in my flip-flops comes to mind. Or as Gracie Cavalieri says to discount critics of her prolific poetry production:

> "I just keep writin' em."

Perhaps you are reading this because you have bought the book. If so, I hope you find something here to like, a little window into how the century turned for me and William and Nick, how things were then, a time you may find nostalgic, a time, in any case, I don't want to forget.

COMES LOVE

January 3, 2000

Black. But soon "a long orange knife will slit the darkness from ear to ear," as William says of dawn on the river at our home in Connecticut in winter. Here in West Palm, the sun will rather drift up in flamingo colors and the day will bloom into its usual aquamarine brilliance. I'll put on my shorts and run bareback under the palm trees along the intra-costal where the Herons strut slow motion, stalking fish and squadrons of pelicans cruise along the water's edge like stealth fighters.

If I open the blinds now on the little glassed-in lanai I use as an office, the red Hibiscus will just be unfolding. The sleep machine (on train mode) is chugging away in the bedroom beside me, and William is perhaps dreaming of the days when he traveled across American as a grandee dancer, a boy doing a man's job, $25 a week, camaraderie and good grub. In fact, he has become a boy again, skin smooth as a girl from steroids against prostate cancer, shrunk up three or four inches shorter than the days he flew off air craft carriers for the Navy in WWII and Korea. I call him the peanut poet now, my senior Ken doll, dearer to me than a son, the focus of my life for almost thirty years. I can hardly bear it. We are both alive, and pretty well, and have made it into the new millennium. The ball did not explode over Times Square, the hostages in India have survived, the second coming has been put on hold for a while. My new novel may not win the Nobel Prize, but I "squeaked it out" as Nikolai Orloff said once of an earlier book, after ten long years. I seem to have a job. And while I am not particularly manic depressive, I get a little worried sometimes when things are going this well, when my heart (chug chug chug comes the cliché) is about to burst with the joy of it all.

I'm old enough to know how quickly things can change though, how tenuous the thread that attaches us to life. Only two weeks ago I sat at William's bedside in the hospital wondering how he was going to survive yet another crisis, watching the drip drip drip of the IV set up, the plastic reservoir like those little glass villas Roman matrons used to collect tears. Nothing to eat for days, his NG tube running black with blood. A fragment from my "Sick Bed" poem read:

I count the drops each

second by second
like a futile rain
on the desert of time.
You float in the perfect sleep
of the silent Buddha.

Distant trains call to each other
through the night,
Clacking their way
to the Carolinas or Key West,
and the soundless weather channel
charts storms in blue and white
drifting across the continent
like waves of ocean, waves of grain.

Tick tock, tick tock, drip drop, drip drop.
My granite forehead runs to lime
with love and grief and tears and time.

And yet miraculously, there we were, two days out of the hospital, winging our way to Pennsylvania for Christmas turkey with my mum, and after, a New Year's house party with ten gay guys in a little palace down in Boca. I have stopped counting the number of lives old

William must have used up by now - bad joss, as the Chinese might say.

A decade ago, I tried to make sense of it in a book called MARATHON. The role of care giver had taken its toll in my own life. For two years William couldn't walk or speak after his stroke. Then a broken hip, a ruptured appendix, surgery after surgery, watching him suffer all those years, trying to keep the house afloat, answer the mail, pay the bills, look after my career. Too fat, drinking too much, too sad, I decided to pull myself out of my mid-life crisis by running a marathon, something I'd never done before. (Yesterday's paper had an early Peanut's cartoon, a sad farewell tribute to Charles Shultz who is folding up his security blanket: Lucy is at her psychiatry booth selling advice, and Charlie Brown describes the deep depression he has fallen into. "Snap out of it," she says. "That'll be five cents.") And it worked. And William won the Pulitzer and the National Book Award for poetry projects I helped him with. And I got a Fulbright to teach in Bulgaria and we were made citizens there by Presidential decree, "et la fête a bien continué," as I said at the end of MARATHON, despite speed bumps along the way.

I'd thought my bladder cancer cured after ten years, but this summer once again the surgeon has needed to go gardening. (Thank you Philip Morris.) And sure there is something out there that will kill me one day, and old William too. "I do believe we all get out alive," I wrote somewhat jauntily years ago, but these days the prospect is a little closer. And while I'm less overwhelmed at the thought of my own mortality, have somehow come to see the illness that begins to show in middle age as part of the process, something to be put on the back burner while you get on with the business of living, at age 53, I guess I have to fess up, despite the TV specials on the medical miracles expected in the new millennium, that I am indeed (gulp) no longer middle aged. My old classmate Bill Clinton will be grinning at me from a twenty dollar bill till the day I die as it were - I guess most people would say my classmate has made something out of himself so far in life's journey. (My mother insisted on buying me an FOB tee shirt from the Georgetown Alumni catalog having worked long hard years to pay for my tuition, though I was never a Friend of Bill in the old days.) Another classmate lives out in Wellington and in Hong Kong and has his own polo team. Life, like poetry, is not a competitive sport - fair enough. But you need to take stock once in a while. It seems to be the present “passage” my generation is going through. At the doctor’s office recently I came across an article that tried to fuse Buddhism and the Bull Market as a way for boomers to have their gourmet cake and eat it too.

I remember when William’s sister was dying and I stood crushed at her deathbed - my terror, like the terror of all young people confronting death arising from the dawning realization that this would be me one day.

“Well, I AM 70,” she said, trying to cheer me up a little. “It’s not as though I haven’t had a life.” At the moment, I seem to be having mine. And God knows, I am having fun. But I keep hearing an old Peggy Lee tune in the background somewhere, “Is that all there is, is that all there is my friend?”

I remember one brilliant fall afternoon when I was teaching at Catholic University a bunch of Hare Krishna devotees were dancing under the trees, their orange robes swaying in the wind under the orange leaves of the trees. They were so beautiful and happy. I was illegally in love with a student of mine and desperately unhappy. And it was not the first time was tempted to enter the temple. You couldn’t grow up in the 60's without confronting some form of oriental philosophy, the need to transcend ego to achieve spirituality. But the few times I did acid in those old hippie days were nightmare for me- letting go of my ego and dissolving into the one, the universal was about as attractive as say, cutting off my penis. The best I came up with in answering life's big questions was Unamuno's notion of the tragic sense of life: reason tells us we die and disintegrate in the grave, while ego refuses to accept such annihilation. The best you can do is build your house on uncertain sands, and make a leap of faith to the afterlife. Just do it, as the Nike commercial says.

Different times over the years I've had the nagging feeling that I'm stuck somehow, that I've done my marathons and taken care of business, but on the old wisdom meter, I still hovering down in the lower quadrant somewhere. The urge to get 'into" eastern religion struck once in London where I had taken William for speech therapy. Our lesbian landlords were so sweet and absolutely charitable- they almost glowed, and their kindness to me and William in his infirmity was simply remarkable. There wasn't anything they wouldn't do for us. And it all seemed to stem from their connection to an Indian guru named Baba Muktananda. We were so impressed by their lives we decided to have a personal interview with the guru. If you paid the maximum amount of money you could have an "intensive" - a kind of high powered zapping experience which provided instant enlightenment. I wasn't sure it would be red electric eyes or what exactly, but we put our money down. In the interim we went to a gathering of the yogi's devotees. They almost floated off the stage and hundreds of people in the audience chanted and beamed. The lead devotee would say something earth shaking like "hello everyone," and the audience would go into rapture. There was no denying they were in rapture. But it seemed so much like mass hypnosis, or psychic contagion, that we canceled our appointment with the yogi, and have stood timid at the temple door once again ever since. Our poet friend Dannie Abse who is also a physician consoled us that this sort of syndrome was common among certain teenage girls who, for example, really can faint at the mere gyration Elvis Presley's pelvis. Cute and reassuring fore the old ego, but I've always wondered what kind of bliss such letting go might involve. I can still see the beaming face of our landladies, but then I think of phenobarbital cocktails at Jonsetown, and the Hale Bob pilgrims all lined up on their bunks, one certain fact being that their husks have been discarded like so much garbage. But the cues won't stop. This Christmas our friend Nancy presents me with a book she's spoken of for some time, THE CLOUD OF UNKNOWING. The dust jacket reads, "The author explains how all thoughts and concepts must be buried beneath a 'cloud of forgetting,' while our love must rise toward God hidden in the 'cloud of unknowing.' " I think of Lear: "Yes, and no too were good counsel." Still, Nancy is one of the sweetest, sanest and most talented people I know...

Last year about this time I was going through some old letters from William as he traveled for the State Department in Israel and India and the brilliant idea struck me that we ought to go to India and look into these questions a little more deeply. So many people seem to come back from such a trip with their lives changed. It happened to my own baby sister. She'd been working with the airlines, in and out of relationships, and decided one day to travel to India here on her own. She came back, married, had two nice kids, went back to school, became a psychotherapist ("five cents, please") and seems to be living happily ever after. Not that I am unhappy, mind you. (Do I protest too much, I wonder?) But apparently a certain kind of osmosis takes place there. Buzz Poverman says so many people have lived there over the centuries the air is thick with ghosts. And perhaps just being there will help answer some of the questions I seem to be asking.

I sat down and wrote the embassy and to my great surprise and pleasure they said, "we would be honored to have you and Mr. Meredith visit India." So here we go, in just a month. We've canceled a poetry class we were to have given in Athens en route so William can fully recuperate from this latest hospitalization. But soon this great mysterious country, this cradle of religion will welcome two American poets. New Delhi, Calcutta, Mumbai, Chennai. Our flight plan is like a diamond superimposed on the map of India. And for a month we will be reading and learning and thinking and wondering just what it is we have embarked upon.

January 6

Back on the porch, my little space bubble, trying to relax into the sort of reflection that can come if I don't read my email first thing or begin the chores of the day. The jack hammers which chisel into our sleep most mornings from the re-construction going on in our building have abated, thank god. The dentist drills and drills you struggle your way out of the dream, run a hand through your hair, and make a pot of coffee.

Hector's comes this morning, just in time for a cup. Every day he brings me a new "loaner" while he fixes up the Lincoln we're going to buy from him. Where does he get these cars? His landlord has evicted him from his shop for some reason, and he is still trying to set up a new business. When we got back to Florida this winter the little ruby sports car I left with him had mysteriously put on several thousand miles and ran like a tank, but Hector promises to put that right too.

We stand around in the kitchen - "Three, sugars and milk," he says, "I'm Cuban!" He talks to me about four inches from my face and occasionally puts his hand on my belly or shoulder to make a point. His eyes punctuate his argument or blow up when he laughs. Sometimes he pinches my "love handles" to tease me and make me think of dieting again. I sit here now in my shorts with the sweet smell of my own sweat, a little hard, thinking of him. I love this guy. One of the best things about Florida, these

Cubans. A whole different way of thinking about life - they'll brush by you at the grocery store, rub right by you without a thought. Latin. "Too international," is the racist euphemism my parent's friends up in Daytona use to describe south Florida , but I love it here. He's something like my Cuban twin- two weeks around the pool and I am just about the same shad of tan as he is. He's trimmer though, works hard through the day. I think I'd move if he every proved to be a hustler. Sometimes when I get too nasty about how long he's taking to fix the car, I turn up with flowers for his wife by way of apology. When he's doing some deal on me, he'll give William a free pair of windshield wipers and put his hand on William's forehead. We have these round about ways of speaking to each other.

Hector wants to take me to Cuba on his boat some winter to show me the life there. He came over in a raft himself - it's surprising how many Cubans seem to have come this way. Hard to imagine it really. I think of that great Crane story, the Open Boat about a ship wreck right off New Smyrna. Unrelenting sun, grey sharks sliding through the aquamarine water, - though that far north water and sharks approach the same color. Today's papers announce that little Elian, the sweet six year old who floated into the Everglades on an inner tube when his mother drowned must be returned to Cuba. He's become a poster child for the anti-Castro forces that run Miami. They're wild to keep him here and poke Castro in the eye every night on the evening news. But to his credit Hector has insisted from the beginning that the child must go with his father. Sensible. Hector's got three kids of his own and he's not an idiot. But he wants to see the father come to the U.S. to pick up his son.

"You look at these baseball players," he says, grabbing me by the shoulder." They sit down there in Cuba and say, "you can keep your fucking money. I don't want your money." Then they get here and then, pffet, they're over the fence in a minute making a million dollars. You want, I'll bring you a nice lady and you can see. She came over in a raft just two weeks ago. All she knew was there was a better life here and more money. Now you should see her. She's a nice lady, good looking woman, married. She drives around with her husband and I say, "how often were you stopped by the police today?" She says, " I don't even know who they are. Where are they?" And I say, how often were you stopped in Cuba. And she says, "Yeah, every day." You see Richard. Every day."

“I love you very much, ”William calls out from the kitchen where I’ve set him up with breakfast, for absolutely no reason. I guess he’s guilty for spilling his weekly pill box all over the floor in a rainbow shower of capsules, gels, vitamins. And I love him back, totally when such serendipity plays out in our lives. Body and soul, as the old song goes - though body is a little less part of the equation these days since his prostate cancer and advancing age. And so, yes, I slink out to Gomorrah on occasion to drink at the polluted well. There were long times when we could not be together in the past decades when it was “understandable” that a healthy young man might take his pleasure somewhere else in the absence of his lover - though I’ve never thought of ours as an “open” relationship as they used to say in the 70's and 80's. Monogamy was a gift William gave me, but never demanded in return - the way to keep the bird is to set it free? But all these years later, I’m still not sure what to make of this freedom.

“Man, you’re still stuck in western polarity,” I can hear my old hippie friends say, “right brain, left brain, body and soul, yin and yang, life and death. It’s all one, man.” And to an extent, I “get” it. “Form and content can not be separated,” I used to pass on to students in the old days. What we say is a function of how we say it. "How to I know what I think until I see what I say," as Auden would have it, if I haven't mis-paraphrased. I will be with William till one of us dies, but I still haven't figured out what it means to be faithful. And as I attempt to "follow my bliss," as our old hero Joseph Campbell used to say, guilt enters the garden like the serpent,. and the psychedelic brilliance of the trees and flowers pales into a flat reality:

I'm stiff as hell from the athletic workout I got two days ago from a Spiritual Counselor I met at Roosters, our local gay pub. "Spare me the details," the gentle reader may now be saying as I consider singing the body electric. One pole of gay esthetics these days holds that gay writers have to write for gay readers - damn the torpedoes, say what you want, slime on down, since the straight world doesn't give a damn anyway and we only have each other in the end. "Richard, why not just admit you're gay and stop putting yourself through the wringer," my housemate told me once when I was just back from the Peace Corps and still trying to figure out my sexuality - a satyr I am not, but I still am forced to wave the flag when some young amazon passes by, or a particular lady smiles my way. "The vagina is a potential space," Danie Abse's anatomy instructor told him once, a phrase that has troubled him since, and one with which I empathize.

But today I am filled with the joy of exhausting myself in sex, getting to know a strange guy through my body, until it is time for breakfast and to take the car to Hector for the new radio he is installing. I'm not sure which part of the soul my spiritual advisor was communicating with as he manipulated the parts of my body through the night, but over pancakes and coffee I was sure I had a new friend, that the sex didn't matter, or mattered enormously, that William was going to love this guy, but doubting that I had made much spiritual progress that particular 24 hours as the blue marble spun through the black universe. Hector looked at this guy in the front seat of the car when I drove to the shop and read the situation like a clairvoyant. "I'm sorry I'm late Hector," I said. "I didn't get to bed till 7:00."

"Hey, you can't work all the time," he said, giving me a little pinch. "Say hello to William." Nice the way he pronounces it. "Say hello to Weilyum"

January 11

Sick, but tan and happy. What has caused this bronchitis? Too much second hand smoke about me over the past few days? Nick has come from Bulgaria for a few weeks visit and still hasn't shed his bad habit. The three of us will likely go to the beach later in the day when the sun comes up and the hibiscus twining through the chain-link fence outside the glass wall of my studio begin to unfold - a neighbor airing an Amish quilt, if you will.

Nick came back from the pool yesterday and stood beside me at my desk in his new bikini - blue with a big white hibiscus almost able to cover the ripe crotch. "How you doing Bubba," he asked, and of course, that was the end of the working day for me.

"Yeah, it's the same flower," I said, plucking one of the vermillion blooms from the fence and handing it to him.

"Really."

"Well, look at it," I said, tracing the outline of the flower with my index finger. "How do you say Hibiscus in Bulgarian?

"We don't have Hibiscus in Bulgaria," he said. Nick's big on a new kind of sun tan oil that has metallic flecks in it. They catch the light on his bronze shoulders or cheeks and you think for a minute Apollo has dropped in for a gin and tonic. This guy has troubled my imagination for five years now ever since I first saw him standing at the edge of the Black Sea, looking a little lost, part child, part god. I guess, for better or worse, I'm in for the duration. He loves William as much as I do, and while I am undoubtedly still number one - or had better be - William drinks in his sweetness as naturally as a man parched in the desert would do. A complex love the three of us have for each other. Some day I must try to fictionalize it and sort it all out - William pushed me to re-write my first novel in the third person years ago to help me shed my autobiographical blinders, even offered to do it himself. How I wish I had taken him up on the offer. The novel might not still be collecting dust.

What joy to have Nick around to help with the dishes and give me a little breather in William's care. The three of us glide around town in the new Lincoln on our way to therapy or out shopping or to the beach, and it's as though God has said, "here you are Richard, here is some happiness for the times you have been unhappy, for the times you have washed William's shorts and changed the bed linen, or worried about the tell-tale blood in your urine announcing the bladder cancer's return, wondered how you'd pay the bills, or watched your friend in pain, suffered your own. Here you go guy. Enjoy." Everyone has his own list, of course, his story to tell. But, to paraphrase Billy Holiday, "comes grace, nothing to be done."

We gave the old sweetie his 81st birthday party on the 9th, a small affair with some local friends in for dinner. In an hour and a half we managed to buy the food (giant shrimp, mussels, and swordfish steaks), shower from our day at the beach, prepare the dinner, set up the bar, wipe off the last bit of shaving cream and welcome the guests, flushed with the minor radioactive glow you feel when you've had just a little too much sun. Jivi y Stravi, we say in Bulgarian by way of a toast, health AND life, the one without the other wouldn't be much good, the implied joke.

My friend Douglas says he wouldn't want to go out with a tube down his stomach, lingering in a hospital bed for weeks. So, he lives somewhat dangerously: rides his polo ponies around in season, sticks his nose down diamond minds and plots revolutions off season to make a buck. But we can't always arrange for a death of our own choosing I tell him, and surely there is more to a good death than merely terminating life functions quickly and painlessly. You'll want to have finished your business well, have savored the experience, have understood it, I guess. Little deaths, orgasms, or so it seems down through the centuries for poets, the little "dyings away" some intimation of the larger last release.

I still do not comprehend Dr. Frued's notion that the aim of life is death, and hope not to have to for some time yet - though it isn't as though I haven't heard the bell tolling for me on occasion. You'd have to be pretty deaf at age 53- is that what I am now - not to have had that deep klong resonate through your soul at some point or other. I'm sick, for example, I remind myself. The yellow green sputum tickles my chest and produces little nagging volcanic eruptions, as though I had just lost my train of thought or misplaced my car in the parking lot somewhere. If I turn around real quick, death will have disappeared into the shadows or the dark heart of the hibiscus bloom. I'll catch him one day. That's one certain thing. But today, I'd prefer to go to the beach with Nick and William.

January 25

Cold. The rains have gone but it is still cold by Florida Standards. Cold in my heart. Like a Cuban love song. Corracon. Is that the word? It seems like every other word on the Spanish radio stations here is corracon.

Nick has flown back to Bulgaria like the two grandmothers - they have become The Two Grandmothers in the press like the Three Tenors - who flew to Miami but finally went back home and left a rug of carnations on the streets of little Havana when a meeting with little Elian couldn't be arranged.

I drift through the photo album of Nick's visit already missing him lots. There he is shooting skeet off the stern of casino cruise ship, gliding by the mansions of Palm Beach in the white hibiscus tank suit, cap turned backward on his black curls, standing on the water taxi touring the island, arms on each other's shoulders triumphant in front of the double loop roller coaster at the South Florida Fair.

“Use the telephoto,” I called to him from the surf, and of course he didn’t. William and I bob like two Styrofoam cups far out in the blue green water, waiting to be pecked at by curious seagulls. But the distance is charming too finally, the distance between us as he flies into the arctic winter of the Black Sea even more poignant - the way his goofy way of doing things so often brings an unexpected result - foreign, charming. The delight of a person’s otherness, how they shave, how they take things, the mystery of another person who has become a friend. I finally give up the little mini- dreams I have been in and out of since five am and dutifully begin to fire up the coffee machine.

This morning Nick is nodding off in Vienna waiting for a connecting plane to Sofia I imagine, not spread eagled like Endymion on the pull out couch, deep as death in sleep the way only the young can sleep. This morning I do not have the pleasure of coaxing him out of his sleep and William has anyhow managed to burn up the Mr. Coffee last night doing the dishes. “I really love Nicky,” William said before we went to bed. “Every day two kisses.” A European habit, a kiss on each cheek when first you meet. How delicately Nick would kiss his little son when we visited with him and his family in Bulgaria. How gentle a way to start the day. But today the three Musketeers have dropped to two and that task will fall to me. What was that old classic notion Sister Margaret taught us in Latin class all those years ago, the greatest value in friendship is that friends inspire each other to the good?

Last week after many years I got a letter from Sister Margaret. Amazing. A little retired nun who feeds the birds and looks after stray dogs in Betty's neighborhood on Staten Island gave me her address about a decade ago and I sent her all my books and a long letter to catch up on my life. Apparently she wrote me, but I never got the letter and assumed that she didn't approve of how I had turned out.

A number of us were in love with Sister Margaret in high school. Rumor had it she was the daughter of a protestant minister and had converted to Catholicism and entered the convent on the eve of her marriage. Better than a Jacqueline Suzanne novel. But she looked far too Italian to be a minister's daughter. Black hair peeking out from her bonnet, black eyes and rose cheeks. I wrote her letters demanding to know how she could give up sex - how one could love without sex - my hormones and hedonism dovetailing very nicely as we read Virgil and Catullus.

How could she deny the body? She was the one, after all, who astounded us by calling hell into question: waving away the notion of an all-powerful, loving god who would go to the trouble of creating a creature destined to spend eternity in hellfire. Her long letters back to me explaining the nature of baptism, and a love that transcends the body never really convinced me I guess, and I wasn't sure what she would make of this middle aged gay guy still struggling to come to terms with his sexuality and the nature of love. But there it was, the same sure hand at the end of her letter - she must be nearly William's age by now - just as breezy, just as astounding as her letters nearly forty years ago:

"And so my very cherished friend, I celebrate with you all the grace-filled moments of your life. Continue to experience the beauty in yourself, in William and in the world. In times of quiet and serenity experience within your own special depths, your true self. Therein you will experience God's presence. Truly, so!"

Talk about the "wind beneath my wings." I'm not sure what she'd make of me if she saw the whole picture, but I'll take it Sister. I'll take it till I can think it through just a little better. Now it is time to give William a kiss on each cheek and begin the day.

February 1, 2000

“In a cold sweat,” as James Brown would say. Woke up this morning having dreamed through all the possible nightmare scenarios that yesterday portended. William’s been unable to pee, an emergency I’ve always kept a catheter on hand for as we traveled. But it looks like the bladder has become atonic and he’ll need to be “catherized” twice a day for the rest of his life, a nice bit of euphemisms for sticking a red tube through your penis up into your bladder to void. I know from my own cancer how uncomfortable that can be, but William was remarkably placid yesterday as the urologist demonstrated what would be needed. “Just get four tuperware boxes he explained breezily, outlining the regime needed for keeping a sterile supply of catheters available. “We even do it in pediatrics” he assures me, “a lot of parents do this twice a day for their kids.” He’s young this urologist, but sweet. I see what he is doing, minimalizing the question, challenging me to match a good parent’s dedication, helping me to take on this work without too much fuss.

But how shall I carry my Tupperware boxes to India I wonder? I'm willing to take on this expanded role of giving William care, but how to keep from thinking it a set back, a daily reminder of the inevitable. "Anticipatory grief," has been such a constant part of my psychic makeup for so long now - what bright expectations, what projects can I cook up to fend it off. Well, he is a good patient, and we'll just get into the routine, just do it quickly and in a dignified way, one man helping another and get on with life. This is how I must think of it. If he can go through the discomfort without becoming depressed about it, I can't begrudge him the work and bother of it. We all have our work to do. "Keep your nose up," as Nick says in his wonderful mis-use of the idiom when he wants to encourage someone. Nose is better than the chin when you think of it, gets in a certain pride as well pluck.

Yesterday, the embassy sends the final schedule for our trip and it is as I feared. They have taken every single topic I gave off the top of my head when William was in the middle of his last crisis, and scheduled a lecture tour only Harold Bloom could contemplate. Doctor Professor

Harteis is to enlighten the academic world from Delhi to Madras, Calcutta to Bombay. I've got twenty days to become an expert in contemporary American poetry, the poetics of Robert Penn Warren, poetry between the great wars. I always thought it would be fun to study the work of poets William counted as good friends in the old days. He was an intimate of Lowell, and Berryman, Warren and Rukeyser, often acting as editor and confidant. I got to know these poets and their work a bit. But now I am to be the expert and I have visions of a young brown students a the back of the hall like a formation of Gurkhas pointing out somberly that I am wearing no clothes. Ninety minute lectures? What have I done to myself?

Last winter when I was sitting around wondering how to use up all the frequent flyer miles and my finger landed on India, I had exotic dreams of elephant headed-gods and temples, spicy foods, Moghul castles, high tea at the Oberoi. Our friend Buzz Poverman says that so many people have lived on this land for so long that every square inch is so saturated with the souls of the dead you can hardly breath. Karl Shapiro apparently got off the plane, took one look at the poverty and misery and turned right back around and went back home. But often, it's just the opposite, apparently. Could it focus my life the way it did for my baby sister Jude? I don't see how, given the schedule I have been presented with. How in the world am I going to get everything done that needs to be done before we leave? I'd like to crawl back into bed and just pull the covers over my head. How to get over this panic attack?

Watched my old classmate Bill Clinton the other night in his state of the Union speech - I have not, it seems, become President or even a senator and as long as we are both alive I will somehow be comparing myself to him as we teeter into old age - if we make it that is. Silly to make such comparisons, of course, but that won't stop this baby boomer's competitive drive. We seem destined to a mid-life crisis psychology right up into our nineties and hundreds, a kind of spiritual keeping up with the Jones from our parents generation. How long have I been wondering "what have I made of my life? "

I had to hand it to old Bill. Even the bitchy former speech writer for Ronald Regan had to admit Clinton looked better now than when he entered office. What a joy to see Henry Hyde and his sidekicks, all grey and silent, stewing in their own juices as the Congress applauded Clinton's long legacy of achievement. How hard it had been to watch Clinton go through everything he had to keep his job. So worried, so ashamed, so beleaguered, so guilty, so unattractive looking for so many months. And yet there he was in front of the congress, beaming, having beaten the bastards hands down. You had to hand it to him, no matter what you think of his morals or his politics. Talk about the little train that could. He just kept rolling that rock up the mountain like Sisyphus till one day it rolled down the other side and flattened the opposition. That's his working method, he explained to the country, just stays focused, chip away at the problem little by little, day by day. Get up every morning and do your work.

I've got to take my cue from old Bill, but do I have enough days left to chip away with? "If it doesn't get done, it doesn't get done," my mother advises from retirement when I worry about how much is on my plate. And that's a comfort when I look at the pile of mail to be answered, the translations I have promised the poetry festival in Paris, the catalogs to be sent out to raise funds for next October's exhibition of our Bulgarian friend's paintings. But, in my dream I am standing on the podium in Calcutta and when I open my mouth to speak, nothing comes out. Time stop wringing my hands in print I guess, and get to work. Right Bill?

February 5, 2000

Dear Brian,

I've been trying to reach you this morning and the constant busy signal means I guess that you are on the internet? As you will see from the letter I'll append, we are about to go to India for the USIS. Or not. William has recently developed a neurogenic bladder which means I must chatherize him twice a day. This morning, problems. I hope the doctor will see us. Well, Brian I am in something of a desperate state to prepare these lectures they have assigned me and wish to plead with you for some help.

HAPPILY just spoke with you. So, I shall keep you posted on William's condition and our plans and will in the interim be sore glad for your help. The following letter will give you a sense of how I am approaching them and the following schedule shows what they have in mind by way of lectures. Anything you can send my way will really be appreciated, especially stuff from the archive documenting William's friendship and interaction with Warren, Lowell, Berryman and Rukeyser. Wish me luck, and love from us both. R.

Dear Ms. Olsin-Windecker,

Thank you very much for the help in mailing the letters and your letter this morning. We are very pleased and honored that there is to be a poetry reading at the Ambassador's residence. These are very busy days for us as you can imagine given the preparations necessary, William's recuperation, and all that will go into this voyage - voyage seems the only word given the mythic scale of the country we will be visiting, the schedule of readings, the distance we will travel. But here we come, "ready or not" as the children's nursery rime would have it. With luck it will be a lot more "ready" than "not ready." I am little nervous to be frank, but we have made such visits before and we always manage to be prepared. William is really a kind of saint - I know I am biased here - and audiences feel it in his presence and his poetry. But it is important for you to realize that his continuing aphasia after the stroke makes formal lecturing very difficult if not impossible. What we have done in the past is a kind of team teaching approach where I take the lead and he joins in as appropriate. I love the challenge of speaking to the various topics I listed rather hurriedly when I was asked for suggestions in the middle of William's hospitalization (You've chosen them all!) I guess what I am saying is that I don't wish to mislead in any way and that your audiences should expect that we will both be "lecturing" at each event. Mind you, I don't plan to be overly formal in these meetings. I hope for an interactive approach with the audience, perhaps posing as many questions as "answering" them. I will have a number of poems with me that I would wish to duplicate for example to share with the audience as we look into the subjects. I do not plan to make these poetry workshops, and there will be an "academic" component to the talks that a university audience might normally expect. And the readings of our own work will be a great pleasure for us, something William does very movingly. In any case, we will do our best, and I'm sure lovers of poetry will appreciate meeting my remarkable friend and poet.

I should have mentioned earlier on that there are two websites that provide a great deal of information on William's life and work that will be a valuable asset for the press and organizers of the various events. William taught at Connecticut College for nearly 40 years. His literary archive is there at the Shain Library and an endowed chair has been established in his name. Two years ago they set up a website with biographical information, examples of his work and so on. It can be found at:

www.conncoll.edu/meredith

For many years William was a Chancellor and Director of the Academy of American Poets, the premiere organization for poetry in America. They do a great deal of educational programs in the U.S. beyond awarding prizes in this art form. On their site you can actually hear William read a couple of his poems. You can also find out about a number of other poets. It is a great place for students to visit.

www.poets.org

Ms.Sahgal had earlier requested that I suggest poems that the media might wish to reproduce. A number of our books will be sent shortly from Greece where we were to have been teaching this semester and will include William's latest, EFFORT AT SPEECH. "The Jain Bird Hospital at Delhi," is a wonderful poem he wrote after his last visit to India for the USIS. It is a cleverly adapted sestina where the repeated words in the formal structure are often synonyms. The poem may be a little long, however, for some purposes. A much shorter poem, "A Major Work" has become something of a signature poem for William - very short, but profound. If you do not have his work at hand I will try to type out these poems for you as well as a couple of my own. I've just called the publisher to ask if they could send a file of William's book that I might "cut and paste" to email you this material. For the moment, I should get back to work on postmodernism in American poetry!

Again, thank you for writing. We too look forward very much to meeting you.

Sincerely,

Richard

Harteis

cc: Pam Sahgal

ALL INDIA SCHEDULE

SCHEDULE FOR Voluntary Speakers PULITZER PRIZE-WINNING POET WILLIAM MEREDITH

AND WRITER RICHARD HARTEIS

Feb: 27-March 10, 2000

Sunday, Feb. 27:

1900/2130 hrs --- Travel Delhi/Chennai (Madras) via IC-540; Program

Manager D.

Subbaram will meet at airport; Accommodation at Hotel Quality Inn Aruna -

Phone: (044) 825 9090; Fax (044) 825 8282; E-mail: qiaruna@satyam.net.in

Monday, February 28:

1100 hrs-- Dr. William Meredith lectures on "The Life and
Works of Robert
Penn
Warren: A Personal Account" and Mr. Richard Harteis
speaks on his new novel
"Sapphire Dawn" and reads excerpts from it; Venue:
English Literature
Department of Madras University (Audience: English
literature faculty and
students of university and city colleges); 1630 hrs
Exclusive Press
Interview with both by a leading English newspaper at the
Consulate; 1800
hrs "An Evening With Two American Poets," a program
cosponsored by the South
India American Studies Network - Dr. Meredith lectures on
"Contemporary
American Poetry" and Mr. Harteis speaks on "The Making
of 'Partial
Accounts," Pulitzer Prize winning work of Dr. Meredith;
Venue: Seminar Room
of the Consulate (Audience: Members of the Network,
poets, writers, book
lovers and journalists)

Tuesday, February 29:

1500/1645 Travel Chennai/Mumbai via 9W-466.

1835/1935 Travel Mumbai/Ahmedabad via 9W-323.
Stay at Hotel Holiday
Inn, Near Nehru Bridge, Khanpur, Ahmedabad 380 001.
(Tel: 91-079-550-5505; Fax: 91-079-550-5501).

Wednesday, March 1

Afternoon Representational lunch for small a group of invitees from
the literary, academic, artistic world.
1830 hours Joint reading of their works (60-70 minutes) at the St.
Xavier's College. The audience at the reading will be eclectic and will
include academics, writers, artists, literary critics, journalists, and
students. The reading will be followed by discussion and question answers.

Thursday, March 2

0715/0815 Travel Ahmedabad/Mumbai via 9W-322.

Stay at Taj Mahal Hotel,

Apollo Bunder, Gateway of India.

(Tel: 91-022-202-3366; Fax: 91-022-287-2711).

1830 Joint readings of their works (60-70 minutes) at the National Center for the Performing Art followed by discussion, question answers.

Friday, March 3

1030 hours Talk at the S.N.D.T. Women's University on Robert Penn Warren, John Berryman, Robert Lowell, and Muriel Rukeyser along with reminiscences about them and selected readings from the works of these four writers. Audience will include academics, literary critics, writers, graduate students, et al.

Afternoon Representational lunch for a small group of

invitees from

the literary, academic and artistic world.

Saturday, March 4

Free day

Sunday, March 5

1630/1850 Travel Mumbai/Calcutta via IC-274.

Embassy car will receive.

Stay at Hotel in Calcutta : Oberoi Grand (Phone: 249 2323)

Monday, March 6: Seminar on American Literature.(exact title to be determined.) The following sessions will be addressed by the American speakers

1000 .--1100 hrs. Talk on Postmodernism in America by Richard Harteis followed by Q/A session

1115 .--1215 hrs. Talk on contemporary young American poets by William Meredith

1330 --1430 hrs. Poetry readings by William Meredith

and Richard

Harteis

Tuesday, March 7:

1000/1110 Travel Calcutta/ Guwahati via IC-229. Stay

at Hotel

Brahmaputra Ashok (Phone: (0361) 541064

1900 hrs. Poetry reading for poets of Assam

Sahitya Academy

Wednesday, March 8

1100 Half-day seminar by Meredith/Harteis at the

English Department,

Guwahati University

1100 .--1200 Lecture on Postmodernism in America by

Richard Harteis

Followed by Q/A

1215 hrs.-1315 hrs. Lecture on contemporary young

American Poets by

William Meredith followed by Q/A session

Evening FREE

Thursday, March 9:

1550/1815 : Travel Guwahati//Delhi via IC-890. Met by American
Embassy Car and escorted to Hotel Maurya Sheraton, Sardar Patel Marg. Tel:
6112233; fax 6113333.

Friday, March 10:
Late morning: Media Interview.
7:00pm-9 00 p.m. "An Evening with American and Indian Poets." Readings
from the works of Meredith and Harteis. Indian poets to be confirmed.
Venue: to be confirmed. The event will be followed by dinner with invited
guests.

All India Program Coordinator:
Pam Sahgal, American Embassy, Chanakya Puri, New Delhi
Tel: 4198819; E-mail: psahgal@usia.gov

Chennai:
Program Officer: Mr. Madison Conoley, Deputy Public

Affairs Officer,

American Consulate General, Chennai; Phone: (O) (044) 827 3040; (H) (044) 493 7632; Fax (O) 826 3407; E-mail : mconoley@exchange.usia.gov

Program Manager: D. Subbaram, Public Affairs Section, American Consulate General, Chennai; Phone: (O) (044) 827 3040; (H) (044) 474 8247; Fax (O) 826 3407; E-mail: subbaram@exchange.usia.gov

Mumbai:

Program Officer: Jennifer Zimdahl Galt ,Tel: Home - 91-022-364-1787

Email: jzgalt@usia.gov, The American Center, 4 New Marine Lines,

Mumbai 400 020 (Tel: 262-4590; Fax: 262-4595)

Program Manager: Saroj Merani ,Tel: Home - 91-022-215-1284, Email: scm@usia.gov

Calcutta:

PAO Patricia Sharpe, American Center, 38-A Jawaharlal Nehru Road. Tel:

91- 33-2881200;

Cultural Affairs Advisor, Pradip K. De, Tel: 91-33-2881200;

Program Manager, Smita Basu, Tel: 91-33-2881200;

New Delhi:

Hilary Olsin-Windecker, Assistant Cultural Affairs Officer, American Embassy

Shantipath, Chanakya puri, New Delhi -110021

Tel: 619-8815: 619-8000

Usha Balakrishnan, Cultural Affairs Advisor, American Embassy, New Delhi

Tel: 619-8817/ 619-8000

Pamela Sahgal, All India Program Coordinator

Public Affairs Office, American Embassy

Shantipath, Chanakyapuri, New Delhi 110021

Tel: 91-11-419-8819 (direct); Operator:91-11- 419-8000;

Fax: 91-11-419-8826

E-mail: psahgal@usia.gov

February 18, 2000

Can we really be leaving in two days? Exciting to

thinking that it is going to work. I've gone into a kind of trance with all the subjects I am to teach in India - stealing hour by hour as William sleeps and I entertain my sister and George who have come on a golfing vacation. We were to have been in Greece, of course, but now we are all camped out here together. I have still got to Xerox pages of poems to carry with me to illustrate my points, but for better or worse, I have pages and pages of notes which outline modern poetry from Eliot on with all sorts of subdivisions and categories sufficient to satisfy any Anglo academician we might run across in India (I hope.) The key is always to over prepare I guess, and never let them see you sweat.

At one point over dinner in a nice restaurant a couple of days ago, poor William began to throw up like Niagra Falls, all grey and clammy. Just what we needed, a viral gastroenteritis just before we leave. But he's back on track now and Dr. Raymond has called with the blood results which monitor all the medications William takes. "You're all set," the doctor pipes in his cheery 8:00 A.M. voice. How do these people get to their office so early. Will this sort of early bird routine ever seep into my habits as I get older.

Poor William was so sick. What a hero he is. I felt awful for our guests and George kindly said, "anyone who has had kids understands. Not to worry." Sweet of him. But God, the pressure as we leave. Little time for spiritual advancement. Last night I cooked a great steak - Texas style the way Mackie Jarrell taught me: "sear an inch- thick hunk of meat in a hot frying pan lined with salt, turn it twice and slice it up like London Broiled." Works every time. After dinner we walked under the swaying royal palms and stars along the intercostal, admiring the houses, talking of the future. At one point two exquisite greyhounds came out with their owners, a tan beauty named Daphne and a black mate named Hector. A magical moment, their great dark eyes as they slid right up along side my legs to the hip joint to be petted, like gods who deigned to drop in and bless us with beauty and grace. Such splendid creatures.

For all the extra effort, Barb and George have been a happy distraction from my neurotic preparing of these lectures, forcing me to focus on something else from time to time other than the ax hanging over my head. I tell Loretta Cobb my recurrent nightmare as I stand at the podium in Calcutta and open my mouth, and nothing comes out. “Oh, I used to get that all the time darlin,” she says, “only I was naked. Women are always naked, why is that?”

Though I am still not finished, I at least will have something in hand when we get on the plane. It has been wonderful at times to read of the lives of the poets William knew and loved so in the old days, get to know their poems better. Warren, Lowell, Berryman, Rukeyser, Jarell. Their letters to him that Brian Rogers sent from the archive in a spectacular gesture of friendship, make it clear how much these poets loved William and depended on his opinion: “With Randall and Delmore gone, I don’t know whose judgment I trust more than yours,” John Berryman writes. “ ”All I can say at the moment,” William chides Robert Penn Warren “is that the poem is wonderfully alive and I can’t for the life of me see why you have to use the word “fucking” twice on the first page of a poem that lifts your scalp off quite independent of that.” When William is sick, has survived two hours of cardiac arrest by CPR and then emergency surgery, Warren writes, “All I can say is that you are constantly on our minds and in our conversation. Your are of inestimable value to us, and we count you among our great blessings. But if you’d don’t know that by now, there's no way to tell you, and if you don't know you are too stupid to understand anything said." The archive testifies how for years William was a kind of eminence gris in American letters, providing long, detailed editorial comments and suggestions for these writers and a host of others. It is an amazing record really. And it was my good luck to hang out with such writers over the past 30 years, a fortnight with Auden the summer before he died, visits the Warren's in Vermont, dinner parties with Jimmy Merrill, swimming nude with Maxine and Victor in their New Hampshire pond - a kind of de rigeur checking each other out. How hip are you, and what sort of equipment do you have? Funny. Someday I should put some of this down. As I read through William's correspondence I see how interesting it can be. Of course, his is an exquisite account and in close.

This forcing myself to take American literature into account has been a little step perhaps on the road I hope to travel in this journal. I've had the chance of reading criticism such as this, for example, from Paul Marian speaking of Warren's "Heart of Autumn": *

"It is fall and the great geese are heading for

warmer waters, though some of them - thanks to the hunters - will never reach that destination. Death comes unexpectedly; the wounded geese do not even know what has happened to them. Unbeknown to them, the poet suddenly realizes with a shudder, they are enacting his own story. For they have risen into autumn skies to cry out with their "imperial utterance," calling out the joy of their nameless tragic destiny. In this, the poet has come to understand, they seem to know more perhaps that the poet knows himself. And if it is the path of some inner logic, this pull to the south, or merely the path of folly, where the hunter lies in wait, what matter finally? What does matter is the great wing beat across the heavens. Wing beat, high beat, the poet hears and for a moment imagines himself transformed and following their wake. And now his heart

> is impacted with a fierce impulse
> To unwordable utterance --
> Toward sunset, at a great height. "

Each of the poets I've studied, how each has approached their own sunset - some cruelly, sadly, in fear, in madness, resignation, grace — is something I must ponder for myself and William too. One thing is clear from this study: how essential is it to take the joy from life when possible - carpe diem has never been stronger in my soul.

We walked the bird sanctuary at the Wakodahatchee Wetlands with Barb and George, a beautiful boardwalk among Great Herons, blue and green, egrets, moorhens, American coots. At one point a little flock of Ibis flew in a white vee across the moon as it rose and the sunset fell across the black waters in neon pink and purple stripes - electric.

I mourn the dead poets I have been reading of, these friends of William who so often ended so badly. He's had some tough times over the years old William, but oh joy, the old sweetie is still with me, and soon we will be hitching a ride with the Ibis to India.

From ROBERT PENN WARREN, Modern Critical Views, Chelsea House Publishers, 1986 ISBN 0-87754-662-2

February 21

The day after we were supposed to have left...Saturday night Barbie said, "are you sure you don't have to have any vaccinations before you leave?" And just to be sure I checked the web page for the Indian embassy. To my horror it informed me of the necessity of visa, that the US embassy will be of no help should we arrive in country without one and that one can not obtain one in any country other than the country of origin. I felt like the Shirly Jackson story about the cow mother who simply doesn't believe all the stories they tell about the slaughter house until the sledge hammer comes crashing into her forehead. Staggering to think all was lost. Again, I went into a trance of action, pleading: got the embassy to give me the home number of the visa official, pleaded my case to the airlines to get a reservation to Bombay at least since New Delhi was now impossible, called the program officer from here by 3 A.M to tell her of the disaster. "Oh my Got," she cried like an Indian bureaucrat in some old Peter Sellers movie. - Douglas says I have to get this accent down for when I lecture - not very spiritual of me. In any case, now I wait to see it the new little house of cards I've established will hold. Will the embassy really turn our passports around in a day? Will the new tickets come on time. Can we possibly still meet our first obligation at the Madrass University?

My visitors have mercifully and kindly taken a hotel to let us pack in peace and deal with this emergency. Just now finished a nice dinner with them. I've spent all day finally finishing the lectures and Xeroxing all the poems I'll use to illustrate my points. I've cleverly worked in previous interviews and articles William has written on Berryman and others as well as his poems dedicated to these friends as well. And after nearly thirty years I'll have something to say too about these poems - the time I saw a ghost in the house and William did a spontaneous exorcism asking the ghost to be kind to me as a guest of the house, waking one morning on a camping trip to find William's "Accidents of Birth" on the picnic table outside our tent. The poem he wrote for me and later stole for HAZARD THE PAINTER. "The Season's Difference" where he refuses to accept my vision of a life together in Florida. Our old dog Mikey swimming through his love poem "Crossing Over." I won't get into these much if at all. We took Auden and Chester Kallerman as models I guess early on when it came to how we would manage our different professional lives.

And one of my obsessions is back to spoil the progress I've made: ruminating all day about the old man who died in William's room the day he was admitted to the hospital just before Christmas. The nurse was taking his blood pressure when she started calling to him in a loud voice. Seems his eyes rolled back in his head and that was it. By the time another nurse came in and they ditzed around the code blue couldn't do too much for him. At least that's how it looked to me sitting beside the bed next door. Why didn't I jump up and say, the guy's dying girls, why not start CPR, or why not start CPR myself. All sorts of logical reasons to keep out: perhaps he had requested no extraordinary means (but then they wouldn't have coded him,) perhaps he was only having a seizure (I didn't take the pulse myself), the hospital would have thrown me out if I had started some intervention and ruined what care William would get (they did throw me out a following night when I caught them over-dosing William by a 100% and insisted they call the doctor to correct the faulty order. The old gentleman was well into his 80's , perhaps 90's. I'd overheard the doctor say he would have to have a catheter in permanently for his bladder cancer. Still, I wouldn't want that sort of care for me or William. Well, nothing is going to bring him back, and my culpability is clouded. Now William has wandered back to the office having done the dishes and it's a much better thing to go spend some time with him and just relax. Ha.

Dear Natalie,

I wasn't able to access the website you mentioned last time. Don't know why. I presume it would tell me something of the program on Saturday? I'm sorry to trouble you, but could you give me some directions and the time on Saturday should Nancy Frankel be able to come on Saturday.

I've been at my journal on India again. I'll tip in this morning's entry. Love, R. and W.

Black Hole, Wormhole

Crisis. A hole. How to get out of this black hole. How can I pick up this story, after the event - how to remember it, imagine it, interest you, dear reader. Until, again last night, I dream of Ganesh, the Elephant-headed god. The god comes to me chubby, smiling, the sort of Walt Disney incarnation that children love in India, Like Santa Clause. The god of education and prosperity, sometimes a youth walking arm in arm with beautiful women, their saris trailing after. But most often a little fat guy, someone who'd share his Snickers with you and would just as soon sit on the bench watching than try to play right field. A little like Spanky in those Saturday morning re-runs of Our Gang.

And in the dream I am young too, sitting beside him, our legs folded under us. His thick trunk rolls down over his belly into his lap covering his private parts. I stick my finger into his belly like a doubting Thomas. He laughs like the Pillsbury Dough Boy and I know everything is going to be okay with the certainty of dream. Like a very old person for whom short term memory is completely shot, but for whom events 40 years ago are as fresh as rain water, I know I will be able to go back to India and relive that voyage, physical and spiritual. Tell of the time I first met Ganesh, sitting forlorn in the deserted courtyard the day after a wedding ceremony in Ghuwati over near Burma, huge crows swooping down from the trees to keep him company. I can close my eyes hear and hear them talk together, gossiping about the guests and the future.

Past collapses into present like a Proustian tea party. Is it real, is it Memorex? The Jain monks in their bird hospital are healing the feathery sick who have crashed into windows, releasing them to illusion from the rooftop of their temple on a Sunday morning. William is back, twenty years later, climbing the stairs after his stroke to visit the broken victims. Forty parrots green and pink, one large peacock, and a platoon of pigeons all complaining about their illness the way the sick do. The old head nurse takes a mourning dove from her cage. She is having some kind of fit, head convoluted under her wing, spinning round in her cage. He smiles at us, embarrassed for the interruption of this emergency, and takes her upstairs to intensive care. Above the door to ward two, a painting like a stained glass window instructing the illiterate in a medieval cathedral proclaims mercy. A king sits with his amputated limbs on one side of a scale balancing a white dove on the other and the legend reads: " Brave and merciful king put pieces of his own flesh and finally his own life to balance a pigeon (demi-God) in exchange to save him from prey of hawk (demi-God.) Both demi-gods bowed assuming their original divine form and blessed the king for his attempt to ellivate (sic) the pain."

William's explanation of this strange sect in India on his last visit: "They think that/ birds and animals - like us, some predators, some prey -/ should be ministered to no less than men and women..../ We recall the embarrassed fanfare for Francis and his flock."

You see some very strange things in India. Where was I? Am I?

March 1, 2001

No, you are not misreading the date, gentle reader - come to think of it, I hate it when I come across this phrase "gentle reader" in a book. The hackneyed salutation can hardly bring me closer to you, scanning the page, still hoping for a glance of India perhaps in this tale. Shall I call you Bob or Barbara, some gender neutral name like Pat or Jean?

Well, somehow Pat, a year has slipped by easily as a page falling off a calendar in that Hollywood cliché for the passing of time. Yesterday, as I was wheeling William back from the aquamarine Atlantic I heard that song that always makes me a little teary eyed when I hear it "Oh, it's a long long time from May to December... and they days flicker by, November, December...." The wheel chair was loaded with cooler, beach chairs, umbrella, towels - we have the drill down pretty good - as we glided over the quarter mile boardwalk that crosses the lake on the other side of the dunes on Singer island. A beautiful day. His radiant smile under the little white cap - my heart leapt up as Wordsworth might say. “These precious days, I’ll spend with you.” The lyrics filled my soul like monk’s vows, especially now, now that Nick has gone out of our lives yet again, this time probably for good.

And what of India you may well ask? I am sitting in my little lanai just as I was precisely a year ago before we flew to Bombay, stuck a little, physically and emotionally. But you know at least we made home. Ever since our return I have been lugging a suitcase up and down the east coast as we traveled filled with books, maps, notes, photographs - all the raw material to tell my tale - paying excess baggage, straining my back and any number of porters. My passage to India becomes memoir and not a journal it seems. If I had only taken the lap top with me as we went...But the images do not fade. I close my eyes and I am in Ghandi’s ashram, the Hridaya Kunj where the master sat waiting for enlightenment to liberate the subcontinent and create a nation. In the cool shade along the dried up river he realized the power of non-violence and set off on his famous Dandi march to the sea with a conviction that blurred the line between religion and politics. Through the gate a group of girls sit in blue and white saris listening to his words.

Lord of Humility
Dwelling in the little pariah hut
help us to search for Thee throughout
that fair land watered by the Ganges.
Brahmaputra and Jamuna
Give us receptiveness.
Give us open heartedness
Give us Thy humility
Give us the ability and willingness
to identify ourselves
with the masses of India.

O God
who does help only when man
feels utterly humble, grant that we
may not be isolated from the people.
We would serve as servants and friends.
Let us be embodiments of self sacrifice
embodiments of godliness,
humility personified, that we may know

the land better and love it more.

Three monkeys in the garden act out the injunction to hear speak and see no evil. A painting on the wall of one of the simple structures depicts the removal of untouchability as he attends an inter caste marriage. Another shows him at his spinning wheel, the "symbol for a constructive program."

This must be my constructive program, to sit and spin out this tale of India, to see if somehow I can approach the Lord of Humility, seek his help to change my life, face the future by remembering what I saw there.

I came back from church yesterday with black ashes in the form of a crucifix on my forehead to mark the beginning of Lent - "I do believe we all get out alive," I once wrote in a poem, but a faith verging on agnosticism needs to stoke the fires routinely to risk not burning out completely. One by one the congregation filed past me with the deep black gashes - Father Ramon really lays it on - and I thought how strange they had all become, the way a mask can so quickly change an actor if one believes. I recalled seeing the occasional guru with a swath of white paint on his forehead marking holiness, how effectively these symbols produce the very quality they wish to symbolize. A time of penitence and renunciation. Per force, in my case, it seems.

After a month of quarreling and pettiness and lack of charity, love seems finally to have died between me and Nick and I am left alone once again, trying to steal a little time from my care giving chores to sort it all out. Just last year he stood in his hibiscus bikini beside a chain link fence covered in hibiscus calling "hi bubba" - a gift from God I thought then, to help bring some joy into my life with his beauty and good character. Now, after too many nights of too much booze, again, we seem to have spoken words that can't be taken back, ideas that have taken on a physical reality that can't be uncreated - reverberating sound waves out into the universe defining loss and distance. Hello Mars, have you heard the latest of my love?

He had become a prisoner in our house, and I wanted no part of being his jailer. The gods give and they take back as well. And the day after his departure, Dr. Brown spots another cancer in my bladder it seems, something which may need tending too when we get back from a book tour we are about to begin out west. Nasty to face this too in the middle of my loss. Perhaps I can write myself out of this funk the way writers are supposed to be able to do. All I’ve managed so far are some soppy lyrics to put me to sleep with, a little anthology of failed valentines:

I

Florida Farewell

Sunset floods the marsh
neon pink and purple
vulgar, electric, primeval.

We stare at a green heron
frozen among the water lilies
transfixed as you and I, transfixed.

If I could look into your eyes,
bluer than the sky’s reflection
I’d see him standing there,
patient as death, immovable.

Eyes empty of love,

We take in anything
but each other
as the sun dies
its splendid death.

On the far island
an alligator gleams
bronze and copper
with the day's last light.

Moorhens and American Coots
grieve to each other across
the Pickerlweed and Cord Grass.

A Great Egret lifts a star-shaped
foot, immobile; a lone Ospry
spies us from afar, waiting to see
what will happen between us.

It will be nothing. Again.

And like the tortoise stretching
his enormous neck, the
terrible wrenching to shed

a leathery shell he has outgrown,
this year again I'll somehow manage,
sink naked and vulnerable
back into the dark waters,
waiting for the shield to harden,
growing something out of myself
that might at last sustain me
against the night's perpetual loss.

II

Now Comes Dream.

You will slip through the stone walls
I've built around my day
like walking through mist, like
stepping through a film of water.

No savage dogs to keep you out.
You'll have your way with me,
you'll pin me or let me pin you,
your dear head will lie in her lap
while I watch, I'll kneel before you
as you blossom. You will smile at me.

Everything I've worked to clarify
will cloud over, every resolution
melt with your velvet touch -
How I've worked for this sleep,
how my spirit cries for respite,
how deserving of a little refuge.
Yet, will I certainly wake,
exhausted, to begin another day
with the terror of my love.

Bandit, sweet bastard.
Now I lay me down.

III

In Passing

William can't find his finger nail polish
the anti fungal that he uses every morning
when the directions say "apply at bedtime."
"Go to the pharmacy. I can't find it,." he says.

Nick's shoes, my leftovers, show a paper thin

sole when he crosses his thighs. Thighs like
Mercury or Apollo. His feet should be
set in silver wings, his beauty, his dignity,
deserve more than I can provide.

This lost medicine, this flower of a man
blooming in the garbage - my broken heart.

Which god among you will help me?
Ganesh, Shiva, beloved Saravasti?
Which of you will see these things and
heal a heart too much taken by the world.

No, no, no. No more sentimentality. Time for a little snap back ability buddy. Remember lacing up your sneakers all those mornings you trained for the Marathons you ran in the 90's? Time for a little new millennial spiritual training, beginning first with going on the wagon perhaps. How many of our friends like Bill Cobb, and Blanche Boyd and Buzz Poverman saved their lives by giving up alcohol. How much TIME they were able to recuperate from their hangover days, they explained. And even if their best work was done in their drinking days as they sometimes fear, not a one of them would give up sobriety for one more rung on the ladder to the Nobel Prize. So, as in Lents passed, I will go dry again just to prove I can do it - the challenge of a mountain for the mountain climber. I shall take my sobriety to California and visit old friends from happier days, a little sentimental journey for me and dear William. "These precious days..." The new novel, SAPPHIRE DAWN may be my own dawning as I attempt slip back into health and try by curious heart to steer into less troubled waters. And if at last I don't succeed, perhaps this will be a useful record to someone along the way on a journey we all must face, sure as taxes, or life's capacity to bring us joy.

March 2, 2001

Day two of the newly rediscovered sobriety and not so worse for the wear, though each night as in years past I have cheated a little by taking a valium at cocktail time. Take them like aspirin, my doctor merrily tells me when I get the sharp wrenching pain in my gut when I am stressed to the max. This morning, mercifully, look ma, no pain. One morning in my haste I accidentally swallowed all of William's morning pills - heart meds, anti seizure meds - a little rainbow fistful of tablets and gels. “You’re going to have a very calm day,” my doctor said, when I called him to check on the mishap. And so it was last night with William and Ginger. I stood there holding his beer while he ate plantains, black beans and rice, swaying to the Bob Marley tunes, hardly tempted at all to sip the cold Coors Light in my hand.

I’ve made a pot of java, the sleep machine train is chugging away next door carrying William god knows where in his dreams. I hope it is somewhere sweet. He dreams more and more now, or at least remembers the dreams. Maybe one day they will transform themselves into poems again. In the hard times of the stroke, those couple of years when he could not move or speak I imagine the dreams kept flowing like deep currents in a river and saved him, his mind, his personality. How he survived that will remain one of the great mysteries to me.

Outside my door the day has come warm, brilliant in Palm Beach perfection once again - just one season here, paradise. Except, of course when the hurricanes come, by which time these snow birds will have already flown away. The tipocina purpura has shed a blanket of purple blossoms again this morning. A week ago, in desperation with the property manager's promises to spruce up our front entrance, I went to the flower show and found the ornamental tree Ginger suggested to us. The dead hibiscus stump at our door was more like grey driftwood than a live tree and it took hours to chopped away at the deep roots snaking through the clay soil. Back from church on Ash Wednesday, the tipocina weeping its purple flowers, it seemed the perfect replacement for the worn out hibiscus. Pathetic fallacy did we call it in literary criticism the Romantic convention of ascribing the author's emotions to nature? It is not raining, Shelley is weeping.

I called Natalie this morning in Sofia - purple is her favorite color. Will she be the new flower in my life? This fabulous beauty sat next to me last summer at one of those banquets thrown in our honor in Bulgaria - weird to be treated like a rock star there. After a Fulbright year as poet in residence, William and I were made citizens by Presidential decree and the paparazzi follow us around like Tom Cruise and Brad Bitt (I'm Pitt, William is Cruise.) I had the wit to bring her home with me in the fall in slight part to spite Nick who had thrown a fit in the end of the summer and abandoned me to all the work I had taken on.

This book on India lay sobbing in the suitcase for months while I organized four art exhibitions for our friend Stoimen Stoilov, including a book of etchings for our poems called ECHOES shown at the N.Y. Public library.

Natalie came along to make a film of the project for Connecticut Public Television. For weeks I was responsible for an entourage of Bulgarian artists and friends up and down the east coast including the Vice President, his body guard, translators, and other hangers on. I was the fund raiser, producer, chauffeur, cook, major domo. For days our crew worked non-stop stretching and hanging canvases at the Lyman Allyn Muesum, no nonsense Natalie alternating between hammer and camera as we worked.

In the fall before Natalie arrived, we were visiting our friends Mary and Fred in New Hampshire. These good folks are like family - are family in a way. Thirty years ago Fred took his oral exams from William and the following day Mary gave birth to their first born son who became William Meredith Fosher - a pretty cheeky way to guarantee passing your oral exams we like to joke.

I was having coffee with Mary and she showed me

two tiny little toy babies that one of the grandchildren had left. The girl was crawling on its knees, the other, clearly a boy from his tiny penis was standing up, giving a jaunty little wave and smile.

"Do you ever regret having children, Mary, I asked her.

"Oh Richard, it has been the most wonderful thing in my life," and she began to cry in the charming way she has when emotion overcomes her.

"I've been thinking of trying to have a baby with Natalie. Do you think I am absolutely crazy? I've always wanted to have a child. All those years studying pediatrics - I guess they were my surrogate children."

"Maybe you can adopt." The little white steeple out her kitchen window against the New Hampshire mountain was more Rockwell than Norman Rockwell. I've discussed almost every important decision in my life with Mary - my surrogate sister -around that kitchen table. She's about as sweet, and sensitive and non-judgmental as you could want in a confidant.

"Yeah, I know. It's selfish, and politically incorrect, I know, but I just feel this urge to reproduce myself, to see what my own flesh and blood would turn out to be like. To hold my own child against my chest. To have the big life experience. I know it sounds hypocritical. I guess it's just my German background. My parents waited for years to spoil some little tow head of my own they way they did all their other grandchildren. Now my father's dead. I'll be dead myself soon, if I don't get started."

"What about Nicky?"

"He seems to be going his own way these days. He showed me a picture of his girlfriend this summer- I don't seem to be part of the picture in his future. He already has a son and wants to concentrate on his own family, I guess. I mean, I always used to think I didn't have the right to bring a child into the world if I was homosexual or bi-sexual or whatever I am. What did our psych teacher used to say? Being homosexual is like being 50% pregnant? But these days gay people want to have it all and there are all kinds of families. It was big front page news this summer in our town when Blanch Boyd and her partner had twins in vitro. Do you think this is just a mid-life thing? I'm not even mid-life anymore."

"Well, what will William think about this?"

"I'm with him till the day one of us doth part - that's the bottom line. I'd never consider this without his agreement. And I haven't kept anything from Natalie either. She wants a child as much as I do. People are going to talk no matter how we live our lives and we'll just have to say the hell with what they think as long as we're honest and try to know what we are doing. They haven't looked after William these past two decades since his stroke. It's our life, after all. And the motivation won't be hard with Natalie, believe me. Here, look at her picture."

At the opening receptions this fall Natalie sometimes wore a black wool sweater dress, a turtle neck body stocking down to the hem at her high heels, her blond hair pushed high up on her head like Minerva or Juno. The hour glass effect was ravishing, despite the slightly stoop shoulders that women with very large breasts sometimes bend to out of shyness. At one point a matron approached her wide-eyed and asked, "are you a model?"

I felt flushed with stupid, high school, heterosexual pride every time she took my arm and we made an entrance. This Playboy bunny, this Penthouse daydream is with me and every guy in the room is trying to get close and pry me loose from her. Amazing. There have been other beauties in my life, but this sensational creature was a whole other class. I felt like I was one of the guys in the locker room after football practice bragging of their exploits, lying through their jock straps. But there she was, Sharon Stone's younger sister.

Dannie Abse, our poet doctor friend from England told me once that when he was in medical school a professor had introduced a phrase that troubled him for the rest of his life: "the vagina," he intoned, "is a potential space." I presume Danny has been fulfilling that potential for the rest of his adult male life. Robert Penn Warren describes it as a dream of velvet as I recall. I've dreamed that dream often enough in my life I suppose (he says preening, toweling himself dry in the locker room), but I guess I've always felt a gay guy's mild aversion to the female parts as an idea? Being there is one thing, but the mystery of that anatomy.... One morning, lingering with my love after a shower, I had the epiphany that has struck poets from the time the little engine of metaphor first began to work its way in language, I suppose. It's a ROSE, I thought to myself. It is a beautiful, beautiful rose. Petal, on petal. I open, I enter this beautiful rose. My love is like a red red rose. Gather ye rosebuds while ye may....

And from the bed stand beside Natalie's bed, the boy with the little penis waves encouragement to me and smiles and I am falling out of myself again through rose-gate, lost in a perfect natural fit of pleasure. How does the Spanish poet say it, we are all angels with but one wing and can only dance by embracing each other?

How will I ever show this rumination to the world - reveal such privacy. Writing to myself is so easy, what would Natalie think of this? Surely she must give me permission if this ever sees light of day one day. "That was Boy ko, I joked with her once after a particularly athletic session working on "the project," punning on the name Boiko, a common first name for males in Bulgaria. What will Boyko, (or girl ko) make of this book if the book and the baby both make it into the world one day.

Natalie's production company has gone bankrupt she says this morning from Sofia. The old Communist joke: We pretend to work, they pretend to pay us. But she is a hard working girl, very professional, very no-nonsense and intelligent. I remember once talking with John Hersey in Key West about this new "creative non-fiction," and how he despised the idea. The whole point of journalism is to tell the truth or as close as you can get to it, he said. Creating facts only muddies the water in the worst possible way. Yet, I have sent some of these pages to the NEA for a grant in Creative Non Fiction to help me pay the bills and take some time to finish this story. Hersey would be turning in his grave to think the "genre" has so established itself in university departments and institutions like the NEA. But it enables me to make a strategic disclaimer here now: TODAY'S ENTRY IS ENTIRELY FICTITIOUS, GENTLE READER, IT IS ALL A BUNCH OF BIG LIES. YOU CAN'T SEE THE WHITE STEEPLE OF THE CHURCH FROM MARY FOSHER'S KITCHEN WINDOW AT ALL.

"I'm gup now," William says in his early morning aphasia-ese for "I am getting up now." He is painting his fingernails with the anti-fungal medicine. Time to see about his breakfast. Saved by the bananas and Kellogg's Corn Flakes.

March 6, 2001

Tickets still haven't arrived for our book tour to California tomorrow. Wonder if we will make it. Two new books out this past year have not had their fair share of attention and we plan to combine visits with friends and family and a few readings and university appearances, starting with Ed Hirsch's class at the University of Houston. Looking forward to it all is more real somehow than actually getting on the plane and flying away. Why does it seem impossible for me to live in the present, to have always the future or past in mind. How well I have learned the Proustian lesson that Andre Aciman writes of that helped me drift into sleep last night: "'what is' should always be turned into 'what seems; what seems ' must become 'what isn't,' and 'what isn't, what was.'" "What was perhaps and might have been," has more meaning than "what just is" in what he calls the "imperfect-conditional-anterior-preterit." Things acquire meaning when they are registered, processed, and understood through memory and wishful thinking, he tells us. This is real life. It is only retrospectively, after the present has slipped away that one finally begins to see the big picture, how close we came to bliss or how needless were our sorrows. As Emily Dickinson would have it:

> Except the heaven had come so near,
> So seemed to choose my door,
> The distance would not haunt me so;
> I had not hoped before.
>
> But just to hear the grace depart
> I never thought to see,
> Afflicts me with a double loss;

'Tis lost, and lost to me.

And so I look back to the last month with Nick, last fall with Natalie trying to see a future, my life collapsing into the present on this page. "One measures time not in units of experience, but in units of hope and of anticipated regret," Aciman says. "Burrowing in a cork-lined room re-inventing your life is life, is the present." But longing for one of these beautiful friends to be in my arms this morning is hardly a present perfect. Time to take the laundry from the dryer, pack my bags, and water the plants. A change in the psychological landscape will do me good. I'll let the future take care of itself for a while, divining lessons by looking at the past.

March 9,

On the plane to LA - William sleeping at my side. The visit to Ed Hirsch in Houston has gone extremely well, his energy and good will carrying us through a stellar visit, an auspicious beginning to pulling myself up by the bootstraps. In the car on the way to airport, Ed suggests I consider therapy, prefacing his remarks by "I may be crossing the line here." He assures me this is only based on how depressed I had told him I was before we came, not, on my performance with his students or the visit. He sees well enough how frustrating it can be trying to understand William in conversation, the excruciating silences as he struggles to remember a name or an idea, the thousands of time I've lifted that wheel chair like Sisyphus, the illnesses, the worry. Showering him, dressing him, day after day - my senior Ken Doll, our private joke as I drape a towel over his head - the big smile, the pleasure of the shower, even his skin soft and sweet now like a baby. The painful pleasure of a leg massage, almost sexual in a body long since absent of that pleasure. And never a complaint. Never. It makes me ashamed now even to be writing this.

Everyone has his own story of course, his own burden. But it has been almost two decades now, and I begin to see the price of the monastic life I have chosen. I remember telling a friend once who was struggling with the choice of staying with his ailing friend or starting a new life on his own: we are responsible for our own choices, for our own happiness.

"I always assumed you were enjoying your life in the middle of it," Roger said to me recently as we discussed details of our visit to him. And yes, there have been triumphant moments. The Pulitzer and National Book Awards which I like to point out he won after the stroke, certainly a unique story in the history of American letters. Our many travels. The Fulbright year in Bulgaria, reading our poetry in Morocco and India, this present trip out west to promote the new books, but more importantly to help me find my swing again, help me get my mojo back. We've been two gypsy kings these past years since William's stroke, but running from or toward something, I can not say. Mary sent me a greeting card recently with two men in Bowler hats, walking down a road, hand in hand, just two black silhouettes in a grey landscape ambling toward the horizon. Beautiful, and sad too. Why this terrible loneliness as I watch William take deep breaths in his sleep beside me? I've studied the syndrome - anticipatory grief - something the care giver must learn to live with. At William's age and health, love is a holding action, and there are few silver linings in the clouds on the horizon.

"Janet found that she could speak honestly to a therapist in a way she couldn't even to her best friends and me," Ed says of his wife. It is a solution he is willing to recommend to others, but would never permit himself, he admits. Ed has a genius grant and can afford to pay to help solve his own family's tragedies. How could I afford therapy? Wouldn't it ruin all the efforts I've made to tough this winter out, wouldn't I have to consider myself in trouble and go to the bottom of the ladder again if I were to start in with a therapist? Doesn't the alcoholic first have to admit he is an alcoholic before a change can be made. "Hello, my name is Richard, and I'm...."

"Remember the old joke about the guy who asks after the queen mother's health," I ask him.

"Yeah?"

"Well, she falls down and cries a lot. But other than that she is okay."

We both laugh. Humor is key to pulling yourself out of a funk, if you can get there. But it can be a false cosmetic, I guess. "Oh dear, here I am with the lava pouring over my feet," as Woody Allen might say. But you are still burning. Perhaps it is unrealistic to think I can write myself out of this hole.

"This trip was a good idea," he tells me, encouraging me with a big smile. And for sure, I needed his friendship, some of the glamor of the old days. Lunch with Bob Phillips, Cynthia MacDonald and student poets trading gossip. James Dickey's scandalous behavior, Muriel

Rykeyser in the hospital.

"We need to get a better urine sample," the young intern informs Muriel. "It is a simple procedure. We just feed a little tube through the penis into the bladder..."

"Your penis or mine doctor," the gay woman visiting Muriel asks him.

How sweet the students were sitting around Ed's living room, so fresh, so gentle, so admiring and courteous of William, and of me. Ed tells them William is "a living treasure." They ask about Berryman, Lowell, and Frost with wide-eyed attention. When William falters, I read from Ed's Paris Review interview William gave just before his stroke.

"I wait until the poem seems to be addressed not to "Occupant" but to William Meredith," he says. "Poetry and experience should have an exact ratio. And astonishing experience doesn't happen very often. Daily experience is astonishing on a level at which you can write a poem, but astonishing experience would be the experience would be the experience which is not the astonishment of reality but astonishment of insight. Robert Frost used to say, 'How many things have to happen to you before something occurs to you?'"

Ph.D. candidates in creative writing. Auden would roll over in his grave. No courses in contemporary literature were offered at Oxford, he'd say, that was an area it was expected students to teach themselves. But for Ed, poetry is as essential for life as oxygen. His flame burns bright. Fueled by that pure atmosphere, his students hover about like beautiful luna moths.

"I don't know quite what I expected," I tell Ed, taking in the azelas and palm trees blooming incongruously as we approach the airport, Houston shining like Oz on the horizon. "I guess I thought it would all be cowboy hats and long-horn cattle."

"There is a sort of Texas component, but we don't have anything to do with it," Ed says.

"I'll let George Bush know."

"Right, all of our Houston friends are gay poets and art historians," he laughs. His energy is that of a manic teenager, the class clown."

"It's been a wonderful visit, Ed, wonderful to see you. I guess I'll figure it all out eventually."

"We ought to write a book: Things they don't tell you about middle age. Like, you're going to put on weight and not take it off."

"You will be stiff in the morning."

"No, you will be lucky if you are stiff in the morning."

His big Jewish head, bushy hair and sad black eyes swoop in and he kisses me as the airplanes roar in and out of Texas.

March 10, 2001

A bay window in the living room looks out onto the California hills, bursting into green with the rains and purple heather. Yesterday, we finally escaped the creeping sprawl of Los Angeles and drove along the verdant hills along the pacific with trophy houses and corporate headquarters buildings gleaming silver on the uppermost ridges. King of the mountain, California style.

Million dollar mansions hang on bolder ledges oblivious to the fire burning in the belly of the earth, waiting to belch them off. A light rain comes and goes. Palms, Jacaranda, cactus, daffodils all vie for space on the hillside where my sister and her family have moved up to. At seven, the guest room reverberates with an air compressors as the boys check the gigantic tires on their all terrain vehicles and pack their pick up trucks for a weekend in the desert. Beer, tent, gas cans, and the huge atv, like a lunar landing vehicle, or a great insect caught in the bed of the truck

I stand and watch them with a cup of coffee, asking questions to try to engage them. I think of Willam's poem to his students:

"I have become fond of this class. Dressed and coiffed

and intellectually equipped like so many Kaspar Hausers,

they struggle into the Nurnberg of my Tuesdays,
taxing my powers of invention."
"I study them hard, but they will barely consent to
leaf through me, their stereotype for me."

"Do you like having two earnings," I ask my older nephew. "I'm thinking of getting another myself." He's a sweet kid, still hugs his mother and father before he goes out. I'd like to know him better. I show them a copy of William's book - they look at it dutifully for a moment and then pile into their trucks. "How the old lady watches and listens," William says of his imaginary mother-in-law in HAZARD THE PAINTER. "How the children unfold like paper flowers, watched and listened to."

Not.

The boys turn of their pagers and cell phones and drive off to the desert for the weekend with shot guns and six packs of Coors Light. Can this be good? Could I possibly not get into a row with m y hosts if I ventured this unsolicited opinion.

Judy has thrown in the laundry that the Mexican housekeeper has accumulated throughout the week and gone off for a manicure and pedicure. John has gone to a tanning booth and the bank. But these are hard working yuppies, up by 5 each morning of the weekday off to their demanding jobs. They work damn hard for what they have.

"Oh she'll get the dishes," Nancy Galbraith told guests once after a party, pretending that a maid would come and clean up after when there was, in fact, no housekeeper. I think of how I do the laundry, the cooking and cleaning up, have become Maria in our little household. I envy Judy and John their normal jobs, their big salaries. I work hard too I think, very hard. Who sees it though, who credits it save for a couple of very old friends who have gone through the rigors of old age together. "I don't know how he does it is," is the dismissive, back-handed compliment a care giver sometimes gets, if anything, to help him keep up his spirits as the years of work drift by. Like writing, I guess. The job has to be its own reward, something you do privately despite what the world credits as worthwhile, useful work. You're down there with the Mexican immigrants, changing the sheets, looking after the children in day care, pushing the wheel chair through the shopping mall.

The morning papers are filled with the latest school shoot out. El Cahon will have it's fifteen minutes of international fame, politicians will wring their hands about the violence in Schools. GRIEVING TOGETHER, the San Diego Register proclaims for the two boys who have died. Santana High School is covered in flowers and teddy bears. In the photo, Governor Davis presents one mother with an American Flag as though the boy had died on the battlefield - and indeed he has. The same front page reports that the twelve year old boy in Florida who beat his six year old playmate to death is sentenced to life in prison. "The culture is in late imperial decline," William's alter ego, Hazard, says of America in the 1970's. What would Hazard think now, twenty years later.

"The cat is taking notes against

His own household. He watches.
Hazard would like once to see
Things with the cat's eyes, flat.

Is it the early morning wake up, the desertion over breakfast only that has me so sour this morning. Look at it flat, Richard. Are you not the least bit jealous of the busy, affluent life your baby sister and her husband have created for themselves. All the toys and gadgets, the 900 television stations - laid back materialism, a la California? Would you not be just as proud if you sold a movie to Hollywood and could afford a million dollar home on the top of a hill? Would you be any less snotty about the bad taste, materialism, sentimentality, violence, and emptiness of what seems to be life in suburban California? There's a line that will guarantee an audience for this book in the great state.

A call to Barnes and Nobel just now and I finally get to speak with a young guy named Eric who is the manager. "Are you ready for us Eric, do you have a microphone set up? "

"No, we don't use a microphone," he says. "They're too loud. If you want one, you'll have to bring it yourself."

So much for being lionized on our triumphant California book tour. Even our hosts have better things to do today. Judy is having a big surgery next week and wants to get her work in order. John plans to go to a nursery to buy some shrubs for planting. This morning though, we did have a jog together in the misty rain and it was fun. He's just coming back after a six weeks course of interferon for hepatitis C and I took a little guilty pleasure in being in slightly better shape at ten years his senior. The injections have left him shaken, but optimistic now that the nausea and depression from the injections is over. He really is a good guy, tries very hard to be a good father and husband.

"Golf is a game than can not be won, only played," the sentimental message of the film we saw on the plane coming to California. I remember William making a conscious effort not to be back biting with colleagues, holding his tongue from delivering the snide barb. A kind of moral training that paid dividends when he had to put up with years of forced silence after his stroke.

"Man and artist, he is working on his ways
so that when he becomes set in them
as old people must, for all that their souls
clap hands, for all that their spirits dance

his ways will have grace, his pictures have class.

I've got to try to be a little more like Hazzard, try like Auden to see, "What grace of spirit can create" as I get older.I've got to keep up my training the way I did in the old days for marathons, day by day, shower by shower, illness by illness. I seem to myself, no where near the finish line, staring out into the California spring.

March 13

Yesterday as I drove Sunset Boulevard up and over the mountains of Los Angeles, I began to see the attraction of living in California. Like any place it seems, money covers a multitude of sins. The last time we visited LA, William had won the Los Angeles Times Book Award and it seemed all we did was spend our days on fog-shrouded freeways in a huge recreational vehicle, a floating cocktail party carrying the winners to readings in different parts of the city. But yesterday, as we made our way to the new Getty museum floating like a marble space station atop the mountain, we seemed to be driving in a new car commercial, the only car on the road as the sun set in the mountains and the freeways below turned into rivers of light, red in one direction, diamond white in the other. I felt like God or Cecil B. DeMill cruising past the zillion dollar houses perched on toothpicks along the canyon walls. We were returning from our meeting with a prospective film agent for my novel, SAPPHIRE DAWN, which I dream of carrying me to Hollywood one day, beret over my balding spot, megaphone in hand.

"This is going to be a tough sell," she said, shaking her head as the birds in the aviary surrounding the office raised hell over her chain smoking - a standard tactic to underscore her talent as an agent if she did indeed pull off the miracle of selling a property to the movies. "AIDS is death," she said, with not the least hint of irony. "That market peaked in the early 90's."

She offered us herbal tea and filled the rest of the day with stories of the coked out old days, what really nice people porn stars were compared to the bastards who actually ran Hollywood, how the upcoming strike was likely to affect my chances of selling my book. (Not good, not good.) She'd seen a lot of years of hard living since her student days in Berkeley, but she's a likeable, gravel-throated, 60's survivor about as street smart as one could find on Hollywood and Vine.

My would be agent lived on the other side of town

from our hostess, however, who lived just down the hill from Whoopie Goldberg and Anthony Hopkins.

"Can't you just see her up there," Betty said, imagining Whoopie's take on the Pacific Palisades spreading out before us from her upstairs balcony. "I'm gonna have the biggest damn house on the highest part of this mountain and look down on everybody in the whole damn valley."

Betty walked hand in hand with Andy Young from Selma to Birmingham, so I knew not to take it awry, just a statement of fact from a person long used to observing human behavior. In the war Betty helped her husband catch German spies for the OSS and sat on them till they lured in the rest of the spy's contacts. In the 50's Ava Gardner and Kenneth Galbraith were her best pals, but she got fed up with the social zoo in Madrid and took her four boys off to Morocco to raise corn. She's as close to being a real live Forrest Gump as anyone I've ever known, with as much integrity. It took a lot of convincing to let her son build her a house out here finally and give up the modest cottage on Staten Island we used to visit when Betty and I trained for marathons together. Cathedral ceilings, marble baths, she seemed a little embarrassed as she showed us to our guest room, more like the night manager at the Ritz than a notable denizen of west LA.

"Anything that can be solved with money is not a problem," she once opined, as opposed to health problems, love trouble, or what have you.

"Easy to say when your husband is a billionaire," I teased her. But Betty has never made much of money. She's a kind of secular Mother Thressa who abhors pretension and loves the earth, its peoples, and the challenge of improving any situation. The story William used to tell about the President of Yale could be apocryphal for Betty as well. Was it Kingman Brewster who looked at the words on the gate above a revered graveyard in the middle of New Haven which read, "The Dead Shall Rise Again," and said to his secretary, "Indeed they shall, the minute Yale needs this space for a parking lot."

Our reading at the Midnight Special Bookstore in Santa Monica had me more nervous than any reading so far on this tour, Carnegie Hall west as it were. Betty sat listening politely to the adulation of a fan who recognized her from my marathon book. Poet friends such as Judith Hall, David St. John, and Rex Wilder chatted with each other as the audience began to enter and take their seats. Jackson Wheeler trooped in with a group of friends from SOLO Magazine who had come down specially from

Ventura. Finally, a big fat guy in long hair and tee shirt got up and made a long pitch for independent books stores and passed around a can for contributions. Almost as an afterthought, he said, "Tonight we have William Meredith and Richard Harteis," and pointed to us.

I thought of telling the story about the big wind bag introducing Rosalyn Carter once who finally gave up talking about himself pointed to the First Lady saying she was a person who needed no introduction, causing Rosalyn to begin:

"Jimmy and I have been traveling all over the country this past month and of all the introductions we've had, I can certainly say that that introduction was the most ... abbreviated."

William and I our well-practiced dog and pony show, alternating back and forth in a kind of poetic dialog.

"I never mind," I told the silent crowd, "if the audience sometimes mistakes one of William's poems for my own." Polite laughter.

When a reading goes well, when the audience is with you and loving the work, it is a spiritual experience of great power. You feel them warming to you, you rise on a wave of self confidence and love for them and the words you deliver can have you on at the edge of tears. A kind of psychic contagion takes over and you feel like Leonard Bernstein dancing on the podium, cajoling the orchestra into rapture.

I remember such a reading last year when we visited a very rural university in Gawhati far to the east in India, almost to the Burmese border, as exotic a place as I've ever been. The airport security involved a virtual strip search before entering the province. Rebels had set up snipers and were blowing up government buildings in an effort to secede from India and maintain the illicit poppy industry. Anything useful to that effort including camera batteries that might go into a bomb were confiscated before we put our bags back together at the airport and headed to the university.

The local tea plantation owner drove us out in his "limo," a mini version of the low-lying, black sedans the SS is always roaring around in in films about the Nazis in the 30's. Darth-Vader-Mobiles. We wound our way through the ubiquitous sacred cows meandering over the school grounds and asked directions of a group of ravishing young women dressed like butterflies in their bright saris. They were so exquisite I asked Smita, the guide assigned to us, if I might take a picture. "I'm coming back to marry that tall girl we spoke to, "I told her."

"Why not," Smita said, completely serious. How I'd come to love this Indian woman the embassy provided to manage our tour. So bright, so self assured. Genuine, with a lovely sense of humor and dignity at the same time. I felt the affection for her I would a sister. All the "local hires" were like this in their own way, in fact. In the matriarchies long before Mrs. Gandhi arrived on the scene, Indian women seemed to have maintained their feminine side and still find an equal place with men in the work force, at least at this level of work. Their American counterparts seemed so shrill by comparison, so territorial and competitive. I asked Smita once in an indirect way after it became clear we were becoming friends, how an intelligent, well-educated person could believe in the phantasmagorical pantheon of Hindu gods, demi-gods, devils and all the rest. She could have dismissed the question by saying they were merely symbolic of man's aspirations, the good and evil we find in human nature. But the legends clearly took on a real reality for her, as well, the way Joseph Campbell might describe the power of myth. She indulged my assessment, but in a shy way she made it known her religion was both fact and fiction, and that she was not overly bothered by the idea that truth might contain polar opposites.

When we finally got to the end of the long corridor in a run down classroom building, my heart sank entering the empty hall where we were to give our lecture.

"Let's give it a little time," Smita said, registering my disappointment.

Sure enough, the room slowly began to fill with the same beautiful girls we had met along the way. They covered the table in a white cloth and added a bowel of purple flowers, bottles of water, name cards, and two carefully gift-wrapped packages. They set up a large sign behind us on an easel which read:

SEMINAR ON AMERICAN POETRY
Sponsored by USIS
Department of English
Gawhati University
March 8, 2000

After a thorough introduction and warm welcome from the head of the department, we were accorded a custom we invariably encountered whenever we spoke during the tour. Two students walked behind us and draped a white shawl about out neck and onto our chest, similar to the chasuble a priest wears when he serves Mass. I gather it is a symbol of respect for a teacher and his wisdom, and the ritual always left me embarrassed, and profoundly moved.

I gave my lecture on American poetry and began to tell anecdotes from my notes and letters written to William by poet friends over the years. The professors wanted to know about the language poets and postmodernism, who, in our opinion, we considered to be the best contemporary American poets . I felt so comfortable and well prepared, it was a joy to talk with them. William added his recollections and commented as best he could despite the aphasia, ending with a short poem that has become a kind of signature poem for him:

A Major Work

Poems are hard to read
Pictures are hard to see
Music is hard to hear
And people are hard to love.

But whether from brute need
Or divine energy
At last, mind, eye and ear
And the great sloth heart will move.

The remarkable girls took us in with their dark, all seeing eyes, seeing clearly what William and I meant to each other, what an effort he was making to talk with them through the veil of his aphasia. “Nothing is unlovely which takes its rise in love,” William has written, and the girls eyes filled with sympathy and admiration for our friendship, and yes, love. I wonder what they would make of the tale I am writing now. Would they understand my quandary about Nick and Natalie. Would they think me disloyal as I struggle to make sense of everything, make it all work for everybody. Would they turn their eyes away from me. I guess it seems less and less likely that this rumination will ever see the light of day.

Today’s mail brought a letter out of the blue from a poet we met at the Virginia Festival of the Book years ago. Some lines in his letter made me remember the loving faces and frank questions that afternoon in Gawhati:

“William is such a genuine talent, and it if weren’t for you, perhaps he would have been silenced by physicality years ago, and a whole new generation of poets and scholars and readers would have missed out on him. You must be given primary credit, coupled with his incredible stamina, for keeping William Meredith's work alive and well in America and abroad."

Such letters, such encounters can sustain a care giver for months. My brother and sisters all think it's cute the way our mother insists that we honor Mother's Day each, relishes the holiday with the intensity of a Soviet worker drinking vodka throughout May Day. But we all need such encouragement along the way, and I have saved every single chasuble presented to me in India, white silk or the simple white cotton I wore that afternoon in Gawhati.

It is the custom too in India for one member of the class to stand up and give a formal summation of what went on that day, to thank the visitor for their visit and in our case, for coming so far to this poor corner of India. And as so often happens in this country, a co-incidence arose that can not be explained in any logical fashion, troubling the heart and moving the agnostic a little closer to the center on the spectrum of faith: The beautiful girl who I told Smita must be my wife, had been chosen to deliver the closing words of gratitude.

And so it was at the Midnight Special in Los Angeles that evening with Betty and the silent audience taking us in as we sang for our supper. At the end of the

reading a woman stood up and thanked us for our openness, for our lives, for the inspiration of our words. She spoke movingly of her own struggle with cancer, and raised practical questions about how one carries on, how love sustains us, how poetry can help as we walk the road each of us is destined to walk. The applause from our colleagues in the audience finally was like a welcome rain in a summer dry spell as we turned off the microphone and headed out into the night for martinis and pasta.
March 15, 2001

"Et la fete continue," our old Russian friend Nikolai used to say tossing back one more shot of Vodka as we sat around Svetlana's table eating ham and turkey, blini and piroshky after Easter services. The whole congregation would leave the darkened church and make a candlelight procession around the church three times to symbolize the nights Christ lay waiting for his resurrection. Sweet old Svetlana, long gone now. For decades she fought the good fight to keep her family afloat and the white Russian dream of the Romanov's return to power. "I was born in the other century," she used to boast, matching us vodka for vodka, by which she meant two centuries ago now that we have turned the corner of the new millennium I guess. How I wish she were around this year when I finally break my fast, and let the spirits carry me into whatever spirit awaits me this Easter. I've managed this Lenten sobriety, for better or worse, as we've made our way up the west coast on this tour, but there were times when a stiff drink might have saved my bacon in a way that caused me a little concern: a danger sign when wanting a drink is actually more like needing a drink?

It would have been great to have a glass of merlot or pinot noir with Fred and Anna in Los Altos, catching up with our lives as the sun illuminated the spectacular garden outside the wall of glass in their living room. Birds of Paradise, Kiwi trees, exotic grasses, persimmons, bamboo, lavender wisteria framing the picture window. These were our best friends in the old days those times William played hooky as the Poetry Consultant at the Library of Congress and came to visit his lover in Morocco. I think Stewart Udall was the only Congressman who ever used the Poetry Consultant, a fact that Robert Frost appreciated and enabled William and Stewart to talk Frost into reading at Kennedy's inauguration the time William drove his old friend through Tucson for a visit at the Udalls.

Fred worked as a quality engineer on the radar system we were building for the Moroccan Air Force and

Anna created sculpture and incredible flower gardens, even though she'd have to trust them to fate and Fatima when we all returned to the US. Their beach house outside Rabat was the only place we could have an adult conversation since they too were without children and not caught up in the sort of family life at the club which preoccupied most of the other expats on the project. They still held the line against boredom and apathy as they settled into retirement and old age in the hills of Los Altos.

Fred sits facing the window by the hour reading the latest texts in sociology and history as Anna installs the new sculptures in her garden that she has created while her students work on their own projects at the local community college. As I waited to see Dr. Brown last week, an elderly couple came into the waiting room that made me think of them. The guy wore a blazer, lime green pants and loafers without socks; the woman, a little too much gold jewelry, a well-tailored dress, and a Gucci bag - standard Palm-Beach-going-to-the-doctor's-office drag. But they were sweet too, pleasant with each other, and cordial to the black lady who admired the woman's handbag. I thought of Fred and Anna reading side by side in their living room, quiet as the New York Public Library, each with their own reading lamp and a glass of wine beside them, silent, but bound together by years of shared experience, exotic travel, gardening. A civilized life and comfortable, with each other for comfort as the rigors of age and infirmity began to darken the bright life they have made together, Fred's cancer, Anna's MS.

"Bandaged comrades," William calls the two trees at the edge of our field down by the river he has used to describe our friendship:

> "How perilous in one another's V
> our lives are, yoked in this yoke:
> two men leaning apart for light,
> but in a wind who give each other lee."

But I miss my comrade since his stroke. I look at Fred and Anna and wonder who will sit with me one day when my time comes to sit in the sun. Not Nicky certainly, who has his girlfriend and plans of some future married life with more children.

"It's too much," Carmen proclaimed to me once when I told her William was twenty five years my senior. "It's too much," she said, "it was not fair of William." Would it have been fair of me had my friendship with Nick worked out - I am about the same age William was when we met. Am I playing out the pattern my own life has fallen into with Nick?

"He's not going to want to spend the rest of his life with some old guy," Ginger summarizes with her usual, brutally honest take on things when I lay the question at her door. And what of Natalie? Is it any fairer to start a new life with her at my age? Yesterday's paper has a photo of Clint Eastwood and his four year old daughter. And Biography is constantly holding up models of such spring winter marriages. (Think of Picasso, think of Methuselah, he says, to himself, ignoring the fact that these guys had great fortunes to sustain such a "lifestyle," as the expression goes these days.) Perhaps my agent really will get me a movie deal for the new novel and inject a little realism into the picture here.

It was a real effort on Anna's part - the MS makes her tire quite easily these days, but she dutifully joined us for the reading at San Jose State, which, of course, proved to be the sole disaster during our tour. The chair of the English Department finally found a microphone when I convinced him that we really did needed it and promptly left the for another previous engagement. The fancy dinner party I promised Anna after the reading proved to be sandwiches, chips, and Coke-a-cola. And the point of our coming to this school in the first place, a chance to see the famous poet friend from William's old days at the Library of Congress who was writer-in-residence this semester, proved pointless as well as she had slipped in her bathroom and refused to be seen in public with two black and blue shiners passing for eye makeup. The only consolation I had was the large audience of students that had obviously been corralled into the reading and the chance to read a poem I'd written for Fred and Ann from Morocco. A bit of journalism really, but it managed to get a few good laughs from the crowd:

Dinner with the Americans

Fred describes his first attempt at
a goodnight kiss at Harvard in the '30's.
His date was a normal co-ed: rode a bike,
wore a fur and dyed her hair green.
"What happened then, Fred?"
"She lay flat out on the concrete
and screamed until the police came."
"Was that before or after you kissed her?"

"Now don't be mean babe," our hostess

says. “He was trying, for pete’s sake. Here
Fred-honey,have some of this coffee liqueur,
made by real Cappuccino monks.”

Angela commiserates with Loretta
on growing up in the south.
“The nuns came to our house when
I said in school that we had books
with pictures of naked people. Well,
those sisters just demanded that mamma
turn over our copies of the Iliad and
the Odyssey, by Homer? And those books
are practically classics.”

George has acquired mid-east manners,
picks his teeth behind the palm of his hand.
“Did you hear about the Colonel? He
walked across the border after he took his
house arrest to his country house. Told the
guard he wanted to hunt pheasant. Can you
beat it? “To think we made him head of the
air force.”

“Now you just watch out,” our hostess

cautions. "He may wind up being your boss
yet."

So it goes, as the novelist has been lately
at some pains to tell us. Still, the turkey
was superior. The room a little too hot,
the talk a little heavy with tales of the
dead king, the CIA, the good old days.
But a superior turkey.

At a mildly formal dinner with compatriots
I'm reassured somewhat. No one supplied
Our hostess with the name of the President
of South America, I accept these Brazilian
monks who have provided the tasty cordials:
Ad majorem Dei gloriam. I'm sure
we are at least as gracious and
dangerous as any people on earth.

March 18, 2001

Seattle on the other hand was a different kettle of salmon. One of my best friends from the Peace Corps days in Tunisia insisted on meeting us even though Alice and Dave had insisted on renting us a car to make the trip more comfortable. Lovely, zany Roger. In the old days he kept his LSD in an orange juice jar and used a fried egg for an ash tray. The intellectual among us, Dada Roger, arms folded in front of him, bushy black hair, heavy black-rimmed glasses, part Peter Sellers, part Charles Manson. He taught the pilots English out at the airport, and considered himself communication central. His apartment was the unofficial headquarters for volunteers coming and going from villages throughout the country, a place to get stoned, plot the revolution that was sure to follow after the war ended in Viet Nam.

But here he was thirty years later, a tenured professor at the local community college, still teaching English as a Foreign Language, with two great kids he'd transplant his heart for, and a calm beauty of a wife, a foot taller than he, mothering all three of them. Last summer he came east to visit his father and we sat on our terrace under the stars with a glass of wine and talked about the old days, our shared history, how, amazingly, years have drifted into decades of personal history. And as he sometimes does when he talks about his friends and family and love overwhelms him, Roger began to cry.

Years later, of course, the hippie scales fell from our eyes, and all the other baby boomers evading the draft and talking revolution with us became stock brokers, or Congressman, or judges, or Microsoft executives. Ironic that the most cynical among us, crazy, brainy Roger should have been the only one in whom Woodstock lived on.

"Our house, is a very, very, very nice house, with two cats in the yard...." Was it Stills and Croft who sang that sweet song in the days of peace and love. Roger and his family actually still have two cats in the yard of the little Victorian house sitting beside Green Lake as though the Enterprise had beamed back to the summer of '68 and Janis Joplin was crooning that the living was easy.

"So, you see how simple it is, Richard," he said, perched over my shoulder as I drove, "You just take I-5 the whole way into the University. I could take you another way, the way Sarah and I take to school everyday on the back roads, but you'd get lost on the way back to the airport. Also, you have to go across two bridges and go through a tunnel. We don't mind the earthquake risk because it's a lot faster and we get an extra cup of coffee in the morning. We'll take you down to Pioneer Square, though, that's where most of the damage was done. Those old brick buildings weren't made for earthquakes, of course, no one ever realized Seattle's sitting on a major fault line. But we don't mind. It's like hurricane in Florida, I guess, you just learn to live with it." Manic Roger, non-stop Roger. "Tonight Sarah has her foreign policy discussion group, but I call it her menopausal discussion group. She loves that. Dave and Alice want you for an early dinner tonight, but tomorrow night we'll have a dinner party at our house. It's a shared party, really, one of our friends just got tenure and Tyler has been accepted for a summer program in Rome. He was in the honors class of Latin and they let that pass for his foreign language requirement. Isn't that great?"

I Imagined Tyler, a carbon copy of Roger in his thick black-rimmed glasses only a head taller, like his mother, flying around Rome on a vespa, the way Roger did on his junior year abroad from St. Michaels. What would a carbon copy of me look like if Natalie and I had a child. Startling to see those words in black and white.

"Go for it," Roger said immediately, without the slightest hesitation, when I told him I was considering trying to have a child. I didn't need to bring up Picasso, or Clint Eastwood or Dudley Moore siring children in their 60's. He didn't ask if I would want a wizened old papa like Hugh Hefner driving me to my first day at grade school.

Time-warp Roger, we'll always be twenty five years old for each other no matter how old we manage to get. How does Gertrude Stein say it, "we are always the same age inside."

I can put up with Roger's stream-of-consciousness monologs, he puts up with my obsessive rumination. At brunch on Sunday morning, poor Roger and Sarah had to wade through the Nick story with me yet again while we waited for Tyler and Lilly to get out of bed and come down for the hash and eggs and stacks of pancakes Roger had whipped up.

I was irritable after my failed foray into the Seattle's night life.

"Where's the social life in Seattle," I had asked Dave when he dropped us off the night before after an early supper.

"Broadway and Pike, up on the hill," he said, astutely figuring out that it was gay social life, I was looking to find.

I did a computer search using the words "gay bar," and Seattle and came up with pages of photos, maps and advertisements for establishments like the Cuff and the Eagle. With William tucked neatly into bed and the night still young, it seemed ridiculous just to go to bed myself, so off I went. I spent the usual gay bar hours "standing and staring" with leather-clad men in smoke-filled bars watching campy "porn" movies from the 50's. The boys did charades of bunk house muggings, and bank robberies, bad guys forcing the blond beach boys to strip down to white, thong-like outfits which covered their front but showed off their bare butts as the wrestled for a whip or gun. At one point in a back garden, a nice-looking guy offered me a hit of dope from his pipe which I accepted. But whatever he was smoking had me paranoid and catatonic for the rest of the night till I traced my way back to the hotel at 4 in the morning, lonely, wasted.

How I'd have loved the bloody mary Roger offered me as he dropped more blueberry pancakes into the heavy iron skillet. Why had I taken on this Lenten abstinence, I asked myself again for the first time of the day.

The conversation shifted from my love troubles to Tyler's as the hungry teenagers began to dig into the feast Roger had prepared for them.

"That's terrible," Lilly told her mother when Sarah suggested Tyler should date other girls. "They're going STEADY." Lilly added reverentially of her older brother and his girlfriend. "That would be so unkind."

"I just think Tyler is young and ought to meet other people sometimes," Sarah said, defending herself. "There are lots of lovely fruits in the garden."

"Oh Mother, please," Lilly continued with indignation.

"Sarah, stop forcing free love on your children," I teased her.

Tyler's young lady was special, he admitted, though he had nothing against the contemporary category of "friends with benefits" by which his peers meant someone with whom to have sex but did not require monogamy. Was that a way to look at me and Nick, I wondered, friends with benefits. Should I start looking for other fruits in the garden? How I envied Tyler about to start off a summer in Rome, his youth. Could it really have been almost twenty years ago that we first met and I dedicated the poem to him that I wrote during the visit. Later in the day I would read the poem at the fancy bookstore along lake Washington, still thinking of babies and the dear friends in the audience, and Roger escaping the hall at the end of the poem, choked up again with his love and joy in the day.

Serving God and Mammon
In the Great Northwest

For Tyler Bourret

Youngish parents jog with baby
In designer buggy, rack and pinion,
though the course is sufficiently
manicured for bowling or shuffleboard.
Wooden shells line the lake shore
anxious for the downy argonauts
to part their trim little butts.
Golden retrievers stand around
anchoring balloons, sport bright
kerchiefs, idiot smiles, their tails
like metronomes for a Mozart piece.
Indeed, a neighborhood search is on for
Papagaena. "Green body, orange cheeks,"
fliers proclaim from every telephone pole
in case, I suppose, some other parrot
lands at the bay window during brunch.

The yuppies of Seattle take their
pleasure on a Sunday morning. Monday,
they'll return to the antique shops and
City Hall, real estate offices and
university. It will be time to service
the BMW, and call the nursing home to

check on mother. Time to ship back the
nephew who filled the house with amplifiers
and guitars and racket, and complained
all summer of their materialism. Time to
worry about that too, and whether another
child is a good idea, if they've found the
right career, if their cholesterol-free diet
will enable them to beat the odds. They
know their love will tarnish or deepen as
they jog to the grave. They do their best with
daddy's Alzheimer's, they're bright enough
to see the future, what a limited concept
arriving is, and so decide to forgive
themselves, the righteous nephew,
the sweet world.

March 23, 2001

How unlike this day in March from last year when we sat in a restaurant in Athens having dinner with Helen and the President of the university after a triumphant reading at the American Center. In an hour I will must leave for Dr. Brown to let him take a look into the bladder to see if the suspicious area is still there and if he must go gardening for the exotic flowering once again. Your penis or mine doctor? I've waited a month while we traveled in California- paid the emotional price I guess - so that we could travel and fulfill our reading engagements. It is tempting to drape the crape, to follow the ominous predilection I feel in my soul, to deliver myself to tears thinking what the news may bring. "Richard is very tense," William couldn't get done telling our Alex and Sydney and Billy last night through dinner which hardly made me less tense. And instead of inviting their sweet friend Billy who was baby sitting the bonzi while we were singing for our supper out west, I simply put them in the trunk of the old Lincoln and drove us home. How great it would have been to hold Billy, talk to him about my life of late, give him a little emotional support. He's had to start the interferon injections for Hepatitis C and it's supposed to be a tough go. Nausea, myalgia, depression. How nobly he seems to be taking it.

I think of my cousin and his wife, both cancer patients - surviving their surgeries and chemo, living their life in the sun, weekends fishing on their yacht, rising at dawn to meet their heavy-duty professional lives. "You have to be strong," Kate says when I tell her of the cancer recurrence. Her eyes are blue and hard as stars over a glass of Chablis as we cruised the intra-costal one Sunday just after Nick returned to Bulgaria.

“This has been a real annus horribilis so far,” I tell her as we glide past the light house and Peanut Island, a huge white vee in the wake behind us as we drive through the aquamarine waters. “I guess Mick Jagger was right, you can’t always get what you want.”

“Day by day, you have to be strong. You just have to do what has to be done.”

From Kate, it not a platitude. She has more than paid her dues. Will I have Billy’s beautiful dignity, will I be able to just push through April, take the treatments, and get on with my life? Will I ever arrive at the sort of nobility William has achieved overcoming the myriad trials life has thrown him this past twenty years. Once again, as when I first met him thirty years ago and he made his idealistic case for charity toward the students as the Bread Loaf Conference fell apart, I will have to look to him to be my model. True friends inspire each other to the good, this the highest gift of friendship, Sr. Margaret told us in Latin class all those years ago. I will need this gift.

March 24, 2001

Nick has sold the sunflower, making the decision about Bulgaria this summer a little more certain. For six years we traveled all over the country in the little yellow Skoda during the summer, Nick at the wheel, William in shotgun, and me spread out in the back with food and a computer and cd to keep us entertained. The three Musketeers.

Perhaps Nick has taken his cue from me this winter when I sold my little ruby Fiat spider. Nick drove it to Florida the whole way from Connecticut one winter, passing us and waving with a big goofy grin from time to time through the Carolinas as he headed south in tandem on our way to Florida. We fixed a dangerous gas leak in Georgia, bought him a fire extinguisher and finally got the little convertible to West Palm and fixed up as a second car for us and Nick to sport around. The one I had exactly like it in Morocco I had to sell when William had his stroke, so the replacement Fiat was like a time machine for me. When I got behind the wheel it was 1975 again and I was young and happy with the future laying ahead of me like a warm day in summer. I thought to give the car to Nick one day, but like his sunflower, the car was now too decrepit and costly to keep up. "I didn't need it" he wrote, "it was too expensive to maintain and I haven't any money." But how shall we make our way around Bulgaria this summer if the government comes up with the money I've requested to organize art exhibitions this fall in New London for our Bulgarian friends from Blagoevgrad? He has said he would welcome a visit, but how can he drive us now. I answer his cryptic email, trying put the best construction on his decision as I can. A matter of economics, I tell myself. Why not take him at his word:

Dear Nick,

I don't want to make too much of the car business. I know it must have been a difficult decision for you. I remember how hard it was to sell the Fiat. But you seem to make decisions with more resolve than I do. Anyway, God knows there are more cars in the world. And it is difficult to drive a car that is not reliable. You know if I had a million dollars, the first thing I'd do is buy you a new Mercedes. No kidding. The main thing now is to keep at your studies and do well this summer. Keep your nose up, old chum. Love, R.

We'll miss Nick's little yellow Skoda. It sure had a lot of heart - an elegant buggy, the kind a school child would draw a car for the refrigerator door with rounded fenders and a flower growing out of the antenna. He had plastered the dash board with a bumper sticker from The New London Day and other mementos from his visit to America. He glued a lucky stone I gave him, a Tiger eye to the rear view mirror, as well as several icons and symbols for the Bulgarian sports teams. Sometimes as we drove and drifted through the lazy summer hours, he would catch me napping and give me a little pinch. I'd pinch him back and watch him blink in surprise in the rear view mirror. His eyelashes were long thick brushes he'd kept from boyhood. He had a habit of batting the eyelashes in a parody of flirtation - a kind of self mockery which said, "oh yes, isn't the boy beautiful" which nevertheless got a come-on smile back from any girl he chose to turn them on. I guess I will always have to turn off the radio for the rest of my life when that southern rock song comes on about the preacher dressed in "black velvet and a little boy's smile." Strong and silent, black hair and deep blue eyes - Bulgaria is filled with Elvis look alikes, but it looks like this one is lost to me.

In the mornings as we'd be checking out of the hotels, Nick would be in the parking lot tinkering with the engine or strapping the wheel chair to a roof rack he'd found in the flea market. When we got up speed driving along the hot valleys it was a little like surfing and when Nick occasionally hit a bump, the rack would fly off its hinges. But we never lost the chair.

The cooling system in the little Czech sedan was the most mysterious part of the car for me. Rubber tubes ran the length of the car like an arterial blood supply system and they constantly needed bleeding since we always carried far too much luggage over the mountains. Every time we came to a roadside water stop, we would fill tanks from the mountain streams to carry us to the next fountain. Going up, Nick's eye was constantly on the temperature gage as it hovered back and forth on emergency red. Going down the mountain, he kept his head half way out the window, nose to the air for the first sign of burning breaks. Once just as the rains began as we neared the top of the Shipka pass, a huge rock came hurtling into the road. It all happened far too fast to avoid. We drove over it with a crash and continued on until a car pulled up beside us and indicated we were throwing gas. Nick and I pushed the car the several hundred meters to the top with William sitting inside. A minute later when we ran out of gas. Now the rain was really coming as we coasted 5 or six kilometers down the mountain's hair pin curves. We made it to a dilapidated old barn in back of a café which served as the local gas station. William and I sat for hours at the little café while Nick and two young guys jerry-rigged a solution for the ruined gas tank. The Bulgarian's power of make-do invention in a Communist-run economy of shortages is nothing short of miraculous. My countrymen have a patience for such daily disasters that is almost incomprehensible - perhaps the single good thing to come out of the old system. Everyone stops to help a stranded traveler since everyone is at some point stranded. You stand in line 5 hours for some stupid bureaucratic paperwork and the office closes just as you approach the window. Well, you go home, you work in your garden, you have some vodka or home made rakia and come back tomorrow. It is the kind of fatalism or acceptance of what you can not change that drove me crazy as a Peace Corps volunteer in the Arab world. I remember my pet lamb dying in my arms in the taxi as the driver lost his way in the medina trying to find an animal hospital. The driver was sorry for me, but it was God's will after all. It could as easily have been a dead child in my arms and would have been greeted with the same sad acceptance of God's will.

This day, however, we were finally on our way with the help of Nick's clever colleagues. Colleague, perhaps the most commonly used word in the Bulgarian language:

we're all in it together, we are all colleagues in the business of living. "Collegi, how do I get to the museum you might ask a taxi driver. "Collegi," bring another round of rakia," the way American blacks call each other brother.

These Bulgarian brothers had installed plastic cokes bottles in the back somehow as a temporary gas reservoir. Eight hours later, dizzy from gas fumes wafting up the rear of the car, having stopped about every 40 kilometers to refill our coke bottles with gas, we limped into Varna, tired but undefeated Kings of the Road.

One summer I asked Nick to pull the sunflower over by a field of sunflowers and we all got out for a stretch and a pee. We wandered deep into the giant stalks, like trees in a magic forests and came out covered with sap and lady bugs and sunflower petals. Getting lost in a field of corn was a game I knew from childhood, but I'd never explored acres of sunflowers, that much dazzling yellow, that much sun covering the valley. We guillotined ten or fifteen of the giant brown heads as a present for Nick's sister and pushed on to Sopot like a traveling floral arrangement. Later that fall, when Nick and I had ended the summer badly and called it quits yet again, William and I made our way back to Sofia by train, alone. Now the sunflower is gone, and I guess there will be no more pit stops amid the sunflowers.

The Sunflowers

Acre by acre, the sunflowers
shed their golden manes and
turn their heads away from the sun
grieving the end of summer.

In June they grew thick as a forest,
erect with the thick sap swelling up
in them almost to bursting point.

Now their heads bend to the earth
from which they rose, each withered stem
the ghost of a spent summer pleasure -
The morning we ran
the whole way to the cape
as the sun lifted like a
flamingo's pretty head
on the turquoise horizon,
How the fishermen we met
along the way spoke humbly
to you as though a god had

stopped by to chat and touch
the silver bellies of their fish
bringing the evening catch
back to life.

The days we stripped
and chased each other, bronze
and alabaster far out into the
sapphire swell of the Black Sea.

The animal joy.
The silky pleasure.
The surf, the shower,
full moon, foam, your
shining body, now gone,
all gone, summer gone,
you gone, relentless farewell
of the railway clatter
dovijdane, dovijdane, dovijdane
as my train makes its slow way
across the breast of Bulgaria
where the sunflowers stand
weeping in the fields, their
seeds falling like black tears

to the black earth, where
they must plant their grief
in the end and go to bed
like good children. Throughout
the frozen winter they must
dream of the sun, radiant
as the joy that filled our days
the summer long so they
may flower again when the
spring first thaws the fields
with her sweet breath and
bid them rise, rise - endless
as my summer love.

March 26, 2001

Not nightmare really, but woke and woke and woke this morning, each time a different dream trying to resolve one of the questions I had the bad sense to raise all day yesterday with Jackie and Kate: go to Bulgaria this summer and resolve the Nicky affair once and for all, invite Natalie to America this summer and start a family, or forget them both and try to live happy, uncomplicated years with my dear William while I have the chance. Jack and Kate each vote for Bulgaria when I corner them privately between runs for buckets of bait, or helping Kate in the kitchen.

In the dream, Nick is drunk. "Are you drunk," I ask him. He bites his lip and shakes his head slowly, side to side, stifling a laugh, and offers me a glass of tea.

What was to have been a day of sailing yesterday became a day of fishing on Jackie's dock because of the big winds blowing all day. I'd vowed not to talk about my life again to them, but failed. In the New Yorker cartoon this week, a wife says to her nervous husband at the cocktail party, "Relax. You're a famous author - no one expects you to talk about anything other than yourself."

I seem to have none of the fame, but all the bad habits of the would-be famous author, though Jackie thinks I'm a star. He wants to invite his friends in to have a discussion group of cousin Richie's new novel - a writer's daydream: an intelligent reader who loves your work and doesn't want your help with his unpublished novel or collection of poems.

But it seems no amount of talking this through can help me make the decisions which must soon be made. Can I possibly just drift, and let indecision make the decisions for me. At least for the month of April. Can I just toggle switch this obsessive thinking and live the life of a monk for a few more weeks during Lent. Can I make a conscious decision to stop thinking about something, stop fueling the subconscious throughout the day so that dream life runs amok throughout the night? And isn't that precisely the pathology of obsession, that one can not consciously stop thinking of about the question you would wipe from the mind? I remember the horror my patients lived though when I was doing my psych rotations in the old days and all we could offer was shock treatment and drugs. What could be worse than the hellish torture, the imprisonment in their own psyches, my schizophrenic patients suffered? What a tragedy, as the young people drifted deeper and deeper into the quicksand, like an Alzheimer patient slowly dissolving into non-being. Am I at the edge here? Should I try the therapist my family doc recommended when I raised the question with him. Is it only the money that keeps me from looking into "counseling" as the euphemism goes.

"At least you have options," Jackie dutifully tells me. "Some people don't have anything in their lives to consider or look forward to. But if you have a child, you had better be prepared to raise it the way your parents raised you. it's a full-time job, a full-time commitment."

We sat on the dock among the yachts baked in the sun, despite the winds, or because of them and pulled in a mess of mangrove snapper. A joy to have something to do besides clean the house and prepare meals. Later in the day, Jackie taught me how to filet a fish, dolling out a balanced dose of scolding and praise like a good father. "The tip is the sharpest part, let the tip do the work," he instructed. "There you go, that's beautiful, you really got it now." I accepted his transparent praise, just as I would have from an older brother, remarkable pleased with myself as the pink flesh lifted from the skin in perfect slices under my knife. At first as threw in our lines, nothing took the frisky shrimp that Jackie carefully taught us how to bait so that they stayed live and kicking and attractive to the fish.

"Hook them through the back Richie, not through the belly." I'm not usually too good at taking instruction, but he made it easy somehow.

"Well, if we all we get is a sunburn today, we can at least cook up these shrimp and put them in an alfredo sauce," I told him, just to get in a little self protective ego.

"That's why they call it fishing, Richie" he said, taking the bait. "You have to have a little patience. Otherwise, they'd call it catching."

And sure enough, eventually even William pulled in a rainbow-colored snapper to add to the fish flopping around in the bucket.

What a joy it would have been to drink white wine

throughout the day with our hosts - therapeutic, a way of forgetting. I watched everyone get happier, sloppier, and finally, blotto by the time the palm trees glowed black against the sunset and the delicious fish filed our plates on their terrace. How transparent everything becomes when you are not drinking in a crowd of drinkers - but it is little comfort. The handsome widow who had me walk her home before we left kept saying, "the bedrooms are upstairs." Why didn't I ask her to show me those bedrooms? What an April fool I was.

"Zorba says it is a sin to turn a woman away who has invited you to her bed," I tell William on the way home. He grows silent and sad, says he doesn't want to hear, because he can't have sex anymore. I realize I've compounded the sin, broken the rule we established years ago that I should keep such indiscretions to myself. How could I talk to him of the widow, I wonder in horror. And how can I keep everything to myself.

I tell him my dreams again this morning when he wakes.

"Richard likes man, woman, and animal," he laughs.

"That's what I need," I tell him. "A really beautiful heifer. Solve all my problems. Just you and me and Elsie."

I put my arm around him and we laugh together, a good laugh that begins to clear the bad dreams and burn off the psychological fog. I make his breakfast and read the headlines.

"I wonder what Junior will do now? This could be it the first real test for Bush," I say, reading of the downed spy plane and what seems an ominous confrontation with China. "I'm not sure he and Ms. Rice are up to it." It will be time for the Lehrer News Hour if we don't get out on the intra costal soon for a jog soon with William peddling alongside on his three wheeler.

"Get out of bed," Sandy Holland chides, when I tell her I can't sleep in the morning. "Just get out of bed and get moving."

"Can it really be that simple?" Exercise and cutting back on the booze were always the first line of therapy for patients who seemed mildly depressed when I was doing family medicine.

I think of my friend Betty in the 50's in Spain who picked up her four kids and went off to Morocco to raise corn when the social life in Madrid got to be too much for her. How I long for the good night's sleep she describes in the book she wrote, amid her alien corn, about her life in the Luchas valley. What a model of self-sufficiency she has always been, what formidable inner resources. I guess we all have periods of solitude, either forced or of our own choosing, which seen from without can have their necessary beauty:

"I would take a leisurely bath, thinking again that the rough life is fine if one can have a hot bath after the fields. Pilar then served me my dinner on a tray before the fireplace in the living room. On cool, spring evenings I always lit the fire for comfort; the spring air is decidedly cold when the sun goes down in Morocco. Later on in the summer, when it was no longer necessary, I still lit the fire at nights to keep me company.

Sitting there on one of the straw poufs with my dinner tray balanced on another, I would look into the flames and drowsily review what had happened that day. The house would be so quiet with all the boys asleep, and outside, only the lonesome night noises of the frogs and the crickets broke the velvet silence. I would think then of Ricardo in Madrid and all our friends, being joyously noisy and deciding where to go for dinner just as I was going to bed.

Almost before I finished my dessert, my head would be nodding ridiculously and in another few minutes, the whole house would be in darkness, except for the glowing fire."

But there is another vision of being alone in Morocco that haunts me too. I remember visiting Paul Bowels with William a few years before his death in Tangiers. I agreed with critics that his SHELTERING SKY was indeed perhaps the great American novel and used William's name to secure an audience during a state department visit to Morocco a friend in our embassy had arranged for us.

Bowels too sat alone, taking his meal in font of a fire prepared for him by a woman totally concealed by the haik and little face veil. He told us how the maids in Morocco used black magic and often served their masters love potions concocted from psychedelic mushrooms and poisons. "I haven't left my bed for two years," he announced cheerily to us. "I let the world come to me."

His eyes were like the fire blazing before us. I thought of the terrifying image at the end of Zeffirelli's movie, the hero looking at the moon and the realization that memory is all that connects the dots of one's personality, and watching his memory disappear drop by drop as the fever and madness consumed him.

I can not rise each morning to the challenge of four children and a thousand acres of burgeoning corn, but rise I must, to take the day in hand, to savor the precious drops of life I am vouchsafed with my dear William every day. This must be my Lenten vow until the corn rise tall and green and abundant again this summer.

March 30th

What to make of a replenished thing, to turn around Auden's reflection on a diminished thing. It is far too late and we should be in the brilliant sunshine riding his three wheeler along the intracostal. The valium I took for insomnia has kept me in bed late as did William's threat of a seizure in the middle of the night. The odd sensation about his eye and face, the aura that precedes a seizure or another stroke used to send my heart racing with anxiety. But over the past years sufficient medicine and some food when his blood sugar gets low, has staved off the event.

I lay on the table yesterday in the dimmed examining room, legs spread in those undignified stirrups, waiting for the anesthesia to take hold and the doctor to come in for a look into my bladder. As the palm trees waved their slow- motion greeting along the water's edge outside the hospital window, I thought of yet another friend who has died this month. Incredible to think of Mathias, gone in a week, like snapping your fingers, from AIDS, reminding me of Betty's injunction once again of how fragile is the thread which ties us to life. Mathias, so young, so talented. A painting he did as a house gift for our new apartment when we first moved to Florida takes up the wall over our bed, a huge Picasso-like, Cubist cow blowing kisses in the shape of the letters of the name William. "Yoo hoo, Boys," she seems to be saying, as she waves a fractured rose at us each morning, the painting, a joke based on a tired old bit of German bathroom humor. A big painting, like Mathias, full of color, and humor, and energy. I thought again of the ridiculous greeting card I saw in Seattle of an English bull dog dressed in a clown outfit - red nose, rainbow wig, polka dot bow tie. "Enjoy your life," the legend read, "this is not a rehearsal."

In Bulgaria it is the custom to spill some wine onto the earth when one speaks of the dead, a sad ritual, as though the dead would join us at the party. We certainly drank our share of wine together Mathias, me, Vincent and William. No wine now with this Lenten fast. Come Easter, I'll drink in celebration of his life though, and the joy he brought us all. I'll pray the agnostic's prayer that we all get out alive, fulfill the promise of resurrection which still haunts my soul from my youth.

"I knew my prayers to St. Peregine would work," Kate said, when I called her later in the afternoon.

"Who's he," I asked.

"He's the patron saint of Cancer," she said, and I was struck again by yet another friend who somehow manages a life in the real world as well as a life of faith.

"When the doctor told me there was absolutely no sign of cancer, I told him I could kiss him, but wouldn't. He said, I better not. He just had the flu.

"Oh Richard, I am so happy for you. I knew you would be okay."

"I feel like such a fool for agonizing over this this past month. I mean, this is nothing compared to what you and Jackie have been through." The last time I saw her she was sporting a sleeve that went up to her shoulder to keep the arm from swelling after her mastectomy. "I feel like a real wimp."

"No, when you've gone through it once, it is more difficult when it returns. You focus on it even more."

"Well, it's taught me a lesson. Imagine if I had just had surgery and not waited till after our trip. I tell you, I feel like the scales have fallen from my eyes. I don't know what to do with the euphoria. It's such a minuscule thing, but I feel like I have a second chance in life."

"Just enjoy it."

"I talked to the doctor about the baby idea, remember? He said there is no reason not to start a family. "Go for it," he said. And I've talked with William about it again. He'll be the grandpa. We'll start a little family this summer. And baby makes four. Well, life is short. I'll have to give it a try."

The inside of the card with the clown bull dog on the cover reads: "It's ShowTime!"

Winter 1972

I am walking around in William's head. We are making love. My forehead rests against the back of William's head. William has said this in a poem about one's head:

> We pay more attention to the front end, where the
> face is, Than to the interesting and involute interior:
> The Fissure of Rolondo and such queer places
> Are parks for the passions and fears and mild
> hysteria.
>
> The things that go on here! Erotic movies are shown
> To anyone not accompanied by an adult.

The marquee out front maintains a superior tone: Documentaries on Sharks and the Japanese Tea Cult.

I am diving deep like a great white shark, trust and abandon. We are discovering each other's bodies in savage new ways, but within, I am walking calmly as in a forest where mushrooms grow and a stand of Jack-in-the-pulpit gleams green and phallic in a window of sunlight. Perhaps William will come, dressed in the kimono Jimmy Merrill gave him when they were teenage lovers and serve me a cup of tea. I am outside myself and I am inside William. It is strange and beautiful to be so disembodied. For Hemingway, like feeling the earth move, as I recall. For me, like falling off the earth into my friend. But I have always hated trying to fit homosexual experience into the erotic models and social conventions of heterosexual life in our society. I think of the silly New Yorker cover for February 14th recently: the groom on the top of the wedding cake is dressed in a black tuxedo and the other groom is dressed in a white tuxedo.

We need new rituals, rituals of our own like the poem William wrote for me years ago which tried to make sense of the trouble we had gotten ourselves into and which cousin Betsy had copied out by hand and framed like a wedding certificate for us:

Tree Marriage
In Chota Nagpur and Bengal
the betrothed are tied with threads to
mango trees, they marry the trees
as well as one another, and
the two trees marry each other.
Could we do that some time with oaks
or beeches? This gossamer we
hold each other with, this web
of love and habit is not enough.
In mistrust of heavier ties,
I would like tree-siblings for us,
Standing together somewhere, two
trees married with us, lightly their
fingers barely touching in sleep,
our threads invisible but holding.

We thought of getting married in the 70's, there were lots of Episcopal ministers around to sanction unions between two men and between two women. Just a couple of years ago we danced all night at Joanne and Ellen's wedding. But love and habit seemed to suffice in our busy life together and the trees grew taller and stronger on our Connecticut farm by the river.

Would it be a sacrilege I wonder, a little too Druid, to stand with the beautiful Natalie some summer day under the two oak trees William wrote of and bring her into the family. A private, new age ceremony to say to God and man that this is how our circle is expanding. And if there is to be a new life, that we all share in the attendant soul of that new life. I read an article in Time Magazine in the 60's of all places, that credited some radical theologians as saying the parents were responsible for creating the soul of a child, in the same way on a physical level a child will only speak if loving parents speak to the child, will only sense right and wrong if parents show them the way, will only learn to love if they indeed are loved. The genes would be my own and those of Natalie, but these are far from the only things that make us who we are. The three of us could love this baby, and William as my mate and model for 30 years would surely pass his good soul through and with us into this child. Even at the most basic level, it would be he who had put a roof over our heads, whose spirit informed the land for half a century - the land informing his spirit and poems - who planted these trees, who nurtured them over the decades the way we three would nurture a new baby if it were granted to us.

When William's imaginary Hazard surprises his imaginary mother-in-law talking to his imaginary children, he says he "understands what attention/ is. Perhaps only across such year can it/ happen disinterestedly. Perhaps that/ is why we are vouchsafed three generations-/ they are a teaching device.... How the children unfold like paper/ flowers, watched and listened to." Perhaps can help us watch and listen to a new life if it came to us.

"I need a wife," was my harried sister's standard joke when she had toddlers running around the house. I'll be Natalie's wife, or we'll be William's wife or she'll be ours, and all of us will help raise and love a child if God decides it is a good idea in the brave new world I envision beginning this summer. And sure there will be plenty of friends and relatives who will wish to judge, will call us fools or even worse. But no one will be to blame but me if I don't try for the happiness I see before me. No one has offered to walk in my shoes as William's care giver, even for a day, in the years since William's stroke. The fact that they have no right to judge will surely not keep them from judging - that is the one sure bet in all this in the little Connecticut village where we live.

Today's Palm Beach Post reports: "Dylan's secret wife breaks silence." To give their daughter a "normal childhood," Bob Dylan and Carol Dennis kept their daughter's birth a secret for fifteen years, something I would find very difficult: Meredith. There's a name for a new baby if Natalie and William approve, suitable for a boy or a girl, God willing. And what would Meredith Ilieva Harteis make of this story if he or she ever found himself or herself reading these words.

I hope my dear you will know that your were loved for your own sake, that you were dearly hoped for, that we tried desperately to bring you into this world against taboos that remain fairly strong in today's society, but which may have largely disappeared, we hope will have disappeared, by the time you read this.

I can tell you that when my mother told me once that I was carefully planned, that she and my father tried quite carefully to conceive me, that I was not just an accident along the way in their marriage, that they wanted a boy and that they were ecstatic when I was born - her words made me proud, the first, most primal gift a parent gives. I have always loved them back for the work it took to raise me, the sacrifices required, sacrifices which I will now be assuming, for the life they gave me finally, imperfect as they sometimes were, imperfect as I am. I tell you down the years, I am here, already feeling love, waiting for you.

The Day after Easter- Blue Movie Monday.

The lights of the Greek orthodox Church burned bright Saturday night, but I slithered out into the night as worshipers walked about the Church with candles and celebrated the risen Christ. I had kept my Lenten fast, and planned to go to Church sometime during the day Sunday later, but Saturday night, I felt I had to force myself to go out howling. Night after night in Lent it was the same routine - cook the dinner, do the dishes, catherize William and give him a shower, his pills. And then to bed and the perpetual train chugging us into sleep.

I began to think of myself as a monk who rises each morning for prayer and goes out to work the fields, offering up the boredom and the tedium of these duties the way a monk might offer up baking bread for his brothers every morning, cleaning up the rectory every night before vespers. But now, I wanted to get over the loneliness of Lent, the irritability of not drinking night after night. I thought of the promise I made to myself and to my father when he died that I would work hard at happiness in my life, that I would not spend my final years as desperately unhappy as my poor father seemed to be when he died. It had become so easy just to watch the news and slip into bed with the train chugging away. I felt I had to force myself to go out to the local gay bar, to try at least for a little fun, to talk to someone new, to see what was going on in the world.

A sweet guy, a male nurse with a big grin and friendly way spoke first to me. We had a lot in common, he said. He wanted to know more about my writing. He gave me the skinny on life in the ER in West Palm Beach. After a couple of drinks he told me he and his friend were out to score some cocaine. Maybe I'd like to come along?

"Don't get me wrong. I'm not looking for sex. But we can go to my house," he said.

I agreed to follow them to Classics, a huge country western bar with acres of pool tables, cheap women, weirdos, loud live music. I wasn't sure what I'd wind up doing. The couple of times in my life I'd tried it cocaine, I could see how dangerous it was for me, what it could lead me to. And it seemed to take weeks to get it out of my system the last time - a vague sense of uneasiness in my own skin, a desire to have my brain work take things in in the stoned glow - like seeing with added peripheral. But these guys seemed so normal, so attractive....

"We make about 250 thousand between us," the nurse said of him and his friend. "I guess we blow about $500 a week in coke," he bragged.

Somehow I managed to lose them in the parking lot once his friend scored. Disappointing, but I figured maybe my guardian angel was at work here. It took me years of trying to give up cigarettes, something only bladder cancer could finally cure. What's the Viet Nam quote, "We had to destroy the village to save it." Just what my addictive personality needed, a coke habit at $500 a week. The nurse gave me his email address, but I know when I'm well off and will not add it to my address book.

Cupid's was a better bet. I stood watching the old queens stick dollar bills up the naked dancers' butts then drifting off to the side couches for a "lap dance" or a private session in the VIP rooms. One old geezer dressed in a tank top, tennis shoes, and jogging shorts that looked exactly like a diaper stood playing with a dancer's tits and lolling his disgusting tongue in some parody of passion like something out of Dante's Inferno: Ring three - old faggots are doomed to stand for eternity in their diapers unable to touch the tits of the boy turning slowly in front of them like a chicken on a spit.

"How much you charge for a lap dance," a black guy beside me at the bar asked. "

"I'd do a freebee. You're kinda cute."

"I hate it when white people call black people cute. They mean we look like monkeys or something." A nice edge to him. Threatening me or laughing at me?

"Me Tarzan, you Jane."

"No this here's Jane," he said introducing me to his lover, an aging Tony Curtis, sipping on his vodka while a long haired kid in a gee string tried to get a free drink out of him.

"You wanna come back to the jungle room and swing on a few vines with me and Jane," he asked. "Just the three of us."

It was getting late. His teeth were so white, smiling at me from that black Massai face of his. I looked into his eyes like seeing someone looking out at you from behind a mask. He was in there, a live wire, I could tell.

"After you Bwana," I said.

Jane turned out to be quite the cook and Easter Sunday William and I returned to the scene of the crime for ham and pork roast and sweet potatoes and rice and pineapple upside down cake they had prepared for a bunch of gay friends. They were sweet to William and everyone fussed over serving him his food. The more he drank the louder Bwana got about his life and what he had made of himself. He started bragging about his wardrobe, and after a few joints, one of the lesbian couples demanded a fashion show which he and I provided, parading down the run way in fur coats and pimp outfits from the 70's with wide-brimmed hats and alligator shoes.

"You stole my under ware last night," I said to him, when he had striped down to grey Arizona Jockey shorts.

"Yeah, I liked them. You don't mind do you. Don't you think I fill them out kinda nice."

"Naw, I don't mind. Let's go out like this for the finale."

"You got yourself some purple hickeys, boy. Aren't you ashamed of yourself?"

"War is hell," I said before he planted another sweet bruise on my neck and we strutted into the living room like John Travolta and John Shaft dancing their asses off in a Saturday night fever. Not a very religious Easter Sunday, and I'm not sure my dad would have approved of the fashion show. But he must have put a lamp shade on his head from time to time in the old days. This particular night I did not need a Valium or the sleep machine when William and I finally poured ourselves into the old Lincoln, leaving the den of iniquity to fall, like the dead, into our own clean sheets and dreamless sleep.

April 17, 2001

Sitting in Michael's closet the night he has been named Poet Laureate of Maryland. A closeted poet! I have a comfortable chair in the little niche off his bedroom where I guess Michael has occasional 4 a.m. rendez-vous with the muse. I wonder what poems may have been conceived here.

William's asleep in Michael and Catherine's bed. All the family tucked away where they should be, spread throughout the house and annex where Michael has his real studio, except perhaps for me and Marko, the Mexican boy who rents a room here and helps out in the running of the house. I caught his sweet black eyes throughout the night as he cut the ham and served drinks, looking pretty gay from this gringo's side of the border, but what am I supposed to do with those eyes? "Sweet Spanish eyes, da da da da da da da da da da DA."

If this were not Michael's big night I would ask, "Marco, where do you sleep in this big house? So you teach in the morning too? Would you like to have a night cap with me? Can I check your chiminchanga?" Something clever like this. And probably Michael and Catherine would simply say, "Why didn't you?" if I mentioned it over bagels. But I must behave. We flew to Annapolis today for Michael and Catherine's sake. No scandals please.

I imagine Marko is in the basement, having trouble sleeping too, saying "Why didn't I invite him down here for a beer. He kept smiling at me all night. He's got to be a gay gringo. But I must behave."

Sex crosses the adult male brain approximately every twenty seconds, I believe I read somewhere. Do I need to check into a sex addiction rehab somewhere with Michael Douglas: "Pass the salt peter there, Mike. So, do you believe those Rams last night, wadda game, huh?"

I think of the old Bulgarian joke Nick told me once about the cook who improvises the cheese by hand when there is none left in the cupboard for the stuffed peppers. Ivan Jackinoff, cream of the Russian army. Etc. Get a hold of yourself, Richard. No, don't get a hold of yourself! Say a Hail Mary and think good thoughts as the nuns advised in grade school when even the word sex could elicit a raging boner so strident you lived in terror of its crippling effect inside your tight jeans, sitting at your desk, trying to swell down as the class bell approaches or you near your bus stop and face the prospect of stumbling out in front of all the girls. Ah the good old days.

I think of Deacy's story about finding his grandfather's journal and the final notation the old man made on his 95th birthday. Every year on his birthday he notes, "I woke this morning with an erection and I could not push it down." But the last entry reads, "I woke this morning with an erection and I was able to push it down. I am getting stronger!" Now that's putting an optimistic construction on matters.

But the good old days never come back as Helen always reminds me. "Seize the day!" she scolds. But how often is the day merely daydream these days, the sort I had routinely every morning a couple of years ago when William and I were living in France. I woke this morning....

Davinia Non Commedia

"I do envy your trip to the south of France with its many colorful beaches, the mysterious coves, and the spectacular mountains rising up so abruptly behind them. I read somewhere that Dante's descriptions of the Inferno were inspired by his journeys through this awesome terrain."

Letter from George Strong,

19/2/97

"Count Ugolino dead
Was endlessly condemned
To gnaw the archbishop's head
Where the nape and the skull are one."

"The Couple Overhead"
William Meredith

Every morning at eight
Count Ugolino comes to
gnaw the base of my skull -
cervical vertebrae (C1, C2).
He leaves the spinal cord
intact, so I may
feel his appetite.

He's fast this Count,
rivets me to the dream
with machine gun action.

There is the high wine
of the dentist's drill
The hot smell of pulverized
tooth and bone.

Just as luckier townsmen cease
dallying with their lovers and
think of rising for café au lait
or a butter warm croissant,
Ugolino is gone, along with the
workmen next door who are blasting
a new kitchen out of the stone wall
at the other side of my headboard.

The landlord neighbor, Monsieur Bestouan
is brother to the Count, and deft.
He has by heart the letter of the law,
knows the minute by which he may
begin to terrorize the tourists,
the sum, down to the sou, by which
he may raise the rent. This new
kitchen and the view - off the terrace,
the teal eye of the lighthouse twitching,
up and down, the stone shaft rising

as the sea swells to the full desire
of the moon - the place will take the
foreigner's breath away when the mimosa
fades and almond trees begin to flower.

No use arguing with the dusty boy
who tips his sweet cap and shrugs:
"Excusez moi, Monsieur, c'est
le patron..." He throws up his hands,
fills a wheel barrow with broken tile.

I drift back to bed, my own hands
like clouds caressing the earth -
here light, there shade, here a
mountain peak, there, small island
of pleasure. "Why don't you two take
the morning off," the Count suggests,
and we are over the cliff like a shot
to the aquamarine sea below. We can
not get naked fast enough. I chase him
far out into the waves, he is slick
as a porpoise, white tail bobbing
like a fisherman's float, till

I catch and pin him on the beach.
His brown muscles glisten, rock hard
like the rocks beneath us, the smile
is shy but he does not resist as I
arch over him, erect as the sun
and ah, "The sad inadequacy of lust,"
as Sister Wendy would have it, when
I am jack-hammered out of sleep again
taking instead, the day in hand.

Well, " next time," Marko, 'next time,' the charming, madding injunction Nick laid on me so often before he left and flew back to his adoring harem on the Black Sea. "I let it die, I let it die," as James Merrill says of the avocado seed he has watched sprout all winter long in his kitchen window.

Somehow I managed to get up at 5:30 this morning, and got us packed and fed and off to the airport for a 7:55 flight. And, of course, the airplane broke down and we sat on the tarmac for two hours, the bored stewardess lounging around up front, gossiping about the upcoming airline strike.

"We might still make lunch," I reported to Josephine's nurse on the cell phone. "They're bringing out a new plane for us."

"Why didn't they just come earlier," I hear her ask the nurse. At 95, she is not always in the loop, but on the whole is remarkably astute. This very day she has a new poem in the New Yorker about a man who begins to think about his soul finally as the body begins to give out bit by bit.

This dear woman has been my mentor and spiritual mother from the time I roared over to the Library of Congress in my new Porche, calling her, out of the blue, for lunch when I read she'd been made Poet Laureate. I used to take her to jazz clubs and have her read for my students. She'd write me beautiful notes and succinctly solve any particular crisis I was in at the moment. I can't bear to see her swollen ankles on the wheel chair foot rests, the right hand curled into a brown shell from the stroke, her brave new hairdo each time we visit. I think of William's poem, "Parents":

> They get wrinkles where it is better
> smooth, odd coughs, and smells.
>
> It is grotesque how they go on
> loving us, we go on loving them...

This goes on for a long time. Everything
they do is wrong, and the worst thing,

they all do it, is to die,
taking with them the last explanation,

how we came out of the wet sea
or wherever they got us from.

"I look into a mirror and see a terrified, small monkey,' Josephine says of her face these days. But it is not true. She is the "nightly tiger, fierce and wise, working upwind, the moonlight striping his glade" that comes in William's dreams:

And yet, the wonder is, he is afraid.
At the water hole, one look from dreaming eyes,
From sleeping throat the feeblest of cries,
Will prove ambush enough to strike him dead.
A beast in human dream must go in dread
Of the chance awakening on which he dies.

And I shall wake one morning and find her gone, and what shall I ever do then? Small consolation that she will have possibly woken to a different, and finally perfect reality.

"Richard, the thing I can't abide is having to hide the joy I feel when I take the Eucharist," she told me once over martinis, her eyes filling with tears. "A life of faith is simply not creditable in today's intellectual climate." But for decades her exquisite poems drew the fish in the sand for me, as it were, and like Miss Bishop or Maryanne Moore, she stands as one of the great originals in American poetry. If Josephine, as smart and honest as anyone as I've even met, can choose to believe in God and an afterlife, so might I, I have always thought.

Heartbreaking though to see her amid her last possessions at the final stage of care in her nursing home. Who wouldn't wish to be called away with sight mostly gone and the highlight of the day, the hour the nurse comes to give you your bath.

"Richard, I just think it's so unfair, so unkind," she says of the times intruders have come into her room to steal a diamond star burst broach, priceless delft ceramics right off the walls, even a new dress a visitor had brought. "You just lie there and realize there is nothing you can do. It is so unkind."

Monstrous, rather. How she can not fly into rageI do not know. But there she was in her cramped room when we finally arrived an hour after the dinning hall had closed, shrimp and brie and martinis spread out by her nurse for a snack at least, as though we were sitting her and Eric on their veranda in New Hampshire the way we did summer after summer, lifting a glass to the sun as the last orange crescent sank behind the White Mountains. And still she remains a poet of affirmation. Like the old lady with a cane walking her dog in her poem "Hourglass."

She perfectly understands the calendar and the sun's passage. But she grips the leash and leans on the air that is hers and here.

She's too Catholic ever to do herself in, but even better, is too proud - a solid model, a final gift to us all in an age when throwing in the towel and pulling the plug have become the efficient, sensible approach when the final years of the "trail elderly" prove the final test of one's metal.

"Here's a cartoon for you Josephine," I say, reading from the same New Yorker a few pages after Mr. Forrester rumination:

"A doctor and his intern are showing this patient his x-rays, right Josephine, and the intern says, 'Dr. Horton and I have found something we don't like. Our hope is that you, on the other hand, will grow to like it.'"

How I would have loved to speak Josephine the way I did in the old days and not just pass pleasantries the way one does when you visit someone in the nursing home, trying to keep it light, trying to give heart - though we have at times talked frankly of death - her death, the fact that she will soon die, and she is ready and she is not afraid, waiting, a times a little impatiently for God to take her away. I would like to know her thoughts of Natalie, of my hopes of starting a family. Of creating a baby. Of changing my life forever by bringing a new life into the world in the middle of a life that is far from secure, financially, emotionally.

What would she make of the idea? Would she think me disloyal to William, would she think me foolish, would she wish me well? Her favorite grandson, dead all these years now, smiles down at us with his beautiful good looks, sitting in the very race car that killed him. Father Joe consecrated land in New Hampshire to hold his ashes. She weeps still at the very thought of him. Would she have changed anything, were his short years worth the pain of seeing him die so young, so pointlessly. what would she make of the course I am about to set out upon?

Instead, I gossip about the Governor who we are

about to meet. "I hear Mrs. Glendenning has joined the first wives club, Josephine. Do you think she'll be there this afternoon?"

"They haven't divorced, but she has moved out of the Governor's mansion, I understand. He's taken up with a former student apparently. It's such a pity. She's the one who is really interested in the arts."

"Here Josephine, why don't you sign this New Yorker and I'll give it to Michael."

"Oh Richard, darling, why would he want me to sign a copy of my poem?"

"No, he'll love it, Josephine. One former Poet Laureate to another, waving to him on his big day. It has a beautiful symmetry."

And, of course, Michael did love it. I sat and watched the assembled poets and friends, finally overcoming the last of my jealousy for Michael perhaps after all the years I've watched him rise to his present good fortune. He sat like a Hollywood star, his stunningly beautiful boys in the front row with carbon copies of his good looks, with grandma's blue eyes shining at the end of the aisle as did the mirror images of those eyes in his sisters shining faces. And Michael's proud father, dressed in matching powder blue suit with his wife, "a fantasy in blue," he joked, but more like twin children than proud parents sitting under giant portraits of Lord Baltimore and his wife dressed no less sedately looking on from the State House walls.

I took in all the friends who had come to honor Michael as the Governor plodded on a treadmill of dreadful cliches about Michael's ability to paint pictures with words, his poet's eye, his love of nature.

Lucille Clifton, over her cancer, the recent death of her daughter, winning the National Book Award the year after William won it and she was a runner up, beaming with love and equanimity. Grace and Ken, Ken over his Viet Nam nightmares, almost finished the airplane he is building by hand, Gracie about to launch her new play and finishing perhaps book 49 while she baby sits twin two year old grandsons. Stanley Plumly with wife 7, a bouquet of sunflowers ready to present to his office mate. Rolland Flint's widow, the poet Michael was replacing. Jane Shore and Jane Fox. Al Lefcowitz and Ellen Kennedy. Local culture vultures looking to feed on poetry and advance the art locally, Po Biz, as Maxine Kumin calls it.

Michael raises his hand to take the oath of office and I think of the promise he and Catherine made to take William to live with them in their own house so William will never need to live in a nursing home if I should pre-decease William, as the euphemism goes. I have pretty good life insurance, but I ask them to evaluate and renew their promise each year as the children grow and their life expands. Their commitment is a gift beyond measure and has taken a great burden off me as a care giver.

And Jim Beall, the sweet physicist who worked with William twenty years ago to set up the conference on Science and Poetry at the Library of Congress.

"I'll send you a photo of my new rocket," he promises over mini Key Lime Pie pastries and white wine. "It's a 120 feet. And the satellite is still up there!" Salt and pepper hair and beard, he is still a boy. But I am more interested in his family life. The last time we met he had just re-married and was starting a second family.

"How your new daughter," I ask, "or was it a boy?"

"Kerry's eight now."

"God, can it be that long since we've seen you? How has it been, Jim? Has it been tough raising a child later in life? I mean do you have the energy for it and all?

"My other daughter is 28. She was good practice. Neither one was easy. But I love her dearly. I'll send you her picture too. I have to leave early to get her now in fact." We stand looking at each other, just looking, letting all the years between us flow, until he kisses me on the lips and slips away from the crowd.

Michael makes the rounds of his friends, natural, at ease, unpretentious.

“What an angel Jim Beall is, Michael, isn’t he?”

“He’s a great guy.”

Here Michael, sign this for Josephine, would you,” I ask, handing him one of the beautifully printed broadsides of his poem the Governor has produced for the occasion.

“Sure,” says, opening the Black and gold folder and inscribing the broadside within, “For Josephine, Maryland’s true laureate.”

A fine poem, one of Michael’s best. And absolutely perfect for our mutual dear friend:

Brave Sparrow
whose home is in the straw
and bailing twine threaded
in the slots of a roof vent

who guards a tiny ledge
against the starlings
that cruise the neighborhood

whose heart is smaller
than a heart should be,
whose feathers stiffen

like an arrow fret to quicken
the hydraulics of its wings,
stay there on the metal

ledge, widen your alarming
beak, but do not flee as others have
to the black walnut vaulting

overhead. Do not move outside
the world you've made
from bailing twine and straw.

The isolated starling fears
the crows, the crows gang up
to rout a hawk. The hawk

is cold. A cold is what
a larger heart maintains.
The owl at dusk and dawn,

far off, unseen, but audible,
repeats its syncopated intervals,
a song that's not a cry

but a whisper rising from concentric
rings of water spreading out across
the surface of a catchment pond.

It asks, "Who are you? Who
are you?" but no one knows.
Stay where you are, nervous, jittery.

Move your small head a hundred
ways, a hundred times, keep
paying attention to the terrifying

world. And if you see the robins
in their dirty orange vests
patrolling the yard like thugs,

forget about the worm. Starve
yourself, or from the air inhale
the water you may need, digest

the dust. And what the promiscuous
cat and jaybirds do, let them
do it, let them dart and snipe,

let them sound like others.
They sleep when the owl sends
out its encircling question.

Stay where you are, you lit fuse,
you dull spark of saltpeter and sulfur.

April 21, 2001

Bucking through the unfriendly skies yet again. It's true what they say about the deteriorating air service these days, and two trips north in one week is two too many. Crowded airports, canceled flights, you think you've hit the lottery if Barbie comes down the aisle with a bag of peanuts or some animal crackers.

Friday night Doris met us at Logan's weekend mad house and whisked us out to the Boston suburbs. The first real day of spring, we glided past the Harvard boat houses and newly arrived daffodils tracing a golden thread along the Charles River.

“Oh my God Richard is that a magnolia in bloom,” Doris burst out with the joy of a New Englander who finally sees the light at the end of winter’s dark tunnel. “Yes, it is! I can’t believe it.”

Our hostess had reluctantly agreed to share us the first night with Leon and Anne in Concord, and I was glad for the chance to introduce them since they were neighbors out there in Paul Revere land. Anne’s mother and father had been William’s dear friends since Hawaii days during the war. When her mother developed cancer and was told she would not live, Rochelle decided to go to France for the time she had left and try to paint as she had always dreamed of doing. She did not die, happily, but became a famous painter instead, living decades longer with her husband William in the castle in Provence they bought and renovated long before the area became chic. Talk about a happy ending.

In the 50's, a newly constructed dam in the region began to change the climate, and decades later when I began to visit them with my own William it had become a little paradise. The windows of the guest house looked out onto fields of Iris blooming helter skelter amid the fruit trees. Songbirds woke you in the morning or the calls of the great guard dogs romping down the lane to see who the new visitor might be. The walls of the main house were filled with Roselle's heroic paintings and those of painter friends such as Deibencorn and Pollack. You could have a swim in the lap pool before lunch or sit with a glass of good wine and listen to Bill's delicious gossip about life among the local habitués. It was like living in a Hemingway novel. I'd never lived in a house which had a fireplace big enough to walk into.

In the spring of '97, William and I were living a few hours from them at an artist colony in Cassis and were planning to join their moveable feast yet again when Bill's letter came from St. Martin:

> "Very sad to have to report that my darling Roselle died two days ago. 'I want to be buried in the good earth,' she had said, and we'll respect this wish on Saturday. No mass: c'est moi le prêtre. Once lowered into the grave, the coffin will be covered by roses, roses, never a spray of yew...."

I don't recall anyone weeping that beautiful Saturday before Easter as we stood on the hilltop cemetery from which one could almost see the lake which had given life to the region this last half century. Anne's dark eyes were radiant, like her mother's before her, a benediction on the mourners who had come from various corners of the earth for the funeral. I did not read my poem, only passed it to her before letting a rose slip from my hand onto the fresh French earth that had been turned up to cover her dear mother.

Never a Spray of Yew

The red cliffs of Cassis
spread across the evening sky
like the ragged gash in Christ's chest,
sagging on the cross at sunset.
The mountains glow with an inner light
for just five minutes, then wink out.
The stone slides to ochre, grey,
and slate again as the teal eye
of the lighthouse begins, on cue,
to blink a welcome to the lone sailor
making his tired way across the
deepening aquamarine, home.

It is a scene you might have painted
had your own light not failed.

Instead, today we wend our way
through Dante's terrible mountains
"to say an obsequy" as William wrote
once of another friend from Hawaii
whose heart had burst while he
drew the dog a drink in the garden
under the shade of a small-leafed banyan.

At lunch we will tip a glass of eau
de vie and think of the lime green light
under the mimosa tree William planted
in your courtyard all those years ago
when you first adopted Provence
like Gauguin and Van Gogh
and other "sweet troublers" obsessed
by its unearthly light - how things flourish
when tended to with love, and achieve
with grace the inevitable end.

Your own sweet William will serve
as priest - and why not? Cannon law
ordained you both, nearly six decades
ago when you married each other.
The layman may baptize, why not take

our hand to lead us out of life as well?

The cliché shape of my mind thinks of the that lonely sailor coming into port on his own. How hard for William, for us all. I despair of solving this mystery in my lifetime. (Thoug on the radio last night, I came on a sermon reminding us that Jesus, who conquered death, loved his life, and was terrified of giving it up.)
We can take heart too from Bill's fierce pluck, his brave assessment of your life and death.

So, to die on an Easter weekend we shall call handsome, since now when the season of resurrection floods these valleys with peach and almond blossom, we will always remember the farewell in Moissac-Bellevue, the call for roses, the beautiful life that transformed into light that bright Saturday in the mountains of Provence.

Now Roselle's beautiful paintings hang on the walls of Anne and Leon's house in Concord, large canvases, filled with light and brilliance. The final portraits of the flamenco guitarist she was working on, flourish of red and black passion, so totally there despite or because of the pointillist technique she used as she was going blind. The landscape with barely perceptible sun and crucifix at the center of an infinite line of white, the fields of France that the Pope judged "most spiritual" in the show at Monaco. How lucky Anne is to have had these parents. Her Auntie Mame mother who always wore turbans and carried a foot long cigarette holder. Her elegant father with his keen intelligence and quirky tastes - I remember the final coffee table book he was working on, a complete survey throughout the history of art of every significant image of the human buttocks, male and female, ever created.

Occasionally, he'd write me a question about the "butt book" as I called it, and it became clear in his questions and his anecdotes about gay friends that the subject might be a little more than academic with him. Well into his eighties, the night before a cruise around the world, he spent the night with me and William before we took him to the ship the next morning in Ft. Lauderdale. A friend had given him some Viagra as farewell gift to take long on his cruise, but somehow after William had gone to bed and Bill and I had a nightcap, the subject of pot came up.

"Ever try it," I asked, as I made up the pull out couch for him.

"I tried getting stoned with my grandson once, but it didn't take for some reason." I guess it was clear to him even then that the liver cancer he had wasn't going to give him much time to live. But there didn't seem to be much in life he had not experienced.

"You want to give it another try," I asked.

"I think my grandson was smoking oregeno," he said, a little while later, taking the smoke into his lungs and holding it as expertly as a flower child on the streets of Berkeley in the 60's. "This is very good shit, isn't that what they say?"

He sure was a lovely, lively old guy. I wonder what Anne would make of my getting stoned with her octogenarian father, not to mention what came next.

""You really are a handsome man," he told me. "If you got rid of this gut you really would be extremely handsome."

No one can imagine their parents having sex after

age 30, but I bet she wouldn't mind. Did her father speak of it to her, in fact, I wonder, before he died, our little romp? He certainly had an artists eye for the male form which he proved to me with great pleasure before the night was out.

"Mummy and daddy, loved each other so much, but that never interfered with their becoming the people they were at their core...." Anne said to me at dinner. Did she want confirmation? Was this a part of his life she needed to know about to make her love of him, her knowledge of him complete?

I'm glad I had that night with him, for his sake and my own. Hanging out with people older than you has two advantages - you feel younger, and you learn a little about generosity and drinking life to very last drop. He only worried about the pain of dying, but according to Anne, like Dr. Schur with Freud, at the end there was sufficient morphine to ease the pain. I will sure miss him, his wit, his sophistication, his civilized good will. I'd love to be sitting in the courtyard again with him, gossiping, sharing my little occasional escapades.

Note to Bill D.

"You sure you want to do this," the goofy guy asked me a while back, razor blade in his hand, after he had soaped me up. “It feels great down there. Different. Like you’re twenty years old again. And it’ll grow back if you don’t like it. It’s not like it’s a tattoo or something.”

We’d closed down every bar in West Palm Beach and had become brothers throughout the night. A carpenter from Oregon, wintering down here as a maintenance man at a fancy hotel on Palm Beach. A crazy, athletic, zany guy. A nice guy. Just hanging out, sure of himself, looking for a good time. “God on ya,” he said, after our orgasms, and we slapped hands in a “high five” the way the priest does with the little kids on the way down the aisle at the end of mass.

“Yeah, go ahead, I’ll try anything once.” I said to him as he drew the “good news” through the shaving cream covering my family jewels, turning me into a baby boy once again. And sure enough Bill, it feels great down there. Silky smooth. Makes you want to go jogging all day long. The nuns would certainly not approve, but I’m sure you would find it to your liking if you were spread out on our couch, bemused, and life called for a little friendly experimentation.

I remember how we laughed and laughed once at Jim Maue when we were freshmen in college and shooting the breeze about sex: “Yeah, and if you stick your finger up your butt when you come, it feels really great,” he opined.

Woe! Like who IS this guy, we wondered. Is old Jim a pervert or something? We thought it was about the funniest idea we had ever heard. And I'm sure Brian, and Greg and Paul are still doing their standard missionary duty in the hut each Friday night, never having explored the darker reaches of the Africa of their sex lives.

"What I don't get is, I mean, doesn't it hurt? I mean, man!" my brother-in-law asked me once, guy to guy, beer in one hand, barbeque fork in the other as he turned the hot dogs on the grill. He winced at the very idea of being a gay "bottom," all those weenies stoking his imagination.

"You ever take a good 9 inch dump," I asked him in terms he was likely to understand. "Felt pretty good huh? I imagine it isn't too bad. I wouldn't know first hand, of course."

But perhaps my ship is sailing into the wrong lagoon here, my tone a little too river bottom for the elegant old friend who went back to France with his children last winter and died the death god granted him in the bosom of his family. "The living breath is gone and dust returns to dust." What an idea. What an impossible idea. Yet we had come to Boston once again to say yet another obsequy, this time for William's old navy friend, Harry Hull. Not a "flat earth Admiral" he, Harry Hull had waged heroic guerilla warfare under the sea during in the war, as a sea wolf commander. Almost 90, he died on beach under a full moon after a dinner dance party with his whole family on a vacation in Mexico. Another happy ending. How else could one prefer to take his exit?

I almost couldn't stand the love and gentility of these dear friends, manic with happiness like Berryman or Lowell in the old days in Boston - if only I had an equal share of talent to describe the joy. Doris, our sweet hostess, with her dark Armenian eyes and old world manners drove us out to the little Episcopal Church in Beverly Farms where all the Boston Brahmins had gathered to celebrate Harry's life. But how oddly proud I was of these American blue bloods, middle class boy and ageing hippie I, with their chiseled features, grey hair and tanned faces come to lay one of their own to rest. A middle-aged matron stood in sensible shoes and grey pony tail and belted out the purest, most authoritative Jesu Joy of Man's Desiring I've ever heard in my life. Kim spoke of camping under the stars as a boy trying to learn the constellations from his father, not seeing them drawn there on the night, but finally able to find and identify the pole star, realizing how his father had become that same sure guide for him in life. And Kata learning how to waltz and finally how to become an adult with him. Harry junior turning his father's penchant for being right into ripples of laughter in the congregation but noting finally Harry's often-camouflaged talent for loving. An old man stood and spoke of serving with Admiral Hull in the war, the only speaker who faltered, which the congregation forgave, given the fragility of age and all that was between them. "Mission accomplished, Harry," he said through tears. William stood at his place in the pew to read a poem from the war days and the congregation took on the aspect of the aircraft carrier in William's poem:

> "with her sprung creatures become weak or strong,
> she watches them down the sky and disappear,
> heart gone, sea bound committed all to air."

"Now a military salute," the minister intoned as two sailors, dressed impeccably in blue and white uniforms came to the front of the church, folded an American flag into a perfect triangle and presented it to Catherine. Such precision, the stars all neatly tucked away, the way we had assembled to tuck away and carefully preserve the spirit of Admiral Harry Hull, gone now to his maker. "Thank you," his beautiful widow's firm reply, with a reserved possessiveness which seemed to say, “this is mine, this extraordinary man is mine, his honor and history. I have shared this life. We have created new life in our children and been responsible citizens. I shall relish this solemn moment till the day I join Harry one day again at sea.”

And later in her garden, Neptune, enormous and buck naked, stood with his trident in the middle of the fountain overlooking the Atlantic surveying the scene, while friends drank Vodka and white wine and a line of sailors shattered the air with rifle volleys into the air, scaring the newly emerged frogs back down into the depths.

April 24, 2001

The cruelest month as Eliot would have it? A damn site better than last month with its cancer scare and insomnia and broken heart. A late night knock on the door last night helps me put things into perspective. House guests at my sister's apartment have come to ask how the hot water heater works, an excuse, I guess, to meet some locals and find out what's on in West Palm Beach. The handsome, middle-age doctor has beautiful eyes and smiles a lot. He likes us. His wife, half his age, has long beautiful hair, long beautiful legs. We drink port and open up to each other the way strangers do sometimes, getting right to the heart of the matter: she's just had a second surgery for brain cancer. The screws in her skull hurt her beneath the beautiful blond hair, a wig it seems. The second set of children he's had with her aren't even teenagers yet and will likely loose their mother before they finish high school. She can still remember when she was in high school, walking home during the Three Mile Island accident, covered in a fine white dust. Nuclear dust? Who knows? They remember spring break in Ft. Lauderdale from college days. They've come for a little spring break. Have we been to Key West, do we think they would like Key West?

How can they come to us so full of good humor, polite good manners? I think of Trumbull Stickney, dying himself of a brain tumor. How does his poem go?

"Sir, say no more,
Within me 'tis as if
The green and climbing
eyesight of a cat
Crawled slowly toward
my mind's poor birds.

How can the good doctor keep going to his office each morning, how can his beautiful wife keep cooking meals and helping the children with their homework?

My little monastic rituals, catherizing William first and last thing of the day, loading and unloading the dishwasher, coming to this sleepy journal as the train chugs along in the bedroom next door all seem so unremarkable when I think of that doctor and his young wife standing at the precipice of her death, like two children holding hands in a dark room. And I am holding William's hand, even as he sleeps, and we are four for a moment with our Spanish port, singing while there is time yet to sing.

I woke this morning anxious to come back to this Passage to India. It is taking hold of me now and before we leave for Connecticut, I will fall again into the journals to see if I can recover the joy I felt as we crossed that continent by plane, train, taxi and elephant. I must refuse to look at email before I sit down to this new journal, avoid the distraction of bills and correspondence and the demands of the day. "No one asks you what you were doing those years you disappeared," Alice McDermot reminded me once when I congratulated her on her new novel, her third, in the middle of raising four children and a husband.

"I've put my genius into my life;" Oscar Wilde proclaims on the bookmark lying on my desk, "I've only put my talent into my works." Good old Oscar - Fedora hat, and shoulder-length hair, silk scarf and cape, square jaw. In Varna on the Black Sea there is a disco called OSCAR'S where the very coolest young Bulgarians go to chill out and get laid. But the back of the bookmark reads: "Oscar Wilde is perhaps best remembered for the personal tragedy reflected in the poems 'The Ballad of Reading Gaol' and 'De Profundis.'" In the end, it seems, his genius failed him, poor, broken Oscar Wilde wasting away in prison at the mercy of obsessional love.

I think of Death in Venice and Mann's notion of genius, the flash-in-the-pan sort, pure inspiration, electric and somehow magic versus the plodding, stick-to-itiveness of a lifetime's work, monumental achievement by virtue of accretion. That's really the genius of the love William and I have achieved that I must never forget in the dayliness of our lives. Natalie and Nick must never diminish that achievement, that life in which I have grounded my own for these past thirty years. He is still the same person who defended the hippie rebels at Bread Loaf all those years ago, the friend who I drove to Florida in my Porsche when we had had enough winter, the friend who left me a love poem for my birthday on the picnic table as we drove across Canada, the friend who drove me to his friends in his Mercedes roadster for decades of martinis and Connecticut dinner parties, who took me to visit Auden for a week when I was 25, who buried my little dog when I was off in Spain visiting Carmen, who I took possession of, who gave me freedom, who never wavered in his love.

"Is he becoming invasive in the relationship," my family doctor asked me once when I told him the emotional mess I had gotten myself into with Nick. It was a shocking idea, but correct, I guess. "Triangular relationships never work," my mother chided me once with her remarkable talent for occasionally transcending her sweet, grandma-like persona in a Klieg-light burst of accuracy and insight. Has it been any easier, any fairer for Nick, living with two "married" guys, doing his best not to hurt anyone while being a loving friend to both, and thinking too of his own needs, his own future. Even now, I marvel at the sentimental paperweight resting on the bookshelf he gave me several years ago for my birthday with such shy pleasure. A yellow bird is caught in a crystal ball, iridescent snow floating about when turned upside down. But a mirror image of the yellow bird pecks at the crystal globe from without, as though it would release it's own reflection imprisoned within. Which of us is which, which imprisoned which free, Nick? Which breaking in, which breaking out? You never said. You only handed me the gift with a gentle kiss to each cheek and silence. The enigma of our friendship will remain unsolved until the glass shatters and the two frozen creatures fly free.

I must refuse to look at email before I sit down to this journal, avoid the distraction of bills and correspondence and the demands of the day for, first thing this morning comes a simple chit chat note from Nick from Bulgaria, enigmatic for what it doesn't say, talk of the weather and his family. And iridescent snow is falling about my head again, all about my head again. And so a note in return, less enigmatic, but trying to teach myself how to let go:

Dear Nick,

I woke this morning thinking of you. I dreamed about you last night (x-rated), and sure wish you had been here to make my dreams come true. Well, "next time," as you so often and charmingly say. How are you doing old bean? I got a note from you sister on email. She is in Virginia. Surprise. I thought she was going to the mid-west. If she's on the east coast, perhaps we can see her this summer. Still no word from the Government if they will pay our tickets over this summer. Everyone I speak to about it (Dora Boneva, for example) gives little hope. But I still think it may be possible. And, you never know, this new agent may yet come up with a movie deal which will make us more financially secure. Anyhow, I sure would love to bang around Bulgaria in the sunflower again this summer.

I hope you are well and hard at work. I sent a package with photos and notes I have been accumulating over the past weeks - some you have already seen. I got a call from Cybelee Seeds and paid her for your German book. She was very pleasant and said they started off each class with "vo ist Nikolai." Indeed. Well, sweetie I hope you are hard at work on this German (and not some blond German girl! - unless she is also teaching you German.

I am happy this morning. Because of my dreams? William is well and my book is coming along. I got rid of the cockroaches and the house looks great. Last weeks travel to Boston and Maryland were great. And summer lies ahead with the prospect of seeing you again. Love, R.

May 7, 2001

We've finally made it to Key West. Writer friends Bill and Loretta Cobb have come for a long weekend and after the fireworks at Sunfest, we all pile into my old Lincoln and set the land cruiser heading south. Whenever I see an accident along the road and it's clear someone is injured, however, I feel I have to stop. I gave up being a physician assistant some years ago but many sleepless nights have taught me the folly of not stopping at an accident, even if there are other cars already there. Poor young kid. Apparently her Firebird spun like a bottle before crashing against the cement retaining wall. Bleeding from the nose, but conscious and strong, if rapid pulse. Broken ribs at least, and maybe the pelvis. Air bag clearly saved her life. But she'll have months of recuperation and time to think things through. "Honk if You Love a Blond" her bumper stick reads. By the time the ambulance comes, the Lincoln's battery has gone dead and needs to be jump started. A half hour later, I pass a blue hair who has been sitting in the passing lane and run smack over road debris which has fallen from a truck, ruining my transmission. Hours later I get back from Miami with a rental car and on we go, key by key, bridge by bridge and still make it for the sunset in Key West.

All the tourists and locals gather at the pier and raise a glass as the sun sets, nostalgia for the end of day, but celebration too. Let's have a round of applause for the sun. And let the pleasures of the night begin. The atmosphere is that of a medieval circus, with jugglers, musicians, Houdini characters escaping from their chains, fortune tellers. Loretta takes up with a mime artist with magic wand dressed in a white gown and purple wings, standing in front of a plastic swan filled with loose change and a few dollar bills. Her feet are too big and she has a moustache, but after the sunset she proves to be an exquisitely charming Haitian with an Audrey Hepburn manner who has just arrived from Paris. She tells us in her beautiful accent about a tourist who approached her last night before dropping coins into the swan.

"Fairy, I have a wish."

"What would that be my dear?"

"I want to marry a guy with a big dick and a lot of

money."

"Oh, but I am an angel, my dear. You will have to re-phrase your wish if it is to be granted."

"Okay, okay. I want to meet the man of my dreams."

Our hotel, an "adult resort" is an art deco motel done up in lavender, pink, and orange, with 24 live internet coverage of the "bathing suit optional" swimming pool and pier to the ocean. Throughout the day, the intercom around the pool announces, "Jeff, your weenie is up, Mark, your weenie is up." At 12 on Sunday the bar opens with Kate Smith singing God Bless America full blast on the pa system.

"So, the old guy, what is he to you," the Cuban lady serving at the grill asks me.

"He's my lover," I say.

"Oh, you wouldn't be happy if you know what I was going to say. I was going to say is he your father.

Nope for 30 years now.

I had an old guy once. I fell in love with him. He helped me raise my four kids.

So what happened.

"Well, I was still young, you know.

So you left him.

"Yeah. You know I was young. Oh no. Oh no. Don't drink the coffee here. The coffee in the deli is the best next door!"

Key West for the weekend with the Cobbs. A dream of a vacation. Lots of booze, lots of pretty people. Lots of shopping. The nude swimming pool at our little gay resort. Art Deco. Wonderful place. Everything edged with purple waves.

Last night at Blue Heaven, and the sunset ritual each night. The fairy from Haiti, standing silent against the sunset in mime. Still almost couldn't tell he was in drag.

"Isn't it amazing," I said to the hunk in the living room after I had finally found David. You walk into a living room and see the last person in the world you would ever want to see again, ever." Good old Jill, the broad who said to Nick, "Which one of you boys in going to walk me home./" I had asked her if she wanted to fuck us both earlier in the night after far too much booze. Actually, Nick met her first to be fair, one night during the Key West Literary Seminar earlier in the winter. We drank and danced all over town, and then she had to have dinner. After dinner, Nick was off in a shot with her since I insisted on finishing my dinner. Left me and took the car keys with him. I forgave him. And I couldn't blame her either. They each go what they wanted. But I hated the disloyalty.

I should have said you ruined a beautiful friendship lasting 6 years. But I didn't. I did say something like You are very lucky I couldn't find a brick that night as I walked past you storefront window.

June 27, 2001

I've rescued Boiko and Girlko from the window sill where the sun is baking their little rubber behinds hard as a peanut. A spider was beginning to weave its home from Boiko's outstretched hand to Girlko's nose crawling along beside him - a good omen. But I think they prefer standing at the base of the screen on my laptop.

"That was Boyko," Natalie told me once after a we each had a tsunami level orgasm. Nice little joke - playing on the Bulgarian name Boiko. And it looks as though it may yet be. Can I stand the joy.

After ten days, the erstwhile Ms. Ilieva sends me the an email saying she will arrive July 12th if I send $700 by Friday so she can get the cheap ticker and visit her mother on the way. Just when I had given up hope of her arrival. So, July 12th comes my little sweetie, via Warsaw.

It was strange and wonderful to tell her she may visit her mother, to have her so grateful. What will our relationship be if we do marry. My wife. I'd like to introduce you to my wife. No, honey, we can't afford a new washing machine. I know Boyko needs new sneakers, but do they have to be $200 Nike's?

Bulgarian women are not un-liberated, but for an American it is a refreshing to find a country of women who are a little more traditional in the way they deal with men.

Once I was talking with another Fulbrighter in Bulgaria, a handsome American woman who was teaching in a rural high school. "Can you believe how the women dress," I asked her. At night, under the trees, young women paraded in platform shoes, tube tops, and outrageous mini skirts for the boys who sat ogling them from the outdoor cafés.

"Yes," she said - elegant mid-calf jumper, greying hair cut in a sort of modified Prince Valiant helmet. "But don't you think they all look like prostitutes?"

I've never forgiven her for that assessment. I think of that country western song where the kid brings his prom date home and his old man says, "Son, that's a cocktail waitress in a Dolly Parton wig."

"I know daddy, isn't she neat!" the kid replies.

So, soon my Natalie comes in her stretch pants, and body stockings. American ladies will turn up their noses and the men will swarm in like bees to honey. But I won't care. We've made a deal. While she's with me, and while we try for a child, monogyny is the order of the day. It will make things wonderful for me and cut way back on the jealousy that seems to ruin my friendships. "Jealousy is a terrible thing, Richard," Lucien told me last year when Nick and I were both vying for Natalie's favors. How much of my pleasure in her is that I won her hand? Adolescent, meat head high school competition. But as old as time. Why deny myself the pleasure? A lion who fends off a younger male who wants to take over the pride for another year. The buck who claims his rights in the rutting season. I want to have everything it is to be human along the way, even perhaps the lesser pleasures.

This morning driving through the spectacular green of the Connecticut forests surrounding Riverrun, our farm on the Thames, I could not stop praying that I would use my life fully and with great charity to William and Natalie and Nicky. Last week I saw a fabulous wild turkey, red neck like a May pole rising out of his fat compact body. How spectacular the shades of brown in the muted rainbow of their feathers, he and his mate, standing unperturbed along the side of the road. No radio on, the black Volvo cruising through the vaulted trees overhead, I could only thank God for the joy of the summer morning. Dr. Quinn had taken his periscope down into my bladder and given me a clean bill of health once again, a six-month's reprieve until the next check-up. And so I am free to live this summer dream. How anxious I am to use the time well, to share these days in love with William, to find out more about this lovely woman who gives herself to me so totally, so naturally. To wake with her some mornings, to kiss her top and bottom, "his plumage fanning his desire," William writes of the wild swans at Coole Park - I see myself entering her front and back, natural, beautiful, she shy, modest in public, but at home free, free, free. And when I die Lord, when I am facing the pain of death, sickness, for, for certain one day I will need to endure this as all me must, let me bear it well, let me not forget the green summer day full of hope and joy that you have given me today.

July 5th

Plein ete, and up far earlier than normal for the second day in a row with Daisy, the new puppy we have brought home to replace Mikey. Putting our old yellow lab Mikey to sleep last summer was the hardest thing I think

I've ever done. "There seemed no point in making heroic efforts to keep him going," I wrote to Helga Sandberg last year in a letter to share my grief.

At the end Mikey would struggle up from the river bank where he used to chase sticks and swans non stop, 'until the cold would seep into his heart,' as William has written of him. With no sight and little hearing remaining, the only way he knew I was there, had any company at all in his silent life, was for me to lie down on the floor with him, arm over his big yellow chest, maybe feeling my own heart beat as he puffed and puffed. The nurse let me be with him as the terrible blue poison was injected and his life slipped away. I knew it was the higher loyalty to end this life of pain and solitude, but guilt still floods over me when I think of how he peed himself with the shock of feeling his heart stop. You never get over such things Helga wrote back, a poet's daughter and a poet who saw my loss and how it stood for all loss.

He came to our door as a puppy, out of the blue like a gift from god when William was just back from the hospital and his stroke eighteen years ago. I worried that Mikey's death would depress William, living his own age and infirmity now. But William is remarkable clear headed about mortality, including his own. We will be crossing the street in London and look the wrong way when he is celebrating his 102nd birthday and a truck will mow us both down. We'll go up to heaven and that will be it. This is what he tells people his end will come to.

So, a year later, full summer, I take on the challenge of a chocolate cocker spaniel puppy who we have named Daisy and wake with the birds and stand under the fresh trees trying to house train her. Little Daisy, the archetype of an Adorable Puppy, a rag mob who covers herself in cobwebs and dust balls as she bounces around the library, eyelashes about a foot long, long brown ears luxurious brunet film star from the 40's, Rita Hayworth, Ava Gardner locks.

"You have a little family again," mother says when I announce the news. And it will be a kind of mini-trial run to see if I can keep my energy and good will for the baby project if a stork wings its way over our house at some point in the future.

"You can always say what you've done, not what you are going to do," my father always cautioned me and so perhaps it is bad luck to talk of a baby. I have so methodically followed my vision of the summer and the future - "the only way to predict the future is to make it happen," the Madison Avenue rubric I picked up from some Nike ad or Addidas. Am I a boomer or what, living my life to a Nike ad. Like a true boomer I have decided to have it all. Will I make gooseberry jam from the harvest William and I picked this weekend. Yes. Will we travel to York to visit my mother despite the new baby in the family? Yes. Will we invite our six young Bulgarian friends to exhibit their work this fall and maybe serve as a wedding party even if we don't get funding from the City Council? Yes. Will I give in and buy the exorbitant rider mower with cart that William has seen on sale in the paper and take on the job of mowing the vast fields of our old farm all summer long? Yes. Will I get back to India in body or at least in spirit? Yes.

William and I are sitting on a train platform on our way to the Taj Mahal. It is so crowded with sari clad women, tourists, and porters carrying huge bags on their heads as they snake among the passengers you can barely move. An old Gurkha comes up beside us and I ask if I may take a photo. His brilliant blue and yellow turban is crowned with the insignia of his regiment. Turban follows the curve of his grey beard framing his dark brown skin and black eyes. He wears a saber, carries a gunny sack and pulls himself up beside William's wheel chair in all his dignity. The wheel chair gives William a little breathing space, but I begin to grow claustrophic. How will I get him onto the railroad car? The expectancy in this mob is almost a physical threat. It is clear when the train comes into the station people are going to dive for the doors. Perhaps the Gurkha will carve the way for us with his saber.

A filthy dog comes up to us and sits beside our luggage. He is covered in sores, his grey skin hangs on his rib cage like laundry, but his head is erect, ears pointed like Anubis guarding a tomb. The beggar who owns him has fashioned a collar of aluminum foil to dress him up a bit. The beggar has no arms or leg, just some misshapen appendages that he moves along on like some odd piece of farm machinery. The train roars in a cloud of steam like Moses parting the red sea and along with it the brown-shirted police who have come to clear the platform of beggars and make sure no one is crushed or pushed off the platform onto the tracks. A kind woman and her husband take us in hand and clear the way for me to get the chair onto the train after William is installed. “Let these gentlemen by please, let these gentlemen by.” The masses settle down and pull out food and water. William nods off with the clacking of the railway cars. Dusk falls on the vast green countryside. Fires set by the peasants to warm them in the night have begun to dot the landscape like summer fireflies. A single electric light has been strung up here and there at a cross road where children call to us and wave. I sit on the stoop of the railway car, refreshed finally with the cool night air, all of India drifting by in post card splendor. From time to time pungent smoke and exotic cooking smells fill the air. A terrible nostalgia fills me. This vast landscape. The beautiful beggar boy. William asleep in the car, 82 years old, taking his rest on the night train to Agra. I think of his poem "Accidents of Birth" with Wendell Barry's beautiful epigraph:

"The approach of a man's life out of the past is history, and the approach of time out of the future is mystery. Their meeting is the present, and it is consciousness, the only time life is alive. The endless wonder of this meeting is what causes the mind, in its inward liberty of a frozen morning, to turn back and question and remember. The world is full of places. Why is it that I am here?"

And in this body and not that? And in this moment of time of all the moments in eternity that precede or follow it? I think of the woman I saw in Calcutta, who I found there in the hot afternoon traffic who came up to us as though to answer my question, a found spirit and return to my seat beside William to ponder it on the page:

Esprits Trouves

I

They come out of nowhere
like ghosts of children
the beggars of India.

Tap, tap, tap on your car window
at a stop light, the baby has been
trained like a monkey or a cobra
to separate the tourist from his rupees.
Only a coin will free her tiny fingers,
the terror in her fixed gaze.

II

In Jaipur, a filthy dog
who sports a tinfoil necklace
settles beside our luggage
at the station, silent as Anubis.
His master follows after, a kind of
human threshing machine
sloughing along on four

or five appendages.
He turns his face to us:
an exquisite rose
rising out of a bag of bones,
until the brown shirts come
with their big sticks and
herd them off the platform.

III

"And what right have you,"
I wonder at the beautiful woman
who has come to us
in the middle of traffic
with outstretched hand.

"But see how prettily I have
painted my fingernail, a little ruby
growing from the center of my palm,"
she smiles: Leprosy which has perhaps
eaten off all her fingers?

"Come on sir, give it up,"
with the cheekiness of a woman

who knows she is fabulous.
"You could as easily be
standing here in the sun as I,
though it doesn't matter finally
which of us it is."

IV

Through the glass, through her eyes,
through our karma
I accept the blessing.
"Have a pleasant day," she waves
as our car swims out into the sea
of fish which is traffic in Calcutta.

July 31, 2001

Sitting in the lobby our time share in Vail, waiting for the laundry to dry, drying out myself after an afternoon of fly fishing. I jogged up to the next village, parked the car, and began to roll William down alongside a picture perfect mountain stream in his wheel chair. We'd taken a fly casting clinic and my skills were pretty good for a beginner. Such a light weight to be casting about. At first the only thing I caught was grass and trees branches and my jacket - nearly my own eyeball at one point. But by today I was able to curve the three lazy s's in the air before dropping the fly more or less where I wanted it. This was to be our last day and I was sure I'd catch something. The stream was loaded with trout everyone assured me. I stopped this morning as I jogged. I stopped to watch a red-harried boy playing for five trout lazying about just under the bridge we stood on. Picture perfect stream, picture perfect, Norman Rockwell boy. I couldn't wait to try my hand.

In the afternoon, I had packed water, granola bars, camera, rod and flies and plotted out a perfect course along the paved bike trail running along the eagle river crashing down the rocks into the valley. An hour later though huge black clouds rolled in and we made a mad dash for the sewage treatment plant we had passed by. We got to their shed just a hail storm came crashing down. A sweet guy named Stan took us in and offered me a lift back to my car.

"The sign says you can only have two 6-inch fish per person. Do they really catch them here by the plant," I asked him. "Don't the fish mind the smell?"

"This is Vail," Stan said. "It don't stink in Vail."

I stopped on a bridge on the way home and stood in the rain anyhow, making perfect casts into now muddy waters no fish would ever be able to see in. It seems the only thing I will catch in Vail is a cold.

After nearly a week my body has adjusted to the high altitude, but it has been tough. Just as you begin to fall asleep you wake yourself with the need to take a very deep breath. And it has been tough on William too. Shortly after we arrived I sat at a café with William watching the gondola. In the summer, mountain bikers replace the skiers. It didn't seem like much of a sport, peddling the whole way down a mountain after a lift to the top. But I got a chance to see them up close by climbing a patch I noticed beside the gondola going straight up the mountain to a little bluff where the road curves by. I stood there huffing and puffing as the bikes flew by me, 40- 50 miles an hour. As I came down I met a ranger who was working with a biker who refused to go to the hospital despite his bloody limbs from a spill he had taken. Would he take the famous old poet William Meredith up the mountain, I asked him when he'd finished with the biker.

His name was Mark, about 30, handsome and very friendly. He was one of the senior ski patrol guys and loved his job. He really threw himself into our tour, lumbering up mountain roads till the very last trail petered out into fields of wild flowers. I had no idea how the thin air could affect you until William stopped dead and said he couldn't go further. I realized how dangerous an idea this had been, given his cardiac and stroke history. He felt better when we got under 10,000 feet but still was huffing and puffing by Sunday morning and I realized it was Emergency Room time yet again.

"Mountain Sickness." It even has a name. So, until we leave, William is on Oxygen and we have taken on another sophistication on his medical care. Tomorrow Chris comes with 6 portable green bottles, enough to get us to Aspen and attend the conference during the day. The big 24/7 machine we have in the bedroom at night we will carry along too and drop off on our way to the Denver airport on the way home. Mountain sickness can make you depressed too I think, has only made my depression over Natalie worse. Wasn't there supposed to be a beautiful woman with you in this picture you may be asking. Whatever happened to the Bulgarian lady you have been plying us with for the past hundred pages. What about Boiko and girlko. Did she miss the plane or what? How cool I had been about it- "if she doesn't come, if it doesn't work, it doesn't work." That was my thinking I believe, or was it? Mostly, I've done all I could now and I must just learn from it. Not let it ruin my life and this vacation and my summer with William. Think of how often Nick's behavior ruined France, Hydra, and the shit I have put William through. It doesn't always end happily.

August 3, 2001

A noisy airplane on the way home to Boston. why won't the three little blond girls behind me be quiet, sleep pleasantly, little angels. Mom and Dad indulge them, proud of their little loud voices while William and I try to cat nap. Crabby is hardly the word for me.

It has been a spectacular drive back to Denver, despite the detrour which took us along yet another crashing stream obviously filled with trout. Halfway to Denver, I pull over and call the hotel to see if we can have reservations for the next two nights but they are full. Tortured again by bad decisions. Why didn't I call everyone when I got up and make it work. Now we will be missing the conference just as it gets into full swing. And this after our triumphant reading last night. That, at least, was a bright spot in this trip.

At first I couldn't believe they actually wanted us to read twice to the two different rooms that formed the Hickory House, a barbeque restaurant in Aspen where the formal dinner was to take place. But it was agreed that when people had finished eating, one dining room would move into the main bar where the band was set up to hear the reading. Loud cheerful conversation filled the rustic log cabin restaurant, fuelled by free drinks. A very crowded place with conferees spilling out on the side walk café.

William and I sat eating our ribs and chicken, monster, western portions as the sunset burned red and purple over us. The meal was bound to ruin whatever control I had of my breathing I thought. But I consciously limited my drink to one glass of wine. On my left the wife of the Libertarian candidate for senate talked non-stop about the wicked FDA and their efforts to suppress a proven cure for AIDS. She would send me video's of the ozone treatment that completely wiped out all forms of viral infection in fact.

"They shoot it directly into the veins," she said, because the virus is, what is the word? You know, doesn't need oxygen?"

"Anaerobic," I suggested.

"Yes, that's it," she said. "At first the blood is

black, but then it's cherry red!"

So incongruous, this beautiful, older blond woman with lovely well-made up eyes, kind eyes, spouting venom against the government as fervently as David Koresh, absolutely certain of her outlandish opinions.

I tried to change the subject to our host and mentioned that Doug and I had re-connected after our days at Georgetown at a class reunion at the Clinton White House. The rest of the table picked up their ears like coyotes and insisted on knowing what the guru thought of Clinton then, now, at the reunion. I didn't realize this was Rush Limbaugh country and when I mentioned that Hilary was a fan of William's poetry, one fat mean looking cowboy across the table launched into a tirade about her homosexuality, and every slander the tabloids had published since she came on the scene.

"A whore is a whore is a whore," he said, cleaning his nails with a small buck knife he had strapped to his jeans.

I was sick to my stomach with this incredible rudeness. I couldn't believe it didn't know what to do. Invite him to the parking lot. Strom off, and refuse to read our poetry. I thought of the well-crafted, elegant, philosophical poems of William's I'd chose to read. One sweet guy we had met from Seattle, a regular guy and very bright took it hard too. We exchanged glances and let it pass.

Old Douglas took the mike and gave a raunchy toast to a Nordic God he's invented and sometimes drags out to shock with his bad-boy iconoclasm invoking him, tongue in cheek to slay his enemies, help him ravish their women, and generally cause chaos all around. The audience roared its approval. Douglas turned the mike over to me off handedly saying we were old college friends and William was a good poet and here we were. I stood there full of chicken and ribs staring out at an audience who looked like they expected an Armageddon match between Hulk Hogan and Jesse Ventura at the World Federation of wrestling.

"Well, Doug and I go back a long way," I began. "One of his more creative ideas when were in college was to buy up all the left over napalm from Viet Nam, secure all the cocoa futures and then de-foliate west Africa. I'm still not sure just how serious he was about the proposition...." We were his guest after all, and by the end of the reading, a few sympathetic souls took William under their wing and gave us a round of applause. Mission accomplished in the land of the Yahoos.

August 4, 2001

Dear Betty,

We've thought of you lots this summer, and it seems you are fine and enjoying yourself as usual. I'm glad of that. It has been a pretty nasty summer for me- planned for a lot of fun and help and more with Natalie from last summer, but she arrived with great attitude and lots of problems and finally wound up in Chicago, probably for the best for all concerned. We've had a good professional life though with good readings in Aspen and Bread Loaf - very successful readings, new friends, old memories: William and I met there 30 years ago this summer. I almost wept at some of the poems I read there on the mountain.

I've complicated my life by taking on a teaching job - just one course, but a whole new philosophy of teaching that I must instruct myself in and develop a syllabus for in a week's time. But I will do it. The local college - an advanced writing course. And the novel continues. And the Bulgarians come for ten days on September 29th and I haven't found the budget for them. Etc. Etc. But I am gald to be alive and to have William with me - and the new superlative chocolate cocker spaniel puppy named Daisy we brought home earlier this summer.

We've been invited to Seattle November 7-9th for an important reading and would come to you the 12th possibly the 13 too after the weekend with my sister in San Diego if you were home and would like to see us. Now we are in Keene. Perhaps I will tip in the journal entry from today that may or may not make it into the book. Our love to you.R

August 24 End of Summer

Sitting in the cool breezes of a late summer afternoon, William and Daisy both asleep, the plastic blinds flop in and out with the breeze, a summer music. This is the studio where Dorothy lived her last years with her daughter and son in law and the children, a sprawling old Vermont house that used to be an inn. She loved two men in her life, Frost and William and the walls are covered with memorabilia of those loves. A poster sized photo of Frost smoking a pipe standing in field. A photo of William and our old dog Mikey with framed poems set by hand by her daughter in law. She could recite pages of each man's poetry right till she died in her late nineties.

Dorothy could never understand why we loved to visit this house so, she always thought our life so glamorous. We would stop in for a few days on our way home from Bread Loaf with tales of all the writer friends, the goings on, the gossip. William might speak of how John Irving's new novel was coming along, what editing he had suggested. Toni Morrison, John Ciardi, Maxine Kumin who introduced us exactly thirty years ago this summer.

"There's a cute guy with long hair and cut off painter pants at the bar," Maxine had informed William. We had struck up a conversation. I held forth in my hippiese: "Anyone who wants to go to bed with me, has to say out loud, I want to go to bed with you." Two lonely years of too much hash and a ruined love affair with my roommate had me not a little unsure of what people meant, what they wanted from me. Was the lamp making love to the ceiling? Did the man at the train station who asked for the time have something else in mind? I was at the point in life when you realize that people were always saying more than one thing at once, had ulterior motives, disseminated. Nothing about language was sure for me.

"I want to go to bed with you," William said shyly.

"Say it again louder, I said. And he did. And we did throughout the night. I read my poems, I sang songs I'd written, we talked of who we were and watched the sun come up over the green mountains before he drove off with his protégé, Gayle Jones, in the little 180 SL. I was sure that would be the last I would ever see of William Meredith but then an invitation came to visit him at Riverrun, as he had named the little farm and nursery he had on the Thames in New London, and for thirty years we have continued to get to know each other.

A revolution was going on at the conference and long-haired gentle, egalitarian William was hero to the faction that wanted to do away with the hierarchal structure John Ciardi has put in place. And so what began as "star fucking" as Auden said of his early years, became this thirty year friendship that has changed my life. Ed Hirsch writes in an recent email:

".....Have a delightful time at Bread Loaf. I wish I could be there with you. I remember our joy at being there together. Happy anniversary of your meeting William. Sometimes our lives take radical turns, and we follow the swerving road."

How could I have imagined what a winding demanding exhilarating course it would prove to be. When we read in the little theatre, I could barely hold back tears as I read the poems that have sprung up between us over these years. William's account of our love the night a poltergeist ruined the Japanese porcelain that had rested untouched on the shelves since the war, the presence I seemed to walk through late one winter night, scaring me to the point that I refused to stay in the house any longer, requiring an impromptu exorcism candle and all in the dark basement:

The Ghosts of the House

Enabling love, roof of this drafty hutch
of children and friends and pets, and chiefly of the dear
one asleep beside me now, the warm body-house
I sack like a Hun nightly in your service,
take care of the haunts who stay with us here.

In a little space for a long time they've walked,
Wakeful when we sleep, averting their sad glance
When we're clumsy with one another, they look
at something we can't look at yet, they creak the boards
beside the bed we creak, in some hard durance.

And if we're weary at night, what must they be?
Bed them like us at last under your roof,
You who have sternly set all overs to walk

The hallways of the world-hutch for a lucky while,
Speaking good of our short durance here,
Wishing our sibling spirits nothing but good,
let them see these chambers once with the daylight eyes
you lend to lovers for our mortal time.
Or change some loveless stalker into me
before my bone-house clatters into lime.

And my own poem trying to make sense of how we manage this love affair across the years, despite the stroke and heart attack and broken hip and ruptured appendix and the illnesses he has survived.

Einsteinian Love

"I'm sixty-six,"
you said at seventy-seven.
"I'm thirty-six,"
I said at forty-nine.
"you're fourteen," you said.
"You're thirty-six," I said.
We work it out somehow,
over the years, this lovely

mysterious mathematics
whereby we divide our age
and meet each other at the
fulcrum moment of who we are:

there we damn well are,
seeing through stone,
as the brother says,
prisoners of love and time
out of ourselves
infinity equaling zero
and abiding Mobius strip
of friendship
forward and back
my dear, my dear.

So, once again we visit picture -perfect Surry. Little white-steepled church at the foot of the only street in the village winding in the valley. Each house with a bounteous summer garden, stands of sunflowers, quite porches, a fleet of dogs, in this case four border collies to tend to William Meredith Fosher's 350 sheep.

On the day his father gave his oral exams to

William, the first child was born and became the namesake, a sure way to secure a good grade we always tease Fred. And we catch up and share photographs. The white cat who has brought a chipmunk to her friends the dogs is there with the dogs in attendance staring dumbfounded at the chipmunk who is only playing possum. When the photo is taken, he gets up and walks away to the astonishment of dogs and cat. Another shows the bucks all turning on Mollie as she herds the deer off the island for the state park breeding program. Another of dear Dorothy and William sitting on a bale of hay during William Fosher's wedding, William in a straw hat, Dorothy with her cane, like lovers from another age.

How could we not come here Dorothy to slow down, tell stories, run down to the lake, watch the bird life, tour the garden, visit the rams, talk of Frost and our lives and get hard-nosed advice about the tough questions. What do I do now Dorothy. These classes I have agreed to teach are only a week away. This new portfolio method is one I've never used. How will I find the time to grade the papers, who will look after William while I am in class? He will have even less of me now that I have taken on this work. But I will make it work somehow. I look at the new turquoise ring I bought at the Pow Wow when Zona visited.

Indian symbols of life and protection. Beautiful silver and stone. A treat to myself to remind me that I can think of myself as a person who is capable. A person who can accomplish all that is demanded of me, rise to the challenge.

"Haven't you taught long enough to remember how you get these butterflies when the new year begins, "Mary assures me. "Then when the classes begin you are so taken up by the energy of it all, and the work, that you love it and it all falls in place."

I look at the text books on the shelf, the Handbook for Instructors, the blue binder filled with all the philosophy of portfolio teaching. I hear Mary and Fred preparing dinner on the porch, ice tea, corn on the cob, grilled pork loin, salad, cakes and pies and home made breads spread with pure butter. It is time to turn off the computer and help with dinner. It is time to think of the fall, and crack the books. It is time to have a farewell dinner to summer.

August 25

The thing that was irritating my eye was soap I thought as I headed out to throw our old friends' ashes into the ocean. But it proved to be a worm. I was in the lou drying my face and finally at a little ease about the pain in my eye when I found the living worm which had just come from my eye. This after we climbed our way up the hill and brought William's wheel chair and threw flowers and lit candles and watched Zhurich swim out to the little island with his father's ashes and dump them to the breeze as the light grew other worldly and long and the ferries returned from Block island. Good for you Zhurich. Those ashes blowing in the wind against you. Then back home for lobster from Tom from Maine, five each if we wished. And we ate that many and pastries and salad Nicoise and good bread and wine and too much vodka, the best, frozen like oil. And lovely women. An attaché at the French embassy, Zurich's lovely Spanish, Columbian woman, Carmen.. They fought, She cried. So we gave her a book. She said "he will give me nothing." So we inscribed it to her. Kolyo would really have loved it. The funky Sharpe dog a year and half old in Big Tom's lap, Tom says he sleeps with him but he dog pees on him if he rolls over. A big guy. Zurich went to India with him as a boy. They ran hash hish together. Business. Zhurich off to Frankfurt to the book fair for his photography. An artist. Am I? I give out my poems. Give out my booze. Give out my money. I must begin to look after myself the way the Bulgarians do. I am Bulgarian, after all.

September 7th

Letter to Nick today. What in the world to do? I miss him so. I missed him all day on Labor Day where we kayaked together. Rumination all day long. Ruined the day for myself. Now working so hard exhausted. If he were to write saying please let me come to the US. Maybe.

Dear Nick,

End of a long day, I just have a few minutes to write before going to the Post Office before it closes. But I have been thinking of you. All day on Monday, our Labor Day celebration I thought how great it would have been to have you with us there on the beach at Waterford. You remember the beach where we did a little kayaking one day? The weather is at that wonderful moment now when it is still summer, but not hot, and cool in the evenings. The light makes everything look like it has just been washed. Such beauty, and such nostalgia too. You know my life, living with the dear old William who requires so much care who is so noble about what he must endure. Now that I have taken this teaching job for the fall, my life is doubly busy. I am forcing myself to get up early - I have to, to get the work done. But I keep hoping it will become easier as we get into the fall. My new novel will undoubtedly suffer as a result, but I will manage it all, even the Bulgarian artists for ten days, somehow. And the little dog is like having a two year old kid, as well. She wants to have my attention throughout the day and manages to chew anything she can find. So far, the worst has been shoes, but I am sure she will get into a computer cord or some other disaster before it is all over. And I must keep trying to sell the remaining copies of ECHOES and Stoimen's large paintings too. I need a wife badly! I'm actually thinking of hiring someone or giving free rent at least for a little help around the house here.

Perhaps you don't want people asking, but we hope your desire to work on a cruise ship is being fulfilled. Did you have the interview, how does that stand with you? What is your life like these days Nick? Are you in Sopot. Are you working? I got your electronic birthday card signed love, for which I was grateful. But no other word. I know it's difficult to write in English, but think of me as practice! Well, I continue to promise a real letter soon, but for now must print this off and get to the post office.

William joins in sending our love and big hopes that all is well with you and your family. Richard

Rumination

Housman says, " we would never love anyone if we could see past our invention." - Have I learned at last, to give up on my love for Nick, see him for what he is, ie. heterosexual who has not planned me in his future. Nancy says he is the center of my circle, but for Nick I am only on the periphery? I must learn, or accept to put him on the periphery. Housman is a sad image in the Stoppard play we have just seen. He never fulfills his life. Some classic books, some sentimental poetry. What has he to show for his life. What have I? 30 years of friendship with William.

The student in the class room who is mocked by the professor says, I don't mind. "Life," Houseman says, "is minding."

"Love is like a piece of ice held in the hand of a child." i.e. we hold on, but it is constantly slipping away.

"Dust and dreams" are all that are left when we die, and we must indeed gather the rosebuds while we may. But Housman never did. Does his poetry chart my future?

Dear Loretta,

I'll put a set of keys in the mail tomorrow (overnight mail if necessary) to be sure you have the latest set. I made some for the Bulgarian Consul who was there for a few days on his way to Key West recently. Insurance balked, by the by on our transmission blow out - says it was normal wear for a car that age. Piss me off. But I am still fighting them.

Natalie's arrival has been something of a disaster. She is so cynical, aloof, and whining about her future and her problems: her building is being privatized and their subsidized rent no longer applies. Also, apparently she must take additional computer courses for her degree to remain valid. So, she is Nicky ten times over in terms of her needs. How do I do this to myself. The 150 pages or so I have ruminating on her arrival and family etc, seem to be down the drain: aside from that Mrs. Lincoln, how did you like the play? The City Council said no to our request for tickets for the six artists we hope to invite and I've said we will somehow pay it if we can't find the funding. A good local hotel did say they would accommodate them for the time there are here gratis, however. So, I am encouraged by that. And I sold one of the large Stoimen paintings and made $10K.

It's 50/50 if Natalie will stay the summer. Prisoner in my house once again. The lady seems to be on the make big time- the days here filled with silences while she polishes her nails. I can't believe it. We had a wonderful party for her when she arrived, 20 people. She went to bed protesting jet lag about 9:00 before the fireworks I'd arranged even. Well, you asked. I'm filled with the decision of dis-engaging or seeing it through. God I hate to waste the summer on this sort of angst. We had a clear arrangement before she came, and now all has changed. She talks of family in Chicago she might visit, insists on working to make money, casts her glance at any male that comes within view with a view to? Keys tomorrow. William is fine thank God and long suffering, the one sure thing in my life. How I love him. R.

Dear Natalie,

I was glad to hear you last night on the phone, to know you had arrived safely. I tried to call back after we were disconnected and the phone service was not available. I hope it was just mechanical troubles and that you were not unwilling to talk. I said pretty much everything I had to say in the last long email. I guess at some point you will get the emails I have written. But I don't want to be pressuring you. You should simply know that I am prepared to go ahead with the plan of trying to have a child anytime you feel you want it. I feel I am young enough, and young enough in spirit to produce and help raise a child as a good father. I am willing to make that commitment (and while the woman gives birth, it is nevertheless a real responsibility for a father and something one does not enter into lightly.) If we were to marry after you could be a citizen of the US if you wished and work here legally in a professional capacity. My resources are limited but I am working hard to make a financial future. I've told you I have taken out life insurance with you as beneficiary after William. My life is that of a writer, quieter I am sure than playing in a rock band, but there is a certain amount of glamor in my life with international travel, artist friends, and so on I could offer you. I would try to spend more time in my second homeland, learn its language. Cross cultural relationships are indeed challenging, but can be rewarding for both parties. But again, I feel I have said all that I can say at this point and do not wish to put you off by re-iterating all that we have discussed. If the time comes when you wish to return to Connecticut or spend a summer in Varna or what have you to try for a child, let me know. It is normal that you would wish to follow your star and be looking for the best options to make your life happy and complete. If you decide you want me to be part of that plan, just call. Meanwhile I send you all my very best wishes for your happiness and love, Richard

Call to Nick yesterday. He says he is cooking a fish for his dinner and has taken a room in an old house in Kranevo. Imma ojde riba vof cherno mare. He jokes on the idea of there being other fish in the Black Sea. Charming and sad. Brings back all my agony for him again. Says the rector says he can't take the exam this fall, next fall. "One of these years," he'll get his degree. I guess he sees that he won't get the degree. How I wish I were on the Black sea now. But we have a dog now and maybe Natalie will return. The best thing is to get the house in order and try to enjoy the summer with William. Plan for next year. But remember how Nick was this winter. His affair with Kathy, his aggressive separation from us and our household. He'll always want to be with other people. Me too. So we can't be together. So fucked up.

August 17, 12:35 am

Getting close to the big day. And tomorrow Natalie says to call her. I spent the morning on the phone reading my emails to her. If she returns I will give it a real try again. If not, I'll not pursue it and really pursue my other life. My bet with Nancy. At least I won't feel bad about things though. This will be it. I have paid a heavy price, sending her away. But I won't immolate myself if she says she is staying in Chicago. No anger. Let it drift off then. Let her come to me if she wishes and it will depend where I am then.

Drinks on the river. The taches of light are neon pink, like a school of fish when the sun goes down. Thames here, Thames there. We are living in a Turner landscape here.

My little Yaddo here. Nice. I say to William when we read Partial Accounts, "Will he ever be remembered when the present generation of teacher dies out" that's you Michael , but then we got a request for "The illiterate" recently in a child's book of poetry or poetry for young adults. So perhaps there is another generation. William is percolating through the culture. This is nice. I doubt it will ever happen to me, but it is nice to see it in William, to be in close, and part of the process.

September 10, 2001

Indian summer. I'd rather not have it, I think. Perhaps when the fall really comes and the air is sharp and the river banks here are in flame with autumn, I'll be able to put the summer past me.

"How was it," Tony asked me as we sat on his porch with Peggy taking stock.

"Fucking Terrible. FT on the pleasure scale," I told him. "Too hot, too wet, too stress filled, too boring." I recall the vow I made when my father died not to let myself get as lonely and unhappy as he was when he died. I am not quite yet in the springtime of my old age, as Gore Vidal said on the tube last night, but the older we get the more we are it risk it seems for intolerance of the slings and arrows hurled at us, the general stupidity one finds all around you. How did Dr. Johnson say it, he loved mankind, but hated men? Or Harry Truman: "You want a friend in Washington, get a dog."

So, I did. Or so she has become. The little cocker spaniel that was to keep Natalie from getting too homesick for her own dogs, has now become my own companion.

I remember the photo Natalie showed me of her

dog, a mongrel big as a wolf, lying on his back with a penis the size of a banana and a little American flag tied to his paw, waving. So like a Bulgarian. No explanation for the odd photo. Witty, ambiguous. A little un-announced Rorschach test. I am the American dog who has invited her to the US to sex her up? An innocent snap shot of a beloved pet, the way a little girl would dress up a kitten in baby clothes? What do you see in the picture, a beautiful young woman or a wizened old hag, the psychologist would ask.

"Byzantine," my friend Stoimen says of the Bulgarian character, in his polite, Byzantine Bulgarian way. Even the most uneducated peasant in Bulgaria is like a master chess player compared to most Americans from centuries of getting and holding what you want. A nation of masks, as another Bulgarian friend put it. Just as Bulgaria was forming a modern nation after four hundred years of the "Ottoman Yoke," in came the Russians for fifty more years of repression (accounting for another national trait, the sense of victimization to account for any failures on the road of life.)

In a world where Big Brother really was watching you - sometimes through the eyes of a neighbor who would report any criminal, "deviant," or antisocial behavior like criticizing the government or blowing your stack at a fellow worker, it was best to maintain a flat affect as defense mechanism. With no chance of getting out of the country, no California on the distant shore to which on could escape, you did not burn your bridges with people, because you would be living with them the rest of your life and you could never be sure what power an enemy might hold over you one day. Give him enough rope to hang himself, don't make waves. Never give evidence that you can be caught on of how you truly feel about anything.

I remember how sarcastically she raised her lip, an actual snarl, when I opened my desk drawer to get a pen for Natalie and she spotted some gay pornography there. It was embarrassing for me, even though she's known my bi-sexual nature from the very beginning. Part of her beauty for me was the way she accepted that as natural, even attractive perhaps as though I were one of those androgynous rock stars in a band like KISS or something. Her look said, "ah ha, I caught you, you hypocritical faggot. Just what I thought. Men are pigs, finally." But how do you pin someone on a look?

"So what Natalie? It's a dirty book. So?"

"I didn't say anything. You are too paranoid Richard."

This would be the engine running the rest of my life

if we had had a child with her, I guess.

"Marriage is difficult enough without adding cross-cultural differences," I counseled a friend once when he was divorcing his French wife. Adding gender complexities to the mix couldn't have made it any easier. And, "Just because you're paranoid, doesn't mean they aren't after you."

What would a child have meant in our life, how would it have developed if affection was all I felt for the mother, not real love. "Her first child should be with a man she is truly in love with," one female friend told me once when I was trying to make sense of what happened with Natalie. "She shouldn't be denied that." I think of how often Natalie would close her eyes when we had sex, indulging the act it seemed, for the sake of our shared goal of a child. I would have let biology solve the question and hope for the love to grow...

What a mystery another person is in the act of sex. I think of the joke about the genie who agrees to build a bridge to Hawaii rather than be able to grant a man's wish to understand what his girlfriend is really thinking. It ain't over till it's over, the great yogi says, to which a friend has added, "But when it's over, it's OVER."

Natalie arrived in July desperately wanting to work,

to make money to solve her problems. There she is in Chicago, working full time as a waitress, living with a friend from her ex-husband's rock band presumably. "This is Nasko," he says on his answering machine, polite, coquettish. I can just see him, thin, pale, long hair, with beautiful Bulgarian eyes - eyelashes too long, eyebrows too thick and dark. A kid, with Natalie sitting patiently like a Raquel Welch band aid, chain- smoking, at some second rate club where Nasko is tossing his greasy locks around and the band climaxes in an East European rip off of some hard rock 60's number by Arrowsmith.

I hear all the stupid teen pop songs of my youth celebrating adolescent sexual jealousy: "I want to have Chucky's girl... She's loving him with her body, I just know it." "Is she really going out with him?"

"Guilty, yes I am guilty," I would tell Boiko if he were here and counseling me.

Jealousy is the cardinal sin in the new "Generation X" which has grown up in post Communist Bulgaria, personal freedom and looking after your future the cardinal virtues. Natalie could barely hide the scorn she felt for crate-training a puppy. She had thrown off the shackles of marriage, the way her country had thrown off Communism. "I am free!" she would say protesting her right to do anything she wanted to do. “Like playing tennis without a net,” Frost says of Free Verse. Free living too, my dear. But there she is, going after what she wants with the passion of a Marilyn Monroe, or Madonna. What can I do but wish her luck? What kind of spiritual progress can I make if I hold this burden within? She IS free and what kind of life with her would I have had if we lived on the opposite trench of sex, selfishly going what each of us was after. At some level, people are always using each other, but the level must at least, be subliminal. This rumination won’t really help me get my mojo back. Better to launch into the fall, new projects.

I look at the photos from that Fulbright year in Bulgaria. Me and Beautiful Nick in speedos having swum across the channel, sailing on the Black Sea, visiting the soothsayer Vanga, having an ice cream with Blaga Dimitrova and some other poets at a café in Sofia, standing with William and President Zhelev in his office the day we were made Bulgarian citizens for our work in the culture. Why does my life in the past always seem so golden to me, how to learn to live in the present. Why the constant anticipatory grief for dear William as he moves into his 80's and faces a certain future.

There are new students this fall, people to love as I

have loved students in the past in Bulgaria. One boy, a man really, comes up after class to have me sign a voucher for free tuition. He's served in the Gulf War. Just in communications, but he, like his father who served in Viet Nam is filled with great ambiguity about what he has done. It will be an honor to help him look into that darkness. Do I risk showing him my poem on the Gulf War. What would he make of it. Would he think I meant to insult him personally?

Briefing

"Anyone who dares even imply that we did not achieve a great victory obviously doesn't know what he's talking about."

H. Norman Schwarzkopf

I

The monster reigns.
The day is lost.
The last peasants
take to the hills.
No one is blessing
loaves and fishes.

On the front page
a man in a beret
holds a wrapped baby
like French bread.
Even this littlest
will join the myriad ghosts
who supersaturate
the desert air
and fall into Paradise
like black rain.

It's time to get back to work. Daisy is finally asleep at my feet, werewolf at rest, bear puppy taking a break from chewing every single object within reach that catches her attention. Her legs have doubled in length as though she's on stilts from stretching up to clean off the coffee table of newspapers, magazines, and the notes I've made for my class. We could hire her out to the Pentagon for a paper shredder.

But when she is good, when she is nestled on the arm rest in the Volvo on a trip, the ac blowing her eyelashes back like butterfly wings, no longer nipping at the feathers teasing her from the dream catcher hanging on the rear-view mirror, her chocolate coat so deep in color it's almost black, regal, smiling up at us as we make our way over the mountains of Pennsylvania to visit grandma, then she IS a joy and worth all the effort it has taken so far to house train and civilize her. (Would I had done as well with Ms. Natalie, ha and ha.)

"If there are ashes in your mouth," Daisy says to me with a wisdom beyond her years, "all you need to do is spit them out. Why don't we stop for a pee? You can buy me a hamburger and have a have a big diet coke for yourself."

September 12, 2001

The day after America changed forever. The sun has come up, a perfect early fall day just like yesterday, but the world has changed forever. Just back from jogging yesterday, I turn of the tv to see the breaking news Bettie Chu has called about, mesmerized like some rubbernecking-necking driver gliding by a chain-reaction horror on the turnpike. Filled with the energy of the run, I am oddly objective about it. "Oh boy, we're in for it now. This is bound to mean a world depression. How did the terrorists manage it?" And even, "this will keep William occupied today and maybe I can get some work done."

But throughout the day the images came to crush the heart. It began to sink in that the Grade-B, calamity film shots of an airliner slashing through the World Trade Center in a wall of flame was real, that thousands of people were being destroyed. These were not anonymous peasants drowning in floods in far-away China, earthquake victims in Afghanistan, or Africans dying of famine that every so often catch the world's attention, prompting rock concerts and self-congratulatory relief efforts. Thousands of well-dressed, well educated, young business people were being crushed to death in a river of destruction falling from the sky. People in wheel chairs unable to use the stairs. People jumping in desperation, hand in hand from a hundred stories up.

Nick writes from Bulgaria, just a note: "It is so cruel." And Pancho sends a note of sympathy for what "the monsters" have done.

I remember taking Nick to the fancy restaurant, Windows on the World to show him the mural a friend had painted over the bar: Emily Ellman's clouds, extending the ceiling right up into heaven with a meteorologist's accuracy. The glass windows by our table went right to the floor, and looking down made us dizzy, like stepping out of an airplane. I felt like the devil tempting Jesus with all the world spread below us, the vistas those seen from a mountain top. To be so high filled us with awe. You could not believe it was a man-made thing, this enormous city rising into the sky. It was like a natural wonder in the natural world: the Grand Canyon, Niagara Falls. I remember the pride I felt as an American to be showing my friend from a gentle, rural valley in Eastern Europe this symbol of the modern age, this science fiction tower to the future.

We are not used to taking condolences in the US for such tragedy on our own soil. By the end of the day my eyes fill with tears watching the stunned New Yorkers, thinking of the 200 firemen extinguished when the second tower went down. And a nationalistic anger begins burn in me, and the hope that such an anger will flame into action through our government. Can the world not mourn these innocent civilians, regardless of our nations' politics around the world?

The Cardinal prays at the altar for the dead, but also for the living, that we not now cast all Arabs into hell in our national consciousness, that the principles of democracy and civil rights be maintained. I think of the Japanese internment camps in WWII , MarCarthyism, Selma and Little Rock. Will we keep some balance in our reaction to this evil. I think of how pro-Arab I have become over the years. My Peace Corps experience in Tunisia, working with normal Arab families who were trying their best to be good Muslims, so lost in the modern world, so forgotten by the west. Will I be able to maintain my emotional and intellectual balance as the enormity of this horror becomes apparent. To see the Palestinians celebrating in the streets of Jerusalem...

After the Gulf War, and all that high-tech, sanitary destruction from 35,000 feet, I imagined the serpent in Eden winding its slow way like a random Scud through the empty chambers of the Arab heart. That missal has found its target in my own heart. I worked for ten years on a novel which tried to give a sympathetic portrait of their cause, years which tonight seem wasted. Silence and sadness.

The whole world will suffer now: economically, as depression encircles the world, and in the curtailment of freedom of movement of all people, the fear which has been planted in the heart of the world. And the retribution will undoubtedly destroy more innocent victims. The rules have changed, Americans will have lost their innocence, but this act will leave us all diminished.

On the late night news, Governor Rowland suggests we hug someone. Stupid, sentimental and accurate. My mother has tried to reach me all through the day while my computer is tying up the line. She is remembering Pearl Harbor, needs to be with someone today. But my father is dead. Years ago he sailed out under the Golden Gate Bridge to the Pacific, one of Tom Brokow's "greatest generation," to defend freedom. What would he make of this new challenge to our nation? William's poem from his days as a Navy aviator on carrier ships during the war comes back to me:

> Although not yet a man given to prayer, I pray
> For each creature lost since the start at sea.
> And give thanks it was not I, nor yet one close to me.

This night, we go to bed. I hold the old guy, sweet, shrunken a few inches now by age, dignified and engaged throughout the day in the tragedy unfolding on the screen, in stunned silence. We say the Our Father anyway, and sleep.

September 17,2001

"Life is short, William," I say in preparation for running by an invitation for Nick.

"For me especially," William interrupts. "Funny joke?"

And it is funny, the sort of tone he has taken to his predicament. How can I be so long faced these days given his pluck? The fall has come with its sparkling days, we are paying our bills more or less, our health is stable. My class are going okay more or less. If I am depressed at this point what will happen when things become really dire. Imagine what Betsy is going through at this point in her life with a husband undoubtedly slain in the World Trade disaster. On Wednesday after the attack we get this message from William's cousin:

Hello guys,
Thought I'd let you know that John was in 100 world trade center yesterday
morning, on the 100th floor, at the time of the disaster. We have been
everywhere looking for him. He is missing. Please pray for him, and call me when you get a chance. New York is a

war zone. - Love Cuz Bets

Been trying to reach her ever since with no luck. And on the answering machine John's voice says to leave a message in his cheery, self-confident, yuppie New Yorker voice. He'd ridden to the top of his insurance company at an early age, had his offices at the top of the World Trade Center, a new apartment at the top of a fashionable building on the upper east side. A little Scottie who like all members of the breed loved just him. A second wife, younger, with dark bangs looking a little like a Scottie

herself, with the dog's same fierce intelligence. Wonderful young people. Betsy in publishing, also very professional, and witty. Always bragging to William about her Meredith chin, the same chin that his great great uncle, Tyler's Secretary of the Treasury, William Morris Meredith sports on the first paper money printed in the US:

I remember Betsy coming to William's 75th birthday party with John in tuxedo. Her gift: one of William's proems written out in calligraphy and framed like an impressionist masterpiece:

Tree Marriage

In Chota Nagpur and Bengal

the betrothed are tied with threads to
mango trees, they marry the trees
as well as one another, and
the two trees marry each other.
Could we do that some time with oaks
or beeches? This gossamer we
hold each other with, this web
of love and habit is not enough.
In mistrust of heavier ties,
I would like tree-siblings for us,
standing together somewhere, two

trees married with us, lightly, their
fingers barely touching in sleep,
our threads invisible but holding.

Oddly personal a gift, she wanted to recognize our "marriage" the way she celebrates her gay friends in New York. Touching. I remember there used to be line in that poem about love going on like the hair and finger nails of the dead, that William took out and which comes back now to me in this gruesome time. The only possible hope for John is that he died quickly, or had the wit to jump when the flames lapped at their heels at the top of the world.

911

"Hello guys, Thought I'd let you know that John was in 100 world trade center yesterday morning, on the 100th floor, at the time of the disaster. We have been everywhere looking for him. He is missing. Please pray for him, and call me when you get a chance. New York is a war zone. - Love Cuz Bets "

An email from Betsy Meredith the day after.

"Hi, this is John. Leave a message and we'll get right back to you."

John's answering machine 9/13/01

Still no answer John, hello. Hello,
Please get back to me. Or,
are you on the line with death,
John, does he have you on hold -
ominous red button flashing?

Are you falling forever like dream
in a river of destruction, have you
taken your partner's hand and leapt
As the flames licked at your heels
and smoke clouded out the sun?

Wave to us John, wave to us
with your sweet smile brother.
Your little Scottie who loves only you,
your wife, fierce, intelligent, who
loves only you, look up to heaven,
through their long black bangs.

We are here below, John, waiting

with outstretched, empty arms.

Dear Nick,

Late at night now. Back from a day in Boston with Doris looking at leaves and having a picnic at Walden Pond where Thoreau wrote his works. A very nice day. We bought three big pumpkins and carved them up. Then dinner with some other friends. A busy day for all, including Ms. Daisy. I wanted to say that if you do wish to come to us, I have in mind that you stain the deck, possibly parts of the house too with a pump machine we have. We'd add $400 for this big job which would bring your "take" to $1000. Your work would be worth more than that, but it is what we could afford now. Believe me you will be busy if you agree to come this fall, which we very much hope. All best, R and W.

Within a week the same dynamic is back. Me frustrated by his lack of interest in sex, filled with recrimination, silences. After the film, GHOSTS WORLDS, we sit in the garden and he finally tells me that the biography he is describing is that of his girlfriend, someone he has been with as long as his wife who has just left him without any reason and gone to France to work. So, he is on the rebound too. "I am going to bed," he says after his cigarette.

This ends any real desire I have to be his sponsor now. I wasn't sure how it would work in Florida, I thought to have another year with him, in these difficult years looking after William. But this is not the answer. There are fine moments. We did the garden today and we were happy. But I have to use him as an employee. He never initiates sex. He doesn't want me. I guess I am sure of that now, though he says he loves me.

Halloween morning he would not make love. Is that why I had sex in the men's room, unsafe sex, that is haunting me now. Today after the work in the garden, I ask him to have a shower with me. Later maybe. And now, "I am going to bed." It is not a comfortable relationship. But I won't make sex part of the equation. For a month or so, he can work here and do his bloody work. His personal life has had little to do with me over the years I see that in his description that he's been with this girl as long as he's been with his wife. I am a fool. But at least he can help me. Don't expect anything more. Now I am just very tired. So very tired. But Florida will be better. Having Nick there will be too difficult. If he can find housing and get his degree, so much the better for him. What kind of love for me can it be that he would tell me of his despair about his loosing his girlfriend? Now at least he is being honest. I've really got to get on with my life. Begin tomorrow.

Sunday November 25th

Grey grey day, heading north on 83 from Cockeysville and a visit with Josephine. My dear Josephine. How I love her. Her distinguished grey hair, swept back in a classic wave, dignified, civilized. She looked better at 93 than anytime I can remember. Over bourbon she worries about Ashcroft and the risk to our liberties that the September 11 measures are bringing about. Her work is being re-cycled through anthologies and magazines. A Polish woman is in the process of translating her. She is living now for the sake of posterity and keeping up appearances for the sake of the friends who visit her. She never thought she would live this long and is now invading her principal to a serious degree. She is very worried that she might have to accept the nursing home's provision for a reduced rate when patients live longer than the expected income they've come in with. Such pride. Really of another generation in this regard.

Big storm with lightning booming around. Nick following too close for the rain. If I tell him not to, bound to be an argument or kick him into hours of silence like a teenage boy who has been rebuked or embarrassed. How will it ever end with him. Sending him back to Bulgarian on the plane he is scheduled for will seem like sending him off to Siberia - he has told me he must stay here and work, that if I really wanted him to stay here, I would have found a way. And I guess that is true.

He's used to the Communist boss system where a patron gets you what you want in life, the man who has the power. He accuses me of not working hard enough to get him a modeling job. Says I didn't tell him about junior colleges and how cheap they are, that I kept him from meeting people, didn't teach him American currency or how credit cards work. Now a great crack of lightening and he blows three times on his chest so that the fear is gone. Strange to love someone from another culture.

At lunch Josephine quotes Hilaire Bellock's "Ode to a Waiter"" "Bye and bye, God caught his eye." When we catch each other's eye now, a sick sort of look comes over his face sometimes. Mostly, I've accepted his rejection, the fact that he will no longer have sex - he says that's all I want, that and to do my chores for me. Now a sad new Irish song comes on and I risk breaking into tears. How will spend the next weeks, how will I be able to let him go? Over over over.

November 26

Back from an exhausting vacation for Thanksgiving. Nancy so difficult, so passive aggressive about the exhibition. She simply changed the date of the opening to the date she wished without telling me. So, the exhibition is to be on Saturday. I pray we get an audience for Stoimen. But he has called to say he can not come anyway, too many paintings to accomplish in light of new exhibitions. And mother, so neurotic, so impatient. Control freak. Well, enough of that. The important issue tonight is Nick. I stuck my foot up his sweater and he scratched my foot as we drove. And I kissed him when we got home and said let us not waste this time. And I invited him to take a shower and he says no. He doesn't feel like it. He really doesn't want to be with me and this is clearer and clearer. So, don't worry about Florida.

December 12, 2001

Back from a run around the block - the three mile circle of road that runs along the river and back home. How naked the woods are with winter. The Thames seems twice as wide and when the moon comes out it is like a huge lake. Yesterday, there was just one swan on the river. Where was his mate? Aren't they always supposed to be in twos? Perhaps he is a teenager and hasn't found a mate yet. Pretty lonely looking creature in the blue black water, the reeds along the shore firm as a bottle brush against the wind ripping across the river.

The run has almost purged me of the deep dreams of Nick last night, the depression I felt on waking. In the dream he has found another friend, some well-dressed guy his own age and has spent the whole day with him somewhere while I looked after William at the beach by myself. Will it be possible not to care if Nick pursues his own life in Florida, falls in love with someone, marries, makes a zillion dollars and lives happily ever after? Jackie Boyle has said he always got the person he wanted, always made himself available, made times together possible and let time work for him. This will be a final try with Nick this winter. But how will I not care, why have I set myself up again for the pain of rejection. I do not enjoy this pain, I am not a masochist. I am not, I am not.

Life is too too short for this sort of unhappiness. When I've run and come back with my blood flowing and sweated and my head clear and Daisy is growling at her squeaky toy, wild and white eyed then it seems possible to contemplate a winter of happiness, despite the constant care for William. I have to cultivate patience with him, see the courage it takes him to keep his optimism. It is a vision I can maintain. But how can I deny my dreams, the terrible sense of loss I woke with, Nick abandoning me to all the work. Cooking, dishes, laundry, house keeping, showering him and every night before bed, drunk or sober, catherizing him while he sits like a little child patiently waiting for the procedure to be over, then pills, and cardiac patch, a good night yogurt, a glass of water, perhaps a prayer.

I've got be more like Daisy. What a lot of spunk this dog has. Last weekend the neighbor's matched South African Ridgebacks came lumbering down our driveway like two stupid dinosaurs swinging their large ugly necks. Daisy stood in shock for a second as though two deer had come in from the woods to eat tomatoes from the garden. She began to bark her head off at the two giants who lumbered off again, confused, chastened. An amazing little dog. She does not know fear. And I have to learn this from her. You know Nick will fade away this winter, like water seeking it's own level after a flood.

I carped a little about it with real estate agent today, explained my misgivings about having Nick in such close quarters in Florida, without getting into the question of real intimacy. "You just have to do what you think is right and see what happens," she advises. And she is right. You do the best you can with your conscious life and hope for the best with the unconscious.

Patsy McCloy is another good model. I stopped by on my run to take up her garbage can as I sometimes do. Still keeps her own house at 94 after her husband's death, sits warm and toasty with all his art surrounding her, the light in her front window burning through the night like a lighthouse on the river atop her hill.

"I told Margaret's nieces they could bring her ashes up here with us," she explains. "But Margaret wanted to have them put in the "Tems," you know the English how they pronounce Thames." She adds the second hearing aid though it doesn't do much good.

"Why don't you come to the college Christmas party with us," I ask, sweating from the jog, anxious to be back out into the cold before I warm up too much in her over-heated house.

"She used to give those nieces lots of money each year, $10,000 each but they said we have jobs and don't need the money. Now they don't give a damn about her."

"So, why don't we pick you up at 5:00. We'll drive you right to the door."

"I think somebody ought to write up Margaret's biography. She was quite a woman, you know," hoping, no doubt, I will take the hint and not forget her one day soon. How cheery she is, how breezy about her age and the friends dying about her every week like last leaves falling from the oaks about her house before the first show arrives.

Well, time to make a fire in the Yotul and prepare the final class for Friday. I wonder if René will finally pull through. When we met during office hours, I confronted him about his absence last week, told him he was in serious danger of failing the course, he explained that his grandma died in Haiti and he had to go back for the funeral. Then two large tears rolled down his ebony cheeks. Designer jeans, gold chains, flashing white teeth, always so clean and smelling of Dakar or Calvin Kline. He is star of the basketball team and the current campus heart throb. He doesn't have much time for English papers. And who can blame him? No way in hell am I am going to fail this sweet kid if he turns in even the shoddiest effort at a research paper. I don't even care if one of his groupies helps him clean up the English.

"Do you have any beauties in your class," Rob Evans asked me when I took this teaching job earlier in the fall, "giving some lad an A pour ses beaux yeux?" He's a lovely old lecher, Rob. He misses his students in retirement.

Today I must try to sell some gold stocks that Douglas has advised me on and invest in the goey duck business. In Seattle last month I finally saw Jim Gibbons shellfish operation. He's got about $25 million worth of the giant clams growing in the Puget sound that he'll harvest over the next three years. Billions of Chinese can't be wrong I guess: Not only do their big necks look like giant penises (peni?) the clam itself could pass for Arnold Schwarzenegger's family jewels in spades. Jim ships tons of the aphrodisiac to Asia each month, and unless we all die of smallpox, this just may be the answer to my retirement woes. Otherwise, I'll be grading English papers till the day I die. Perhaps Douglas will hire me to carry his bags and cut his cigar tips one day as he travels the world like Robin Leech in search of the ultimate lifestyle. A short note form him today in response to my Christmas greeting makes me wish I'd gone into the stock market or dentistry or almost anything but teaching as I face the prospect of looking after myself in my old age:

Richard-- I'll be in Thailand from the 15th to the 4th, then NZ for the winter. Am in Panama right now. The picture arrived-- don't know about the print. I think the duck deal will work. Best to you both for Winter Solstice. Doug

In a message dated Tue, 11 Dec 2001 5:46:21 PM Eastern Standard Time, Richard Harteis <RiverrunBooks@compuserve.com> writes:

> Dear Doug,

>

> I got an email from the shipper which makes me hope that you have

> received the painting safely (i.e. no news is good news, as the expression goes.) I certainly hope you find the painting to your liking - can't

> imagine that you wouldn't. And you should have received the lithograph

> Nancy Frankel sent as well. You saved our bacon this summer with the

> purchase of that painting as you know. I'll always be grateful.

> Where are you this holiday season, I wonder? Any chance business
> will take you to West Palm Beach this winter? It would be great to see you.
> Nick is already there looking for work. Samantha has given him a lead and we are crossing our fingers. He and I are "just friends" these days, and it was probably foolish of me to bring him to Florida. But after 6 years, and
> given the desperate economic situation in Bulgaria I had to try to help him
> in his day dream of making some money before returning to Bulgaria. He
> hopes to get into a junior college and apply for a working visa - wishes to
> go the legal route. But I am afraid his hopes are far from realistic. Ah,
> the things we put ourselves through in the name of love.
> I spoke with Stoimen last night. He is very busy preparing for
> shows in Europe and so will not be here for the show we have arranged for him on January 5th at the Studio Gallery. I've told him you might join me
> on a trip to Bulgaria this summer. We could stop by Vienna and meet him, or meet him in Bulgaria if he's there

and if you do think it would fit into
> your schedule. That is a happy thought to contemplate.
Whereever you are, we send very best holiday greetings to
you and Ancha. R.

> p.s. Your gold suggestions seem to be doing pretty well,
the Harmony Gold, less so, but still good. I thought of
selling maybe $2K worth in order to invest in Jim Gibbons
goey duck operation - an act of friendship as much as
anything, though I think his prospects as a good investment
are high. What do you think?

Christmas catch up:
> Dear Friends,
>   Where is the time flying? I'm like the elves above
trying to put it
> all together before we head south for the winter. But
somehow it all gets
> done, as we say in Pennsylvania Dutch country. My mum
will be with my
> sister in California this winter and so we will spend the
holiday with our
> dear Doris Carlson and the Hull's in Boston this year.
And New Year's will

> find us with Nancy Frankel in D.C. as we prepare for an
opening at the
> Studio Gallery on January 5th from 5-7:00. Please mark
your calendar.
>
> Studio Gallery
> 2108 R Street, N.W.
> Washington, D.C. 20008
> Telephone: 202-232-8734
>
> Ambassador Dimitrov will open the show officially
and I believe the
> World Bank and American University will also help
sponsor the exhibition.
> It will include 8 Bulgarian artist friends, six of whom
showed their work
> this fall here at the University of Connecticut. It was
quite an
> undertaking for us, but a wonderful, slightly mad time.
We rented a big red van to carry everyone and local
sponsors such as the Aquarium, Garde Art Theatre, Mystic
Seaport and so on provided dinners and outings for our
> friends. This fall I taught a course in writing at our local
community

> college which was a real challenge. How do full-time teachers to it? But I
> managed pretty well, and may teach again next fall when we get back to
> town. Nick Prodanov came back to the US to help me paint the house, clean leaves, put away air conditioners, hide acorns and all the rest of fall
> chores. He also was able to stay with William when I needed to teach or
> hold office hours for students. He'll spend some time with us in Florida
> before his visa is up in the spring.
>   William is well, despite an occasional fall and trip to the ER. We
> had a great visit to Seattle and San Diego last month to give readings and visit friends. His spirit is really remarkable. If we could bottle it, we'd
> solve the world's troubles and make a mint. He joins me in sending love and holiday wishes as I prepare to bath the chocolate cocker spaniel named Daisy who has come to delight and terrorize us this winter.

Vladimir Levchev informs me that it turns out Ambassador Dimitrov is resigning because of the recent elections in Bulgaria in which the former Communists have taken power. More likely, the new leaders have let it be known that his services will be replaced by one of their own men. Yet another prediction from my novel fulfilled. Will my second homeland become a new sphere of influence for the Russians. Here I am crying in the wilderness. Time to stop crying and get to work. Shouting matches with the nasty business manager at Dr. Moorhead's office over Nick's dental problems. Palm Beach dentistry. It is going to take a bundle to keep him smiling. But we will do it, damn it. "Don't let the turkeys get you down." But there are too many turkeys out there, too many turkeys.

December 27, 2001

The day after boxing day - feeling like I've won this round at least. Winter is here at its most brilliant- bitter cold, but sunny. The river is a big glass mirror at the edge of the field, now that all the leaves are fallen and blown away by young Mr. Prodanov. House is painted, and the honey suckle pulled from the Hemlock hedge along the road. The wolly aldegid has sprinkled its powdered death in the tiny stems of the branches like a dusting of sugar or light snow. No time now to wash them down with soap and water. I must close up the house alone, now that Nick has busted his ass to get to Florida. Empty the closets and fridge, scrub the floors, put away crystal and porcelain, make the beds. So much to do. But it all gets done, as we say in Pennsylvania Dutch country.

I miss him this morning, but continue to wonder if I haven't made a big mistake by sending him to Florida and helping him investigate his dream of staying here in the US legally. He doesn't want to "be with anybody" now, his girlfriend has dumped him, he's not interested in gay sex. And so I have an expensive teenage son to look after with all the responsibilities and no real hope of seeing this boy flower into a mature adult.

"You have your needs too," my sister advised as we sat on her new deck overlooking the hills of California. "If he can't meet your needs, let him know that honestly and let him move on."

So right, so California, so easy it seems. But it is not easy.

For weeks now he has not found a job and has had major dental problems - thousands of dollars, and lots of pain while the discount dentist I've arranged long distance tries to help him out. He was the one who insisted in getting down there before the season begins. He's responsible. But that doesn't make it any easier.

His day dream is to model, the way he did one time for the charlatan character who had one winter season before blowing town. I see him smiling from the edge of the crowd of models at the runway, pushed to the back by the third place beauty queens and the too pretty boys hoping for a spot on AS THE WORLD TURNS. A polite Bulgarian boy peering from behind a forest of blond hair, slightly out of it, heart racing, shy smile on his face because he has finally begun to live his dream of America.

Last night, he tells me he has received the red flannel Santa pants and hat trimmed in white I sent him for Christmas. He tells me he has taken a picture of himself dressed in this costume in front of the mirror. He will give me mildly pornographic photo and I will look at it in my fantasy from time to time - that this beautiful guy loves me and is about to let me pull down those red flannel pajamas. Prescription for disaster. Again.

But I couldn't send him out to Chicago this winter. His cousin and the Bulgarian community would give him precisely one week before sending him out to the streets. Winter there. No warm clothes. Hardly enough money to make it. But maybe this is just my own romantic sentimentality. Maybe he would have met up with Natalie and opened a restaurant chain selling stuffed grape leaves or cheese-filled peppers. In Florida he would have an apartment for 5 months. some company, someone to cook free meals or buy him sushi, a car to drive around for work. And some people he knows who are American and a little less calculated and ferocious about securing their own self interest as the eastern European immigrant community invariably is. There's a line that will win me some fans in my second homeland. But after this winter, there won't be enough money to even consider a trip to Bulgaria unless I win the lottery or my mythical literary agent actually does something for my career. If there is a con artist within a hundred miles I seem to have the talent for drawing him to my side - bees to honey, flies to shit.

The vision was to finish my teaching here and escape to sunny Florida with William as we have so often done over the years. This time I am to really spend time with him, read with him, enjoy him, talk with him, give him some happiness. Last night as I catherized him, sitting so patiently on the toilet seat, remarkably calm like a baby being powered after bath and trussing up as I slipped the red tube up into his bladder, he began to laugh: "End of my life peeing!" Laughed and laughed. "Either laugh or cry," he said when I asked him what he meant. Every single burst of frustration I ever give him is met with, "I love YOU." How can he manage these years of pain and frustration and bad luck? How does he do it? How can I not do better with him? I owe him some sort of companionship that will give him real pleasure, not just making it through each trial. This must be the new year's resolution. And if Nick doesn't come around in Florida, I must absolutely let him go, not hound William with the perpetual soap opera. I must really wake up now and seize these days. It is so dreadful when William is in the hospital, I am so destroyed by all that I have failed to do for him, the time wasted, the helplessness in the face of his pain, his old age. I must not ruin the good days with this anticipatory grief that seems to take up so much of my psychic energy.

With Nick it must be que sera sera. I must not do more than I want to do, not let him push me to pay for his education. This was originally my day dream, that he would begin his studies in Florida and share some of these years with me, perhaps grow into my mate. This is what Jackie Boyle has said he has always done, just made the opportunities available, been there so that the object of his love could see him and choose him when the time came. Far from realistic to hope for this, Nick does indeed love women, the idea of women loving him at least - no, he is "a gentleman" as he says, and they fall like crazy for him. But he is a young narcissist too, something not too shocking in one who is young and beautiful I suppose. But I do have to keep my life in perspective now.

And a crash up stairs. I go to find William throwing his brace around and dropping his shoes as he tries to wake. The chocolate dog is there licking him awake. On his bedside is the photo of his mother with one of the champion springer spaniels she used to raise. He is a boy again I guess with little Daisy wagging her tail frantically with joy to see him. The little dog in the photo, the little dog in his bed. Time collapsing in his sweet smile. I think of the poem about that picture and it returns me to my center once more:

The Brother

Printer is so fast,
It virtually thinks for you
as though your soul were a
frantic angel imprisoned
in a computer chip.
Page after page spew forth

As clean as sliced mushrooms.

It would sing your grievance
at high c above z,
assign our tale the
fascination of a soap opera cleric:
will he resist the advances
of the fabulously beautiful wife
of the state's billionaire governor,
will he confess to the Bishop
his hot history of pederasty
while at St. Elmo's School for Boys?
When what there is to tell
Is only poor judgment, the inadvertent
cruelty of a sick loved one refusing
the dinner you've cooked say,
or taking someone's side against you.

My trapped spirit tries to
Make sense of a new subplot,
tries to keep it from turning
into terminal cancer or falling
out of love, when you wander
up to my desk to show me a photograph.

The woman is wearing a flowery dress
from the 1930's, is smiling,
is petting a large spaniel.

You smile back at her,
dead all these years,
as though she would at any moment
stop playing with the dog and
go in to cook your favorite supper.

"That's my mother," you say with such pride
there is nothing to do but turn off the machine
and hold you.

January 16,2002

Took Daisy to school, Nick off to the Clamatis By Night downtown, another fight. He is so strange now. Really sick? What shall I do here. Is he teaching me the lesson of Buddhism, i.e. not to be connected to life. That paradox whereby I will be most connected when not connected. Is this the lesson of the east he has been sent to teach me and to end the book with. A lesson that will help me let William go if death takes him before me?

January 26, 2002

Race for the Cure Day. Let's pray I've been cured. On the 9th at William's 83rd birthday party, Bob asked me to run with him and even though I was up late and drank too much, I sure enough was ready for him when he arrived at 7:00. Still dark here and Nick asleep like Endymion on the pull out bed in the living room. Twice now since being here with him, I couldn't resist the sweet face turned up to the ceiling, cover tucked under his chin, eyelashes a foot long - and slipped into the bed beside him, he mumbling sleepy permission. Just to hold him, still he will permit nothing else. Such frustration. Why have I set myself up for such frustration? Three more months of free-floating anxiety over what to do. But I did what lovers do, or at least I think of it this way. Not to give up, to be there, waiting.

But Bob points out that it is ruining my life in all sorts of ways, creatively, emotionally, financially. He says God gives us our own lives to look after. Nick is turning that job over to me. Can I possibly go through all the work and risk IRS problems by trying to make him my assistant and sponsoring work papers? Can I borrow more money and try to help him enroll in College as he wishes? Can I simply put it on him to do this work and see if he has the gumption and desire to make this happen before his visa runs out this April? I had to force myself to take a shower, pin my race number to my shirt, and organize glasses, gum, a twenty dollar bill, and sunglasses into the running pouch I strapped around my waist.

Bob and I sat over pancakes and grits at IHOP and he helped me shrink some of these questions out. White hair since the day I've known him, but tight body, athletic. I saved his bacon in Morocco when he came down with hepatitis and I put him up in my little clinic rather than risk local hospitals or send him stateside. He's been a loyal brother since, full of enthusiasm and humor. Loves diving, and boating. Used to canvas all sorts of scrub land here to reclaim for the state - fending off rattlesnakes, and all sorts of critters. Runs with the bulls in Pamplona. But the job has turned into management and he misses the old days too, kicking around the globe, into all sorts of exotic places. Now it's movies at the malls and dining out, though occasionally he gets his heart rate going when a Moray Eel comes crawling out of the coral at him.

The sun rose just as thousands of runners arrived at

the tents to register, suck down orange quarters, bananas, power bars. Long lines at the johns. Warm up exercises. The intra costal a flat mirror reflecting the Biltmore and Breakers on Palm Beach. A couple of several hundred foot yachts floated like glass trinkets adorning music box lids. The palm trees formed an elegant arc sweeping up to the north end of the island. Jazzy music blared from the loud speakers as the deejay pumped up the runners. Ladies first, of course, and several thousand women lined up for the start, lithe young phillies at the front, tan, bare bellied. The men all stood around clapping. On ideal runs, it begins to rain just as the ladies begin to run - soaking their flimsy signets and shorts like a bevy of models for the swimsuit edition of Sports Illustrated. One of the perks of racing was to spend time and check out all the beautiful creatures who turn up.

My own passion was a guy named Denis. Most beautiful person I've ever seen in public. Bareback, tiny nipples, a waist that must have been no more than 20 inches, tan, wide shoulders, hairless, blond hair slicked back, grey, skin-tight biker pants creeping into the crack of his perfect back side.

I had the courage to walk up to him and say, "Man, you are my model. I want to look just like you."

He had a heart tabooed over his heart with a shamrock inside and a US marine insignia on his right biceps.

"I gave up drinking and drugs twelve years ago and now I all I do is exercise.. I'm forty three," he said with pride.

I guess he had to have some reward for all the effort to look like that and he didn't seem to mind the flirtation. Sure he gets this sort of chat up all the time.

"You want to be my trainer," I asked him.

"Naw, that's okay. See you around, guy" and he gave me a firm hand shake and a smile. Something anyhow. What a gorgeous guy he was.

A manager from one of the sponsoring companies stood at the starting line chatting with all the ladies on his mike.

"We're gonna kick Cancer's butt," he proclaimed.

I love America. "We're gonna kick cancer's butt." "Let's get that grim reaper! Show him what we're made of! Good guys 5, Grim Reaper zero! Go good guys, go."

Bob and I ran easily for the first mile, a slow, eleven minute mile pace."

"Hey, get back here. How dare you pass me," he joked as we ran and runners pulled ahead.

But at mile two I began to feel strong and pulled ahead of Bob. Wasn't really competing, but felt sure he pull up. Up and back, like angling for a fish. I guess I did feel a little competitive, though I decided I would wait at the finish if he were behind me so we could cross together.

But then that little devil pulled ahead just as the finish line appeared. I bent over to pick up a small American flag someone had dropped. I saw one earlier that I didn't bother with and this second one seemed to be dropped by fate. William's cousin Betsy made us promise to fly the flag after the world trade center.

"Remember the nuns said to offer up the pain for the souls in Purgatory," Bob joked with me at one point before the race.

"I do," I told him.

"So do I," he admitted. "I figure if I can spend some energy and think of them somehow it might do some good, some sort of Karma connecting us all."

I remembered John's voice on the answering machine the day after the disaster.

I picked up the little flag from the street and carried it a while before slipping it into my running shorts, just when Bob decided to pick up the pace. I poured it on - I think I could have really poured it on and caught up to him. But I didn't, finishing 5 yards behind him.

"You beat me fair and square," I admitted as I undid the chip we had laced into our sneakers which would count us electronically as we crossed the finish line. I guess I really had turned it into a competition with Bob.

"No, you had a great race. We crossed the line together," he lied.

But it didn't matter to me. A sweet guy. Lighter by 30 pounds and in better shape. He bought me pancakes and gave me an hour of advice. I love it that it did not matter to me. Maybe this is the beginning of a solution for the sick heart I seem to be carrying around with me for years now. How long ago was it when I first tried to put it into words:

Southernmost Point
I carry my heart through the keys-
failed little lighthouse-
island by island, a hundred
ways of losing you - burning
half as many bridges behind me
as we skim across the patchwork
purple and aquamarine in silence

that private hell reserved
for lovers who have given up
but lack the courage to leap
when they come
to the edge of the world

All the bright day long
the dolphin topiary,
the gay shell shacks
and waving palms
mock the grim cells
we have walled ourselves into.
Yet we push on. Island by island
We must cross the vast
archipelago of loss and solitude.

No need perhaps to leap. Take my sweetie out to the pool and read the newspaper to him. Come back for a shower and massage his legs. Take the little chocolate Daisy out for a walk. Put on your sunglasses and have a gin and tonic. Today, you have run a good race. "Today I am a new man," our alcoholic house guest used to announce to us each morning. But perhaps this really is a beginning. Perhaps God has sent Nick to help me understand the lesson of loss and the necessity of detachment if I am to make any spiritual progress. This seems to be the core of every eastern religion. Learning how to detach myself from the sweet world, may actually enable me to be less obsessed by my pursuit of it. Is Ganesh smiling at me? I shall place some almonds on his altar before I go to the pool. No peanuts here for the moment.

Super Bowl Sunday, 2002

William asleep in the cool dark of the bedroom and Daisy taking a siesta too after a walk to Seven Eleven for some quarters and to see if I lucked out on any lottery tickets. A blond floozie butts ahead of the grandmother and her four gorgeous grandsons out for a slurpie."The line's that way, " grandma says with annoyance. The Floozie has bleach blond hair pushed up into a kind of beehive, wears a pink tube top and adorned herself like a Mayan high priest in a ton of fake gold Jewelry. She adds a couple of cans of ravioli to the pile of groceries in front of her, peers over her sunglasses and says, " I was here before."

"So were we," the grandmother says and throws her money at the cashier, an Indian girl with big ruby earrings who obviously has bought all the fake gold and keeps ringing up the Chef Boyardi. Grandma pays up and adds a parting shot to the blond lady: “You need a pedicure!”

Why can’t I ever think of lines like that when I am dumped on? Sure enough, the lady’s toes turn up sort of like hooks or a falcon’s talons, flying high in the blue air in bejeweled, plastic slippers.

Women are better at this sort of thing. There ought to be some sort of Super Bowl for women where they can show off their aggression too. Super Bitch Tournament. Mud slinging instead of mud wrestling, with Joan Rivers as your hostess.

I had hoped to buy a fishing rod after the jazz concert at City Place this afternoon, but I guess William had a little too much sun and threatened a seizure. It was so pleasant there listening to the cool trio and their sultry vocalist crooning Ellington tunes under the palm trees. But, instead, it’s home to do laundry and put him to bed. I’ve been trying to fill the day with fun things since Nick has been invited out to a Bulgarian party and hasn’t seen fit to include us. Maybe I really have had it to the limit this time with Nick. So willing to take Daisy for a walk when the pretty actress who lives upstairs comes by with her terrier. Who disappears in the flash of an eye to the pool when it seems like I have house cleaning in mind. Does a few dishes, parks William in front of his cereal with a newspaper and is off like a brown Adonis in a speedo tank suit, reading his Steinbeck, aloof and mysterious behind mirrored sunglasses at the edge of the aquamarine water. Maybe I've had it with myself too. This guy has wrecked my self assurance. I feel so inept around him, the stupid little games. My voice actually comes out whining at times. My obsession, my grief, my sexual frustration. The constant rejection. What a fucking looser I am becoming. Why have I set myself up for this sort of winter. What a dumb idea to think I could live this close with a former lover, someone I love still, or am infatuated with at least, and think we could be "just friends."

How could I think that in some Buddhist way I could give up this obsession, or just wait till he came to his senses. I'm as foolish as the old professor in Death in Venice obsessed by the beauty of a young boy. "He loses every shred of dignity," I used to tell my students, "but for the first time in his life he has lived fully, passionately, even if briefly and just before his death, like a preying mantis who dies after mating."

What made me think he would be here to help me if the cancer returns and I need help, someone to look after William if I can't do it anymore? He's so pre-occupied with his future, with making a life for himself and his family, he would never sacrifice for me the way I have with William I suppose. Centuries of getting and holding on to the things of this world have been bred into him. The simplest peasant in Eastern Europe would run rings around most Americans for the subtlety with which they manage their affairs. We are virtual children compared to them.

Sometimes as I jog the intra-coastal Celene Dian comes on the radio with a song that brings tears to my eyes: "Don't give up on your dream, don't surrender...." Am I giving up on Nick, am I to blame? Am I as selfish as he says, as calculating. Is the green-eyed monster ever to be purged from my soul? Can I ever accept the idea of total freedom he keeps preaching to me - absolute freedom, where everyone does exactly as he wishes. Am I a total schmuck being taken by a master at manipulation, am I a small-minded, selfish user who does not know how to love?

I think of that scene in Moon Struck where Cher smacks her boyfriend across the face and shouts, "Snap out of it!"

"What happened, I asked a friend recently when he told me he had broken up with a woman he'd been living with for several years. "That's over," he said. " I don't want to be with anyone who doesn't want to be with me." How strong, how admirable he seemed. And maybe foolish? Nick certainly has the right not to be intimate with me - you can not force yourself to love someone. But I have the right, the obligation maybe, to cast off someone I can not wait for, someone who is killing me while I wait for him to solve his life and fall in love with me again. I think of the mother in the film we watched on Mahler's wife who asks her son if he is willing to give up his creative life for an obsession. But what happens when the creative life becomes the obsession, such as this book?

The harder I try to find ways of pleasing him, of course, the more distant he seems to get. Yesterday, at the fair we took the gondola lift which glides high above the Ferris wheels, and circus tents, food stands and every conceivable child ride for tots you can imagine, swirling strawberries, dragons, dancing elephants and tigers all lit up in the most spectacular rainbow light show below us.

The lemonade and tequila we'd been drinking all afternoon had me in a kind of bliss. Earlier in the day in the cattle barn, two cows lay resting in clean hay, nose to nose, exquisitely beautiful in their silky grey coats, their luminous eyes, big as baseballs, highlighted by a kind of natural black eyeliner. They seemed absolutely to be engaged in a quite conversation, just passing the time as they waited for Lord Krishna to come and take them for a stroll through heaven. I couldn't get over them.

"Have you ever flown over palm trees like this, William," I asked him, arm over his shoulder as our car stopped high above a palm oasis below with benches for tired pedestrians.

"Over and under them," William said. I thought of his years as a navy pilot in Hawaii during the war. The joke ticked the hell out of me.

I turned to Nick in the car behind us and he seemed lost, staring out over the fantastic lights as though he were in hell. Paradise and hell for him both this visit to Florida. Breaking my heart. Breaking his heart. "All of this below, only worship," the devil says to Jesus on the mountain top, trying to tempt him out of his resolution. And Nick floats high above the fair, like stone, just waiting to drop.

Last year, about this very time, when again I was agonizing over Nick, was describing to Cecilia Holland the sharp pain in my stomach each morning as I lay in bed thinking about the situation, Cecilia looked up and said, "Just get out of bed." Just get out of bed. Indeed. Time to take the laundry out of the dryer, get William dressed and ready for the Super Bowl. Just get out of the fucking bed.

February 11

Soon to be Valentine's Day. For me another day of mourning? I wake with a pain in my gut again, and I let it burn for an hour before getting up. "What am I to do, William? This is driving me crazy."

"Three months, okay," he says. And "I love you. Thirty years."

How ignoble of me to be agonizing with William over this. But who can I share it with otherwise?

Yesterday, I slipped in beside Nick and just held him. He let me. But when I tried to kiss his forehead he snaps, "Richard, stop it." If he would just have put his arm over my chest. A little simple friendship. How full of resolve he is. How can he hold out like this? If he would only just hold on to me and love me the entire winter would change, my spirit would change, my joy in life would return. But it is like living with the dead. I am becoming a necrophilliac? Sitting here taking notes against my own household, like Hazard's cat.

"Not healthy for any of you," the neurotic psychologist upstairs informs me. I must snap out of it. I promised myself I wouldn't do anything I didn't want to do when I came down here. I've forgotten that promise to myself. It will be very hard to go on the wagon for Lent again, but I need to challenge myself this way. See if I can really get into good habits again. Up early, writing before William is up. Get myself in shape again. These constant goals. Nick does have a job now and stands to make $2500 a month. I cook every night for him, and we let him use the car round trip 100 miles each day. I guess I should consider this a contribution to the life of another. Even if I am suffering. So, he doesn't love me. I will have tried this winter at least. Followed Jackie Boyle's injunction to make myself available. I have been true to my obsession at least. I've given it a try. But this must be the last time. When Natalie came, I still thought of Nick. But Nick was having a good time with his own girlfriend. He proudly showed me photos of him naked in bed, and the second runner up Miss Bulgaria, blond hair down to her ass, naked. Strange. Like a little brother showing me photos of his conquest? Letting me know that this is what he wants in life?

He's made it very clear for a long time now that he doesn't want a relationship. Yet he continues to say this is possible, maybe in the future. Here, I do think he is using me, using my obsession. Or is he? Is he just psychologically mixed up now, and really does think that one day he will be able to be with me when he has his own money, his own independence? Does he want to be with me in the future possibly. I have tried to nurture this hope now for years. Recall crying at the Black Sea, at Bread Loaf, here. As Deacy says, you'll know when enough is enough. Am I giving up on love, or moving on, out of an unhealthy situation. Give him time, part of me says. Be patient till he comes around. Can I continue to waste the best years of my life, hoping Nick will become my lover, will love me? And ruin my days in this terrible obsession- this grief? You really are doing that. Waking every morning with physical pain in your stomach? If Nick plugs into life here it will be with some chick, and he'll be a constant torture to me. Don't encourage that, part of me says. You'll just prolong the agony.

Ginger says why would be want to spend his life with some old guy, i.e. me? He has said he wants to marry again. To have more children. I certainly don't fit into that picture.

And if William dies. Will I bring Nick back in to my life. Oh, let this all go, even the writing of this book. You are writing yourself into a hole, not out of one. Let things coast now and try to get something done. Don't be mean to him. Sustain him while he is here. How horrible can things be anyhow? You are alive in a beautiful part of the world. You have William and Daisy. Prospects. Pick up your life again.

February 21, 2002

Riding the Lenten wagon. Little good it seems to be doing me. Skin a little less wrinkled about the eyes? Soul a little less raisin like? I don't think so. I watch Nick slip into a dull drunkenness after several coke and vodka's, a pattern his like his father and a million other Bulgarians every night. Drinking that does not give joy, drinking that just dulls details of how rotten their lives are, drinking that let you slip into your own depressive fog and keep you from thinking too hard about anything.

Yesterday, I couldn't sleep thinking of all the possibilities of Nick's staying here. Getting him into school, on a cruise ship, hire him through my agent to work as a translator and program assistant for yet other art shows?

UP at 6, and thought why not send him off this morning. Stood in my white bathrobe, making coffee while he prepared his lunch. Sticking raw hot dogs into buns with ketchup, the way a child would make his lunch.

"You should cook those hot dogs, they're raw," I tell him.

He looks surprised. How many things doesn't he understand that he's too proud to admit.

"There isn't time," he says.

"What about the microwave?" He looks surprised at the idea.

The first time I try it, they explode and the skin's turn to leather. A little bit like ours, I think. Two penises exploding from disuse. Turned to leather in the microwave tensions that fill the house day and night. But I keep the joke to myself.

It seems like the middle of the night. I feel like the millions of mothers awake at the very instant making peanut butter and jelly sandwiches for lunch boxes all over America with a mixture of sleep, and urgency to catch the bus, and love. I put in a bag of strawberries and some cheese and crackers, a container of left over pasta with shrimp, his favorite. Will these little acts of consideration ever bear fruit? What was the lesson on the grade b film we watched last night? Love only blooms when you give it. I have so much to give, but I guess I am a difficult task master sometimes.

Off he goes to his day a stone mason, cutting and polishing marble, returning home tired and dusty after an hour's drive to Miami. I thought the job would make a difference, give him some money and pride in his independence. But he feel's like a gypsy, is given the worst jobs because he is the newest. The others he works with are all younger, better able to handle the hard physical work. He feels old. Will soon be 35.

"I'm 35 and I've got $50. That's all I have in life. $50." He turns on the entertainment channel and watches news of the stars, their luxurious homes, the new fashions, college spring break parties in the Bahamas. It is so sad to watch him seduced by this vision of wealth. Who is watching me, sad for my vision of sleeping with a young lover each morning.

Yesterday I called immigration and it seems he can apply for an extension of his visa. No problem. All these weeks of agonizing about his return date evaporate. Is he happy? No, he doesn't believe me. I could let him stay here this summer and he could take up studies in the fall. If William gets sick this summer, I would have him around to help at least. But this is wrong too. I do have William. I should love him. Use this time with him. And worry about the future when it comes.

Options:

- drift

- let him stay the summer and see how the fall works out.

- send him home

And again, another day in paradise wasted.

February 27, 2002

The sleep machine is chugging away in the next room like something out of the twilight zone - an eternal moment, train in motion, going nowhere, like sleep, like death. Why do I see metaphors for my life everywhere I look. It is like the depression I developed all those winter months in the Peace Corps in Tunis living alone in the medina, smoking too much hash, my heart breaking for love of the roommate who had moved out, my first love after I had finally decided I loved men, loved this boy.

The little black lamb destined for slaughter once it had been fattened up for the feast of Aied that I had saved like Abraham granted a reprieve for doing God's will finally, died instead, in my arms, as the moronic taxi driver lost his way to the animal hospital. I had fed my pet the wrong kind of grasses too young, I had tried to force my roommate into loving me and killed off the friendship forever. The lamps were making love to the ceiling as I stared at the empty apartment living room. The rain wept outside in the courtyard, no pathetic fallacy this. They wept. I was sure of it. The winter winds scorned me, and the blue teeth of the space heater's gas flame were fixed in a cruel grimace. Even the cat had bailed out and a scorpion scurried across the floor with impunity, a little victory dance.

I guess we all have those terrible times in our youth when the bottom falls out, when we despair of things ever changing like a child wailing though the night with an earache who does not know, has no sense of history to be able to hope that the pain will abide, the infection will heal, the morning dawn.

All winter long Nick has agonized in silence over his lot: poor, unable to look after his little son in Bulgaria, living in the land of milk and honey with nothing to his name, feeding his imagination with images of rich young rock stars and models on E and M TV. No car, no job, no girlfriend. Treated like a gypsy when he finally does get a job. He dyes his hair and sits around the pool on weekends, hiding behind his dark glass, having nothing to do with me, with anyone. He does not want to be hurt, he says, like an ingénue with the back of her hand to her forehead in some Harlequin romance.

You can not buy love, can not force someone to love you. His disingenuous "maybe" when I finally have enough and demand to know what is wrong, if we will ever have a sexual relationship again has kept me on the line too long. I think of the little blowfish I caught on the intra costal this weekend. Puffing and wheezing with frustration as I take the hook from his mouth. Golden-eyed, leopard-spotted, pretty enough in his own right. But angry, blown out of all proportion. And Nick, sitting a few yards away from us down the intra coastal behind his dark glasses, silent.

Finally, I guess I am beginning to heal, I suppose. "This is not the life I want," I tell him. "In April, I think we must go our separate ways." And since that awful morning, things have begun to heal. No disappointments when I have no expectations. I am free to plan the summer in Europe with William. Cooking no longer a burden. Looking after William no longer a burden. Every night catherizing him has become as routine as the train going nowhere beside our bed. "Love has become a holding action," I wrote once during a crisis I thought he would not survive. But here we still are, waking to the sunshine of Florida, having our breakfast, following his hero Janet Reno in her little red truck as she makes her campaign trip through the state- Gangly old Janet who seems to have survived the wrath of the Miami Cubans over Elian Gonzales, looking for a second act in her life as a politician despite her Parkinson's and bad polls.

Little chocolate Daisy bounces all over the bed when we wake up, demanding to be let out, groomed, fed. I seem to have arranged dental care for Nick at a clinic to take care of his chronic dental problems. He's getting a pay check finally. March 1st he'll be 35 and I've arranged a birthday party for him. The gold stocks my old friend Douglas has put me on to are beginning to take off and I may not have to sell roses into my old age after all. A handsome older guy tried to take me home when I popped out to the local gay bar for an hour this past weekend.

"There are plenty of fish in the sea," he said, as I sat there crying in my diet coke. "You're a really attractive guy. I came over here when I saw you come into the bar. There are plenty of guys you can meet if you get out."

Things are finally beginning to work. My ship which has been so adrift is setting course finally. Nick can kiss me good night like a sweet child and I can simply accept it without too much longing. Step by step, I will achieve a sea change if I keep on the wagon during Lent and take care of business. "You must change your life." Is that what Rilke says in the poem? Enjoy the train ride while you are on it. I need to be "in the world and not of it," I guess, aim for that Buddhist detachment from the world that has eluded me ever since I began trying to make sense of my life all those years ago.

When MARATHON fist came out, William and I were feted by the American Ambassador in Athens, an old college classmate of William's who we were visiting. An impromptu theater on the rooftop terrace of the cultural attaché's house had been set up and after I read an account of life with William from the book, a very beautiful novelist came up to me, dark eyes shining, bare shoulders a luminescent white in the light of the full moon. Her first words were, "if William should ever die, you must come live with me in Greece." Straight out, flat, immediate, Greek. How we have loved this woman over the years since, despite the distance, the changes in our lives. Yesterday's letter points the way for me as she has done so often over the years.

Dear William, dear Richard,

I was very glad to receive your message and to learn your good news. I have some news me too.

Everything began last September - October. After a horrible summer with too much sun and an incredible isolation in my house because of the distance and the hot weather, I understood that I had to change my life completely, if I wanted to stay alive. So, I went to Paris, I bought a small studio in the 10th arrondissement, I came back, I sold the house in Vouliagmeni which had lost the balance and the charms (noisy neighbors, new huge houses around, distance, age, practical difficulties, etc.) I bought a brand new apartment in the center of Athens with no view at all, but with more space and possibilities, (after two days, I will move there for good), and at the same time I am trying to do some investments, thing that will take a year at least. I was lucky with Paris, because a worker fixes and renovates the studio very well, I hope, although it is not as old as studios in Paris generally are. (built 23 years ago). Anyways I was at least 4 times in Paris after October, but only for a very few days, (things in Athens were urgent. I will be there in April again, I hope for more days, and of course during thesummer, to avoid at the end the Greek sun.

As you can imagine, at that period of my life the distance between me and literature is equal with the distance between earth and moon. That is very nice, because, when I will return to waiting, if I return, I will be renovated from all these changements and I will not repeat myself.

You understand my good friends, it happened slowly, but last September, I was 100% sure that I did not like myself any more, and that I had to change my life' s style completely. So, I began to swim in dangers, new situations, huge efforts. My target is not happiness, but the trip, (as

Kavafi says), and, good or bad, I have it. For the rest, I know nothing

and perhaps I don't even care. But I care for you and I hope that you will be healthy and satisfied forever. Till then, have my love both of you.

March 1, 2002

Nick's birthday, He's 35. And sad to be thinking he

is so "old." He dyes his hair like us now, has developed a slight paunch? How fleeting youth - There's a new idea! I spent whole morning yesterday trying to arrange for dental care for his abscessed teeth (11 and 12) leftovers from bad dental care in the past in Bulgaria. We are all alive, he looks beautiful and has prospects, but why is that the details of his life seem so tragic- to him and to me now. Imagine all the people in the world who have survived torture, or have had to raise a deformed child, or whose mate has contracted Lou Gehrig's disease or some such. The people massacred in Africa's civil wars, the impoverished life so many of the world's people lead. It is obscene not to take joy in the daily life God has granted us. But it is so hard for some reason not to fall into this pit he has made for us all.

I worked hard yesterday arranging our travel to Europe this summer, particularly the Bulgaria leg in which my old college classmate Doug will be joining us and may perhaps spring for some of the cost, since the Bush White House, in its wisdom, has said no to some travel support to France. Perhaps old Douglas will pick up the rental car if Nick is not there this summer. Why do I push ahead this way and continue to try to build a new life, even in Bulgaria that does not include him.

Cleaned the house, ran with William riding his three wheeler on the intra coastal, and prepared a good dinner right down to the cherry pie last night. Nick comes home, tired and dusty with $400 in his pocket for 7 days of hard work laying marble in the rich people's homes. Hardly seems worth it, but it is eight times the monthly salary he would make in Bulgaria. He asked me to watch the rental film with him when William went to bed, but he fell asleep on the floor beside me. Was this the night I was to try again to make love to him? Why will he not just say to me, "Richard, come over here," or "let's take a shower," or "how about a massage?" Last night I was tired too and I got the sense he was frustrated because I did not make the first move. But, sure enough, it would be "I'm tired," or "Richard, stop it!" And I would traipse off to bed angry, frustrated, feeling like an old pervert, humiliated once again. I see over the years, over the summers when he pouted and refused to come to America, or took off to Varna on his own, or stormed out of a restaurant in a huff, or the myriad times he would blow up when I contradicted him that he does have some character issues. But, generally he is very sweet and dignified. I can't deny this. A person whose character I have admired and wanted to imitate the way friends do for his manliness, and his integrity. He is a good person, but he does not love me the way I love him and he will be a frustration for the rest of my life. If he marries, it will be over for me. I've said I would be glad for the years until then, but the years should be joyful, not the sort of awful tension and frustration that has ruled the house this winter. This summer something new, a new experience. We'll be on our own in Bulgaria, and perhaps he will be working here this summer. But he'll have to ask for it. I will not push him into keeping our car and living in the apartment. He'll have to want that and enter into a clear understanding of what is involved. And next winter, he'll have to be out and find a place of his own. This is very unlikely to happen, or his presence in the community is likely to continue to weigh on my soul - Will he visit, will he want to be with us, will I be able to watch his new life here? And I will be lost again next winter. Better in April to go our separate ways? Or drift, and see what happens. It is good to have another individual in my life to take an interest in, to think of cooking for, to wonder how his day went - when it is good. More often though he comes home and it is silence, the enemy, and he leads his secret life outside the house, a house which has become his hotel.

William is not well, very fragile. I don't see much time left for him and I must spend this time with him in positive ways, not fighting with Nick and hanging around in the hopes of taking him in my arms. This is not the life I want, and I must begin to change it now as we have just two month left. Get on the road again with Douglas this summer whose marriage is ending and create some new memories.

Dear Douglas,

Thanks for the quick response. I'm pleased you wish to try the whole enchilada. I know I am going to be very embarrassed when you answer my question (I am having a senior moment) but who is Bruce Meadows? The name sounds familiar (Eris?) but I don't recognize it out of context. "A friend of a friend is a friend," as I believe the Spanish say, so if you wish him along that's fine with me and William. It may make logistics a little bit more difficult. There is room in the rental car (a van, in fact, which for some reason is actually cheaper that a sedan. Your note didn't say if you'd take care of this element of the trip. I'll need to confirm and book the reservation in the next couple of days.) But in the Rhodope mountains we will be guests of Lyubomir Levchev I guess (world class poet and former President of the Union of Bulgarian Writers Union. The first part of his biography is published with Vivisphere Books - WWW.Vivisphere.com - and you may find it interesting: YOU ARE NEXT) unless the first artist of the summer and his family has taken up residence in the house. (We have the right to live there as long as we are alive, but it's main purpose is an artist exchange retreat.) We would be put up by the mayor of the village in that case I guess. I don't wish to give myself airs, but in Bulgaria William is a "celebrity" and we have to keep something of a diplomatic profile shall we say while we are there, at least in some towns. We won't have much to do with the press during this visit though. Varna is a tourist beach resort with all the amenities, albeit East European style, and we can play there with impunity. I'll be writing to the head of the Union of Bulgarian Journalists of which we are members to reserve our time in Varna, so please let me know if it is certain he will join us. I had though of putting you and Boiko - our artist friend who will be driving and interpreting for us if Nick is not in country - as a roommate. The rooms aren't expensive but they are booked early and are in high demand during the season. We usually book a boat for $100- $200 and a crew of three take as many as 10-12 of us out for a day of fishing. They cook the fish right on board. And drinks are included. But more of all this anon. This just to respond quickly and pose a few questions. All best, R.

March 8th

How the days click along. Time, did you say Mr. Einstein, is relative? Why is the truism that time flies faster as we age so true? A subjective truth, but real nonetheless. Is it really really true as well? Don't we make atom bombs based on this science. Isn't science only a way of looking at reality until new knowledge comes dropping, like Newton's apple, onto our heads and changes the paradigm.

How grateful I am that William wrote his journal all those years ago, what seems a lifetime ago now. For weeks since our arrival I have been meaning to look into the journals I xeroxed before we sent them off to Princeton but never got around to it until last night, like the Count of Monte Cristo plunging to the bottom of an underwater cave to find a treasure beyond anything he had hoped for. Now that the stroke has deprived William of speech and even memory, it is a precious lifeline to the William I knew and loved all those years ago enabling me to love him still: Paul Bowles's insight - that memory is the thin line that connects the dots of one's personality, gives it form, making us hard and real, as Walter Jenks says of atoms in William's poem. William was fully aware of this relationship when he writes:

Nov 26, 1975

Last night I read some pages from my brief journal in Austria 1962 and then from one ten years later. I must recognize that a journal is essential to my intellectual life, that I have recently been getting flabby (old?) The two and a half years that were in the book I left on the metroliner last month were among the best of my journal-writing. But in another sense they are not lost, any more than last year's jogging or push-ups are lost - I am somewhat less flabby for having written them, those two and a half years of desultory work in the journal.

Had I lost such a journal, I would have been near suicide. I can just imagine the rage I would have felt. How like William, who man and artist was working on his ways so that when he became set in them, as old people must, his work would have style, class. How clear it become that the way a man responds to life's tragedies defines him and in some ways, defines the tragedy. We are all served up a rotten meal from time to time in life. We are not, however, obliged to eat it. God knows William has been served his share. How does he take it so:

"The proportion of optimism to pessimism in an individual is probably a critical element in the identity. I think it determines, for example, my response to certain destructive works of art - why I am impatiently repelled by what I take to be manifestations of cheap despair - Peter Brook's Lear, the production of Cal's The Old Glory, undercutting the belief in man that I feel in Shakespeare and Melville.

Personal attractions are possible across this difference because personal lives are acts of belief, even the lives of convinced pessimists. Mackie Jarrell, Emily Clayton, sometimes, Richard, have been pessimists I have been very close to - perhaps my optimism attracted them as much as their realism drew me. Is that a clearer dialectic - realism vs. idealism?

My sister's low expectation of human nature, relatively low expectation of generosity from others and from events has determined the responses, to some degree, that she's received. To expect the best of people has proved more or less a source of happiness to me. I am dogmatic about that."

I guess when I picked up the journal I knew there would be things in there that would deal with me and my friendship with William. I wonder if I have improved, changed from the Richard he describes on Thanksgiving Day in 1975 that was so hard to read about last night. Yes, William I say, 32 years later, we Leo's love to be loved. We are generous when loved and give enormously of ourselves when loved. But my journal these past two years has not been the large-hearted, generous affair, one would hope from a Leo. Should I have been to Nick the one William describes himself as being to me:

"I feel even to write in this journal about R is to talk behind his back. But things that emerge to me: one important element in our relationship is that I am The One Who Does Not Criticize. I accepted that role in the early days, out of sheer adulation of the beloved. R is totally dependent on a self-image, an articulated image, which is periled by sudden questions or accusations. Thus Franklin Reeve, Henry Chapin, K, have either challenged him or introduced an image of self doubt into his mind, they were exiled, sometimes for a stated time - Ed Frantz, the evening we quarreled after seeing "Let My People Come," (a silly review, by the way) in the restaurant in Greenwich Village, he (R) said he couldn't see again for six months. (That was soon forgotten, but most others are not). As one who loves and wishes him only happiness, am I obliged to counsel against this? Would he want to change? How rarely does anyone want anything bad enough to want to change himself deliberately, e.g. myself and my drinking habits.

The coming visit to Kentucky should be a time of deliberate attention to one another's needs. It can be kept apart from pressures of approval from outside, and focused on our own seriousness as men and writers. Both R and I are in need of discipline, as men and writers. But I will not be so foolish as to try to change him, I will only try to help him 1) underpin the self-confident image of himself by solider grounds, and 2) make him less self-absorbed by the outward direction of his genuinely kind and observant nature.

It would be a sad account of four years of love if we had not learned to bring out the best in one another. We <u>depend</u> on each other, it only remains to see that the dependencies are enabling, not crippling.

In discussions, many recent discussions, of the relationship between Wystan and Chester, the failure of that for-many-years-successful relationship has been ascribed to inequality between the two. Richard and I are not unequal - I take a whole sort of manhood, the sort that I discovered when I wrote “Love Poem,” (the poem that became a transvestite Valentine in Hazard,) from Richard. He takes an unruffled approval, at a parental level, from me. The sensual part of our relationship, surely more important to me, works because it is a subordinate expression of a larger give and take.

Now I have talked behind your back, dear Richard: if you should one day read this, hope you will see it as another clumsy insistence of my devotion.

Thanksgiving Day

1975 "

How strange to hear these intimate words across thc decades, words that take on the sort of eternal life the words in a poem has: it is always now in the literary present. Dear old William is asleep in the other room, the train chugging away on the sleep machine, which like a wormhole, or Proustian tea cake can take us backward or forward in time. I have him, I have him. Steal the Valentine William. I don’t care. You have not yet fallen off the globe. I am holding you tight here at the edge.

February 14

(Valerie Hazard finds on her desk a strange self-protrait by her husband and a note which she takes to be a valentine and on the whole well-meant.)

What you have given me,
in those long moments when our words
come back, our breaths come back,
is a whole man at last, and keeping me, remembers:

On a deck one night, the moon past full
coming up over the planet's edge,
the big globe rippling its skin,
the smaller already accepting its waning
and talking about vast skyey distances.
I had not met you yet.
Aft, the aircraft folded like mantises,
ahead and abeam, destroyers running like hounds,
and the wind.

A sentry walked off
the rolled front of the flight deck,

crying *oh* as he fell to the sea.
Lost in the cold skin of the globe,
he cried *oh* for less than, panted
for less than love, going away,
the loneliest noise that ever wound in my ear.

I think dear one that one day I'll fall off
this galaxy, leaving husk and canvas behind,
the loneliness I'll take with me made whole,
myself made whole, by what we've said
in these knocking moments, oh,
and keeping, as hearts keep
(husks and canvas being little abandoned houses),
and going away so.

March 29, Holy Saturday, 2002

Daisy is stretching like a sausage in her crate, looking up at me with those clown's eyes, saying it is time to go out as I sit on the little lanai once again. It has been too long, India drifts like some island in my imagination, waiting to be discovered. The room is quiet. I am sleepy. But as Josephine says, the poems don't just come, unasked for. You must sit at the desk routinely awaiting the muse's pleasure. "Stay home and write," she tells me. Why do I take on so much travel. Is it all an escape from my real work?

This summer I've set up readings in Paris, Avignon, Prague and Sofia. Perhaps we will be accepted for the writer's retreat in Switzerland and I will be able to focus there. Once again, I feel like my life is spinning apart. I fall into the kaleidoscope, swirl around, look at whatever pretty piece flies by. Will the pattern ever be whole? I go from one project to the next, and none ever seem to be complete. Now, at Easter, I recall the series of poems I wanted to write, perhaps an opera of Christ in the tomb for three days. Poems for all the characters in the drama. Imagining the process of death, imagining Christ in the tomb, melting into death the way blood pools in a cadaver's body as it lies on the autopsy table. Battling the gates of hell. Just one plum fell from that tree, and perhaps only a prune:

Foreman, Golgotha

Hang him up there.
I've seen enough

men go slack - It's
his problem now
not mine - the beam
will support him,
his bones are fresh,
nail him to the sky,
fucking blue
for all I care -
gravity and death
will look after him.

Nail him into the sky -
and no sweet looks asshole-
I can feel this desert mountain
begin to creak, it's gone
all black overhead.
The scorpions are
coming alive under my skin.
Let's get on with it.

The little financial house of cards I've erected threatens to fall apart too unless I bring in some income. Would I ever have enough, even if I had a billion? This Easter weekend we will "escape" to Ft. Lauderdale, taste the last dregs of a time share we finally sold. Since they don't take dogs, we have an excuse to leave her with Nick and spend a little time on our own. Perhaps I shouldn't even take the computer with me, just read to William around the pool. Write letters, look into my "Urgent to Do" file. Remarkable how fragile he has become, heartbreaking. Yet, I know it must be so.

He insists on walking to the corner and touching his cane to a metal plate covering some sort of water works drain, the way I always tap a mail box, or lamp post, whatever the end point happens to be when I am jogging. Brent, the hunky, movie star, physical therapist who works with William insists we use a belt about William's waist now when he walks to prevent his falling. For a month I was so sore in the chest from supporting William as he walked, over curbs, up stairs, I thought I had a severe pneumonia, costocondritis, something like that. So, the belt is helping us both. But is seems one more step toward his decline.

The chances of his falling will diminish with the belt, so after a two minute objection, William now accepts its use with resignation. It is pink for some reason, with aquamarine stripes. Where did they come up with this belt. But it is remarkable how many outfits William has that go with these Florida colors. One step beyond the black belt, I tell him. You're a pink Judo master.

Nick asleep on the couch in the living room. But I will not go there. That is over. And I am learning how to accept it. A little self-help manual I bought on line at the grocery store check out called "Starting Over" has helped, though I am not sure of the advice. "Don't try to be friends with an ex lover" it insists. You'll only suffer from jealousy when he starts dating others." But isn't the insistence against friendship detrimental to one's spiritual health as well? How many people seem to be breaking up these days, and after decades of fidelity. I listened to David Leisner's sequence of that title again last night with William and Nick before we started a film. Two of William's poems set to music so beautifully: Tree Marriage, He Contemplates Adultery. Has it been 32 years since we met?

The little pamphlet is designed for divorce, end of a relationship, death of a spouse. I sent it to dear Kate, my cousin's widow yesterday, tattered edges and underlined copy though it be. Incredible to think that having survived such deadly cancer, having brought himself up to wealth and fame from living in the woods like Kaspar Hauser as a child when he ran away from home, that his end should come on a bright morning, top down on his new BMW on his way to work and a truck comes from behind to crush him into pulp. Sweet Jackie, offering you a gin and tonic on his little yacht. So proud, so solicitous of William. A little sloppy at the end of an evening of wine and shrimp, kissing me goodbye. What in the world can we make of this, only pray that the dead shall rise again, and try to keep his sweetness in memory to help us as we walk our own way.

April Fool's Day. April's Fool Day.

Which is it? Am I that man? Yesterday, Easter, I mewed around the pool all day as though my best friend had died. Perhaps he had? Nick was to have joined us here at the resort where we've come for the holiday and bring Ms. Daisy with him. I woke missing her enormously. How sweet she is, sitting at my feet in her cage talking to me, rolling her big, frying pan eyes up at me to be let out for a walk. Jumping on the bed with William, chasing her toy. But Nick needed to hang around and wait for a call back from HAVANA, the little Cuban restaurant where he hopes to join the wait staff team, sic. Only an hour away, he could have driven back if they reached him on his cell phone... I guess he wanted some time away from us as much as I did when we left for this little holiday.

So, we went to church and drove to a park to watch the model airplanes scream through the blue sky - little jets among the more conventional flyers. And home to sit around the pool. A lovely woman in a snake skin bikini - really remarkable figure for someone with four kids, took us up around the pool. Her four little ones bobbed around the pool with her husband and she lay beside me on a lounge chair, curious. And we chatted. What a beauty. Where would she have gone with college. But where has she already gone. Such exquisite children. And the only tell-tale sign of age some charming little wrinkles about the eyes as though she had just wakened and was about to make coffee.

“Are any of your books in movies,” she asked?

“Not yet my dear, not yet. But I am working on it.”

Meeting her reminded me of the necessity of meeting people, how important it is to be social. We are all lonely creatures in this world. We need each other, we need any dumb excuse to say hello, to see how another takes the world, how they cook, how they make love, how they play with their children, how they decorate their living room, how they take death, what they use to get over a cold, what little tricks they use to change a flat tire, or keep the garden from freezing.

So, this morning I remember that Ken Hill's brother is in Miami and he's invited me to come sometime for a boat ride. At 1:00 we will meet them and their dogs for a picnic on some island and if Nick returns my phone call in time, he and Daisy can join us. But no more mewing today. I remember Zorba's injunction that it is a sin to refuse a woman who has invited you to her bed. And so too this beautiful sylph of a morning must not be denied.

April 2

4:00 Crazy insomnia from, yes, a little pot, a little pottette, which will not release me from this extraordinary day.

Nick calls just as we are about to leave for a day of boating with Tucker and Robin. Annoyed that he called so late, but thought it would be something he'd like and so I relented with my anger and gave him instructions on how to meet us in North Miami.

Robin was painting a wicker chair set aquamarine,

plump, standing there in her bathing suit, paintbrush in hand. The dogs were all happy to greet us: a Chinese pug named Blossom, a black and white cocker and a basset hound. Daisy made four as we sat around the pool eating locks and brie.

We started out for an island near Miami all dogs on board the little 27 foot motor boat, all comfortable on the sparkling water, making our way against the strong breeze. Nick and Robin sat on the deck chatting, William and Tucker and I at the helm with dogs coming and going all over the boat.

The island was deserted the day after the holiday, with plenty of garbage for the dogs to get into. But various sorts of palm trees and picnic tables. We pulled out the food and enjoyed ourselves - until the dark clouds began to roll in.

“It said in the paper it wasn’t supposed to rain,” Tucker kept repeating. Earlier in Bocca, Chuck had reported that it was raining like crazy and it seemed the storm was blowing straight at us from the north.

“Yep,” we’re gonna get it, we all said merrily as we drank our wine and ate our sandwiches. Tucker and I went to the end of the little island where two Cuban guys and a little girl had beached their little skiff.

"Naw, naw, it's blowing out to sea," the one fellow assured us. "You got any beer man," he asked.

But it did not blow out to sea. We were in the still center of the storm until finally it hit like a bad hollywood movie. William and Robin and I sat under a big umbrella trying to keep from blowing away, all four dogs at our feet under the table. Nick and Tucker just stood under palm trees until they risked it and went to the boat. Thunder and occasionally a great crack of lightening. But the rain would not let up.

"It's gonna get dark, Tucker. I think we should risk it now. Don't you?"

So we waded out and manhandled William up onto the boat. Nick below helping him change into something dryer, and Robin pushing off. Rain and mist so heavy you could only see 50 yards ahead of you at times. I sang sea shanties and we shouted stories and encouragement to each other. At one point Tucker got too close to the channel marker and kicked up sand, but we didn't seem to do any damage.

Ahead at one point we saw a boat that seemed to be parked like an octogenarian under a bridge when the rain gets too heavy to see. But it turned out they had lost power and their bilge pump wasn't working. Five dark skinned guys who spoke no English threw us a line and started giving hand signals about where to tow them. Good old Tucker, to his credit made right for them and didn't think twice. They would have been in some real trouble without us. And he maneuvered their boat into a little marina at 79th street quite expertly. I was sure their boat would hit the rocks - the water was only 4 feet deep as we maneuvered to cruise by the dock and let them drift to it. Diana II I read on the stern as two of them made the dock and one shouted a farewell. Nice.

Nick and I took turns with William below. The cabin was fairly punk with four wet dogs. Dark, the weather booming up overhead, a little like rolling in a barrel over Niagara. At home, hot showers, and wine. Robin made soup, but we decided to push on to our resort. Flushed with the day and pizza derived by Papa Johns. I thought how lucky it was really that I did invite Nick. How much more difficult it would have been without him to help lift William on board, and help with the boat.

"He's sweet, isn't he Tucker," I said to the captain, looking at Nick's strong back and tight blue tank suit sitting on deck with Robin. A little pride. And Tucker agreed he was a very nice guy. But we came home and all went to bed alone, Nick to his own hot shower and no invitation for me.

"I've tried so often with you, now you must let me know if you want anything, you must make the first move," I said. And, of course, this ended any hope of a truly happy ending for the day. But it is true, very true. I can not continue to hound after him when he has made it plain so often that he's not interested in sex. It is unfair of him. Unkind. Selfish. But there is nothing to be done about it. And I must move on.

April 9th

Will it prove to be the cruelest month? Ginger comes by last night for a blank check to arm her in the purchase of a used car from Goodwill. I'm glad to help her finally get a car that might be dependable and cheap. Dinner and a movie, lots of drinks and at the end of the night she mentions casually that she spent Easter night with Nick here at home, watching a movie. She had told me she was too tied up with family that day, he promised to call and never did. William and I sat in the fancy resort alone, I loading him in and out of cars, swimming pools, wheel chairs throughout the lonely, tedious day.

I guess, in all honesty, I had longed for a little break from Nick and the tensions of this house as did he. But it is a nice touch that he would have Ginger over here to spend the night with. And not tell me about it. Let me find out on my own. The guy is a master.

I wake early now, he showering, getting ready for his day. A small thing, his taking the last bottle of chilled water to work with him, a little luxury I had provided for myself to have at the bed stand at night. I pick it up, cold, beautiful in its blue label and consider putting it back in the refrigerator to show my displeasure while he is in the shower. But I think better of it. Several weeks now and we will be gone. It would just be the source of another argument.

Why am I letting him stay here in the apartment for the summer. Just because I know his family and know how difficult things are in Bulgaria now? Just logical to help him out when it is not great problem for us. $300 a month will cover the expenses here - something he might be able to manage, though I doubt he will pay this each month. And in the years I've known him he has never had a car accident. I have put him on the insurance officially, though if he has an accident while using the car for work, I imagine the insurance will not cover it. He's an able driver, even when drinking. I wonder what would go down if he had a DUI while we were in Europe? At this point, is it philanthropy or am I somehow afraid of confronting him, the situation. There is an element of intimidation with him, though when we have had our drunken fights he has said, "go ahead, take your car back, your cell phone." Or is there some part of me that still sees a future for us one day? I told him once that I was sure he would never look after me if I were to be sick, really needed his help. I remember how he abandoned me and William to local transportation, slogging our way on the train across Bulgaria, paying four times what we should have paid the taxi, the time he decided he had to stay in Varna and wouldn't accompany us to the military spa. He's gotten cruder, grown up in his self interest. Was he so innocent when I met him? The beautiful boy on the train who missed his stop and continued on into my life. Was he as innocent and sweet as I remember or was he using me from the beginning to get out of Bulgaria. When we met he was with some Arab, (a Libyan teacher) on the beach and it did seem like he was hustling the Libyan, trying to get out of the country. It is more than just my life, precious years of my life, that I have given him. The money, the incredible efforts to get him his education, his visas. He ascribes this all to my desire for sex. He will always just think me sex driven egoist now - anything else makes him a whore I suppose. Well, as my mother says, not all books end happily ever after. He may need to keep this image of me into the future. But I wonder if all the life we have shared together will have meant anything to him. Have I spoiled his character, made him more cynical? At times, I feel I have been had by a genius grifter.

I woke again this morning with the realization that we are responsible for our own happiness. This situation is terrible or hopeless only to the extent that I let it be. To be bitter or vindictive only hurts me. Me me me. MIMI! as Pavorati might cry. "Always you, you, you, Nick might say." I promised myself when my father died that I would not fall into the bitterness he so often felt about people. It is hard not to be angry about Nick's "desertion." I could wallow in what might have been, my loss. But what would this achieve? I know how to get what I want mostly. This time, perhaps it is just best to say I lost. It may be that Nick will return to Bulgaria on his own if he doesn't get a visa extension. I wonder if he really is as firm about not staying without the proper paperwork as he says he is. Will he get lost in the culture if he doesn't get his visa extension like so many other illegal immigrants? I could insist on his leaving if he is not legal. But I don't think I will. Could I be firm and say, "that's it," you have to leave now. I think I could and if I don't, I hope it will be for the right reason, that I will have given him a model of largess. He says I am only letting him stay on in the hope that things will change between us, that he'll come around to sex, that he'll be there if William gets sick or dies and I need him. What is the truth for me? Certainly, this morning, after learning about Easter, I feel I must make my way without him in the future, regardless of what happens in my life. A few weeks now, and we will be gone. How now to make the best of this, to make this separation have some good outcome finally.

April 10th, 2002

This book does drag on! (There's the kiss of death for any reader who might have reached this point in the narrative with a view toward publication.) What do you suppose the chances are of this book ever seeing light of day, Richard? Very little. I think of all the students in creative writing classes over the years who claimed to be writing "just for myself," like so many Emily Dickenson's, clearing dreaming of immortality when they are discovered someday in the future. long after their trials have faded. Or Britt, my Swedish friend who has filled a library with her journals as a way of not writing a novel. So, this book must become only a kind of therapy for me?

I barely even see Nick now. He comes home from work very late and William and I are already in bed, or at least behind a closed bedroom door. This morning I catch a glimpse of him before walking the dog.

"Well, I haven't seen you for a while." He, surly, eating his cereal. No response, with those big eyes like a Balinese devil mask when he wants to demonstrate his displeasure.

"How's your work going?" I ask when I bring the dog back. She jumps and yaps for pleasure, oblivious to the problem between us like Sammy the dog, in William's poem about the Chinese Banyan, who stays in the kitchen till dawn after his master has a heart attack, "as dogs have agreed to do": "The water had run in the sink/ all night, for his heart had burst/ While he drew the dog a drink."

I went back to bed and put the little chocolate, cockeyed spaniel back in her crate, my own heart bursting a little. Months now, years now, almost twenty, in fact, I have done the lonely work of looking after William by myself when Nick was to have been there to bring joy into our lives, to share this work, at least for a while. "How did it come to this," I asked myself over and over, until I remembered Sandy Holland's injunction from last year when I felt exactly the same way and Nick had gone back to Bulgaria: "Just get out of bed." So obvious, but so difficult to do. House on fire? Turn on the hose. Hungry? Eat something. Got an itch, scratch it.

The only answer to my life is heroism, wildly egotistical as that sounds. Still, since no one is ever likely, really, to read this book, I can afford writing out this prescription for my own life. It is almost twenty years now since I have been William's care giver after the stroke and I must simply carry on for as many more as it may take. I remember all those years watching Natalie Black look after Don as his muscles wasted away with something like Lou Gehrig's disease. "You do what has to be done," she told me when I asked her how she ever managed it: turn on the hose, eat something, scratch the itch. I simply have to keep on, no matter what the cost like someone in the desert struggling toward some dream of water.

There, over my desk, photos of William like an oasis: Head
covered in
a red hood, camouflaging him as he stands beneath an enormous red rhododendron tree loaded with blossoms,

standing in his batman costume, cape and silk tights and all before we go off to a party, sitting in his wheel chair on the Promennade des Anglais in a wizard's hat covered with confetti at Mardi Gras.

I think of the lecture I dragged William to last night at Temple Israel after drinks and Jim Lehrer's News Hour filled with carnage from the mid-East. The article in the morning paper about the lecture promised wisdom from a poet, the redemptive power of compassion for the suffering of others. But the author couldn't really answer the question posed by a lady in the audience who wanted to know how God could have allowed the holocaust in the first place. Nor did he seem to inspire compassion for the Palestinians stacking up like cords of wood in Bethlehem. He could only pose more questions and describe God's infinite suffering, how we approach God in his private room when we share in that suffering. A strange, mystical, Jewish notion. I open his book at random and read as he quotes Maimonides:

"The ancients sages said, 'He who is angry - it is the same as if he worships idols. One who yields to anger - if he is a sage, his wisdom departs from him; if he is a prophet, his prophetic gift departs from him. Those of an irate disposition - their life is not worth living."

We file out of the temple and two very brown old Jews reflect on the lecture as they get into their Bentley on their way back to Palm Beach.

"There's lots of anger in the bible. How else are we going to raise our kids, teach them right from wrong, without anger," one says to the other.

Maybe he'd like to meet the great William Meredith I think, and we get on line to have the speaker sign his book, *THE JEW AND THE LOTUS, A Poet's Rediscovery of Jewish identity in Buddhist India.*

"It's an honor," he says, a little in awe, and I get my slight gratification. "Where are you going to be soon? Aren't you going...."

"We go to California in May," I suggest.

"Aren't you going to be in Prague this summer?"

"Yes, we are. For the writer's conference."

"So am I," he says, beaming, beautiful as a bodhisattva.

Nice, this little co-incidence. And that his words should fall out of the book like lotus petals, to land exactly on my troubled, angry heart.

"Hi Richard, drawers please," William calls from the bedroom. Daisy has shredded the contents of every single garbage can in the house. How can she chew up razor blades without cutting her little pink gums? The day has begun.

April 11, 2002

Another day in Paradise, one which started somewhat wretchedly, but seems to be improving as the phone begins to ring, and whatever humidity remains from last night's rain burns off. Saturday morning, I catch Nick just out of the shower in his blue bikini undies hustling to the dresser drawer for his shorts and tee shirt, walking sideways, trying to hide an erection I suppose? A big smile. God he is heartbreaking. But within two sentences we are at it again. He doesn't have time to change cars, he is off to work. A salutary, "have a good day." William's cotton Bermudas, tight on him, reveal his substantial basket, as he walks out the door. He'll be somebody's day dream all day long. I think of that French painting, les Rabatteur, is that the French word for floor strippers, muscles rippling as they take up the hardwood floors in the impressionist café ,some of the hardest work known to man. I admire Nick for how hard he has worked all week, 9 to midnight 6 or seven days a week, too tired to even eat he tells me when I ask if he saw the chicken and tortellini I left in the fridge for him. The carrot cake untouched. I envy him his drive, his determination. I try to imagine what my life would have been like if he had directed that determination toward me. I seem to myself like the alcoholic mother in last night's film at the festival who tries to buy off her children with gifts and uses her husband as an excuse for her drinking. Nick's energy makes me feel old and decadent at the same time. I am overwhelmed again by the sadness of how much life was wasted this winter, how wonderful it might have been to wake up in the mornings and shower together before he went off to make his fortune and I went to my desk. What we might have done together if he had loved me. The memories we might have created, instead of his secret life with mysterious Bulgarians, this enormous project he's been working on with people who must certainly love him by now. They'll learn at some point won't they? They'll be at the other end of the young Adonis's ambition. But this is too hard. He's a normal person, how can I blame him for going after what he wants. Like Natalie, these beautiful young ambitious Bulgarians. So focused, so obsessed with their future. But neither has been fair with me, really. I offered each of them a great deal. For Natalie, the child she wanted and physical support. For Nick, my love. I think I can say I have loved, that this is not just all sexual obsession as he would have it. Father, older brother, brother, girlfriend, all of these are roles I have played in my imagination, in my emotional life with him. And in his sexual life with me, what did he imagine? Hustler, gigolo, boy being raped, emotional sadist, sweet friend with the gentle kiss and blue eyes so close, smiling into mine. This past week I have been filled with resolve, something like Rob Perkins who insists he doesn't want to be with someone who doesn't want to be with him. I have lived with a sense of rejection, but a strong sense of determination too. "I offered him my love, I waited months to see if he would change and invite me to be part of his life again, to become my lover once again, something I have a right to ask, something he has no obligation of accept, but having rejected my offer, I must now put him out of my life, really out, with no attempt to work him into our friendships here in Florida, to create social events together, to be friends," I told myself all week. I think of the old joke: She offered her honor, he honored her offer and all night long he was on her and off her. Ha ha ha. We have three weeks left here before we head north. I cook, clean, write, do the mail, catherize William, walk the dog, give him his pills, set up the schedule, try to sell our art, shower him, take him to therapy, exercise him on the intra coastal. Days full, full. Too full. I leave Nick's supper on the stove. He is too tired to eat it. The rugs are so dirty, I've asked him for weeks now if he might lend a hand by cleaning the bathroom. But he's working 15 hours a day installing someone's carpet. None of this will get done unless I do it. If the dishes pile up too high, he sometimes does a few before bed. Wonderful. I can't imagine that he wouldn't offer to do more, I can't imagine that I let myself work like his servant here in the house. I've determined that when the month is over, we will let him stay on, but have nothing to do with him next fall if he is around. Nothing. It will only ruin next winter as well. The coyness, the seduction. I'll be at his mercy again emotionally if we see him on occasion. I knew this was a bad idea when I invited him down this winter. Don't try to be friends with your ex, You'll just break your heart when he starts dating others. What, I should be best man at his wedding, having worshiped the very cock he's about to present to his bride? - I guess that does sound a little "sick." Well, it is not. It is very human, and I think mental health would require that I take this stand. A little streak of masochism is one thing, but if I am to achieve some sense of personality, some sense of myself that others will find attractive, I have to disengage from this obsession and move on in my life.

It ain't over till its over, the Yogi says. To which the wag adds, "Yes, but when it's over, it's OVER." I have to really accept this. And when I get out of bed, and begin to set up things in my life, he does recede to the background. I'll never not love him, but it doesn't mean I will build this little time bomb into my life every year by having him around. The best will be if he does not get a visa extension and must return home, the best for me. The best for him, the opposite. And I will accept what is in his best interests. I have a career, friends, financial security for the moment, a friend who truly loves and needs me in William. Thursday night, William and Daisy and I went to a street festival and watched the children play in the fountain. Lovely. I bought a ring of Laborodite, blue and brown semi-precious stone in a fine silver setting. Not expensive, but very beautiful. The woman who sold it to me goes to Nepal each year, I guess, to buy her things and gave me the eastern blessing when she sold it to me, palms folded in prayer, a little bow, "Namaste." And later we met a stunning beautiful boy who I had to embrace before we left. He knows William's poetry, he was not put off by the fact that I was obviously smitten. He introduced us to his exquisite girlfriend. Biologists both, traveling all over the world to protect whales. Wonderful young people. We have made a date for a jazz concert and brunch on Sunday.

Yesterday, we picked up the final copies of the broadside that Florida Atlantic University has published for us as a gift, to thank us for bringing ECHOES to the university for an exhibition. The sweet librarian in charge of special collections said, "what a beautiful ring." One hand is crippled from birth, but the ring fit beautifully on her good hand. "In the Arab world, you must not admire something or it will be given to you," I said. I liked teasing her about Arabs, she so intensely involved in oral histories of holocaust survivors, the Jewish tradition. I guess I really am a passive, aggressive little prick as Nick might say if he'd had any training in psychiatry. "You keep it Dee," I said squeezing her hand, and kissing her good by.

April 23, 2002

Up early, day bright. Insomniac with ideas for the calendar of William's poems from WWII and the photos of ships from the Navy Historical Foundation. The broadside Florida Atlantic University did for us has been a tonic, but a distraction too I suppose. Will I even fall into that dream again? I have finally unpacked the suitcase with memorabilia from the trip to India that I have been carrying around now for two years, put everything in order in the library and now it is time to leave here once again. “Why don’t you just sit still and write,” Josephine has asked me in the past. Why this gypsy spirit. A way of running away from the blank page? “And she’ll have fun, fun, fun till her daddy takes her T-Bird away...” Caught a glimpse of the ghost living in the house this morning. Puffy eyed, surprised to see me, a grudging “good morning.” He’s eaten the dinner I put out for him last night, I see. It’s like getting up to see if the deer have come in the night to strip the cherry tomatoes from the vine. I risk a question:

“Have you heard from immigration?”

“Yes.”

“Yes! What did they say?”

“They said my request is being processed.”

“That’s great. That means you’re legal until they make a decision. That could be months!”

“I’m going to be late.” And he’s into the shower.

Why didn’t he share the good news! I guess he really does see his life as separate from us now. As do I. But I still love him and if I can help him, it will be something good at least from all this. Every night I cook his meal and there is never a thank you. I pay his car insurance, cell phone bill. All as though this is somehow my obligation, the way, I suppose a teenage son takes such things for granted from a father. But that is okay. This may finally be the lesson I'll learn, how to give expecting nothing in return. I suppose I still have some future in mind if William pre-deceases me as the awful euphemism goes. More likely I'll go first. But it is clear to me that if I am alone in the near future, Nick is not about to step in and become the lover with whom I will live happily ever after. So, enjoy William and these precious days and let the future to itself. Live the way we did this weekend in New York, the old glamor. Staying at the Bulgarian Consul's townhouse, the brunch in our honor at Bill and Margaret's, dinner with David Leisner, the lovely composer who has set William's poems to music. Send the broadside to Bill Clinton through Margaret. Finish the calendar. Meet the President and Prime Minister of Bulgaria this summer and Ivan Stancioff who has agreed to help me find funding for Stoimen's large painting as a gift to the UN in Geneva and set up readings for us in Varna. Enjoy Michael Harris and his beautiful daughters in Prague at the writer's conference. Rear your poems and work with Sooky on a new book in

Paris. Read your work at the festival in Avignon. Visit Casey in Aspen in August for the Eris Conference. Visit the Bread Loaf Writer's Conference this summer. Michael writes that he has finished the first draguht of his translation of Medea. Get working on your own new book, SCUDDER. Love, work, play. The three key ingredients in a life. Lots to do and pleased to have the chance.

April 26, 2002

How I wish I were like Daisy, my little chocolate cocker spaniel. She chases the tiny lizards into the bushes so avidly on our walks but she never catches them or bites them. She always seems so astounded that they are there. Throughout the day, constant attention to her toys, to us. Non stop play. Such a happy little dog. Just takes whatever comes her way. Will I ever regain that simple joy in being alive. The sheer physical joy in being alive in the world? It has been a wasted winter, but I have to recoup somehow, and start anew. I have no right to blame Nick for rejecting my advances, but I do. It could have been a wonderful time this winter. This morning I can't resist lying beside him, hand on his face. His ear so soft, like a baby's. Everything about him is so immediate a turn on. I catch a glimpse of his sex as he heads to the bathroom, come back, come back. But he's late for work, angry at my advance. Why can't it be sport, just two friends finding release in each other?

Two weeks ago I met Arnold in a leather bar, older than me but in good shape, with pierced nipples, blue eyes, and a big open smile. Beers are a buck at Saddles and Spurs if you go bare back, and despite his age, he looked as good as any of the half naked gay guys lining the bar. A retired lawyer, divorced, grown children, working as a doorman in a fancy building on Palm Beach. He's been around. And it was lovely to sing the blues to Arnold about Nick and have him take me home. Fuck buddies. An idea from the 60's and 70's. Just someone you can indulge your fantasies with, get yourself off with without having to get yourself off. Someone, paradoxically, who becomes a friend to whom you can confide at a very deep level because no commitment is required, like a priest confessor in a strange city to whom you can tell all for the sake of his anonymity. What an absolute perversion this would seem to someone like my sister who takes all her homophobic cues from the church and no doubt prays for my damned soul every morning at 6 when she goes to church. I'll have to re-read Jean Genet, sexual outlaw who turns perversion into a kind of religion. Is getting into the gutter with Arnold from time to time bad for the soul? What a joy it is to lie there and have him attend to every single part of my body with his mouth, to get myself hard, totally in him and just hold still as he asks while he looks into my eyes looking down at him. I've never had this sort of wild sex, even when I was young. Nick would call me a slut, no doubt, and guilt does cloud the picture. But why should it? Haven't there always been Geishas in the straight world, Courtesans who could talk politics and art and business after a night in the sack? Arnold is a friend, civilized, lively, caring. We lay sweating, laughing, exhausted after our romps. My burden gone for a while. Why shouldn't I accept this as a gift that God has given me at the end of this troubled, lonely winter. How's that for sacrilege Barbie? But isn't that what god really gives us sex for? A way to get out of the ontological loneliness that is man's plight trapped in our bodies as we are on this earth. And William? How would anyone reading this believe that he remains the love of my life, that my tenderness for him, my grief at seeing him age and suffer the trials of old age remain the very core of my soul, that I am able to go on living only because of him, his need of me, my desire to make life a pleasure for him in his last years, my gratitude for the life he has given me, our life together.

I remember Mackie Jarell's astonishment at the menage a trois that seemed to be the social life of James Merrill and David Jackson when Peter Hooton entered the picture. Sophisticated as she was, Mackie just couldn't see how such an triangle would, or should work. She might be able to superimpose the heterosexual model of marriage onto two men who shared their lives, but a live-in mistress, or whatever role Peter was playing in the relationship was beyond her comprehension - and that of most straight people I imagine. But as I age, I see there are many strange accommodations people make in life, lots of ways of getting through. This dear Nick I will have to let drift out of my life now. It's what he has in mind, no doubt. I couldn't get an answer about his plans after we leave - I suspect he will take an apartment of his own. When he has a difficult day, I will be the scapegoat, the source of all his miseries in the usual, weird inversion of logic that always seems to dominate the end of a friendship. The years I have invested, the energy, affection, and yes, the thousands of dollars will all have been for nothing. But one is not permitted to worship at the god's temple for nothing, I suppose. "Do you think you can touch my ear, or look at my body at the river's edge without gold, without flowers to place on my altar?"

How many summers has Nick run the little sunflower Skoda through the Rhodope mountains at the northern border of Greece with us in tow. It is said the god Orpheus was born here. His cult survives in secret societies. Not hard to imagine he has re-incarnated himself in the shape of this beautiful Bulgarian boy who has troubled my heart for so many years now. Hard to imagine though that he is about to move on and give grief to some other poor bastard at the aquamarine edge of the ocean here on the palm beaches.

May 2, 2002

So, here it is, what the Nick experiment has finally come down to again this winter. A tidy letter to Nick saying "bye bye fat ass." -- The old joke has become our standard parting: General Patton, impatient that his orderly has disappeared, calls the motor pool himself and says, "Bring General Patton's car around immediately." The corporal at the car pool says, "you can tell that fat ass, I don't do nothing immediately."

Son, do you know who you're talking too? This is General Patton."

"No, says the boy, do you know who you're talking to?"

"Well, no, I don't, " Patton admits.

"Well then," says the corporal, "bye bye fat ass."

I guess at any minute throughout the fall and winter Nick would only have had to say, "Richard, come here" and given me a kiss and in a flash, I would have been back in the saddle all over again. Can it really have come to only this. I guess life sometimes does. Like Marty.

I go to funky Marty upstairs to talk about the new carpets and house painting he has said he will take care of this summer for me. How I've loved having Marty around this winter. He's worked for months turning his mother-in-law's apartment into a showplace, but he always has time for a chat and a Pepsi. He jump starts the old Lincoln when it dies. Offers to go buy me a cheap battery and install it for me. Can't understand why I let a shop do it. His 1956 ford truck just keeps on going. Never locked. Pink dice hanging from the rear view mirror, pink dice on the radio controls and gear shift knob. "I had to make it look Spanish," he explains. "Nobody will touch this truck in my neighborhood, believe me."

I track him down at his mother- in-law's, drill in hand, since he hasn't answered the note I left on his windshield.

"Rick, I'm sorry I won't be able to help you this summer. I'm.... sick," he says sheepishly.

"What's up Marty?"

"I've got liver cancer."

"Oh, Jesus, Marty. I'm so sorry." I hug him. Strange. Like the odd feeling of hugging a brother. And we have a Pepsi, and we talk about it.

"I'm on a list down in Miami, but I don't want to take a liver from some kid."

"First come, first serve, Marty. You let them decide. You just take you're damn liver if they offer it to you."

"Yeah, that's what everyone says. Well, I want to spend some time with my son this summer, you understand? He took four ribbons last week - he jumps horses. You understand."

"Of course, Marty. Sure I do. How old are you Marty?"

"Fifty one. How old are you?

"Fifty six."

"Yeah. Well, I guess everyone gets his turn."

"Yeah."

"Why don't you and William come over this

weekend. I want you to see my garden. Lots of things are in bloom now."

"Sure Marty."

"Say, how was Bonnie Raitt last night?"

"Man, she was fabulous. You wouldn't believe it. And let me tell you. I had Daisy sitting in William's lap in the wheel chair as we entered the gates, right? And the guy says, 'You can't bring that dog in here.' And I'm thinking oh man, now I have to walk her ten blocks back to where we parked the car and I can already hear Bonnie singing on stage, so I say to the guy, "This dog is blind, this dog is handicapped." And the guy says, "This dog is handicapped? - Daisy is sitting there with her little pink tongue out, panting, looking right at him with her big bright black eyes, right? And the guy says "Wait a minute, I have to get the supervisor." Well, this tall black girl comes over dressed in a skin-tight uniform, badges, hair pulled back, American flags painted on her fingernails, right. and she says, "This dog is handicapped?" And I say, "Yes, mam." And she says, "Well, you can go right on in." I thought I'd die Marty.

"She went for it?"

"Yeah, either she was really dumb, or really sweet or both or something. I don't know. But Daisy was a hit.

The only dog among ten thousand Bonnie groupies. Talk about a chick magnet."

What can you possibly say. Remarkable, beautiful Marty. Such equanimity. His lovely wife, his mother in law. His son. His garden. How can he stand there with a drill in his hand, offering me a Pepsi? How can I return to the laundry, how can I do anything but wish Nick well, and try to help him find his way this summer, provide for his family. But have I really signed my letter to him "all best." All best. All best. How can I work toward and believe in "all best." All best to you Marty. All best to you Nick. All best to you Richard as you say goodbye to the person other than William you have loved the most in your entire 56 years on this earth.

Dear Nick,

As we prepare to leave for the summer, I wanted to take some time to write you in case we don't find the time to go over things and to be sure we are both "on the same page" about our leaving and your taking over the apartment for the summer. There is lots to say, but I'll try to keep it short.

Last night I mentioned to you that looked at

objectively, and if you were to ask for my advice, my recommendation would be for you to return to Bulgaria to take your final exams if the dance studio doesn't work out to your expectations (or even it if does.) You have spent so much time, energy and money on your studies it seems to me you all always regret not having given it a final try at least. I don't mean to cloud your mind with any uncertainly here, but we have taken a serious interest in your studies and I felt I had to tell you how I felt. In spite of the events of September 11th, I still feel you could obtain a visa to return to the US if you returned to Bulgaria to take your exams. I would be willing to write a letter of invitation if you wished to return.

As you know, yesterday I spent the day working on the I-127 to obtain an H-IB visa for you to work with us on art exchange programs for a year beginning this September. It is an extremely complex process. I am waiting now for a response to the form I sent yesterday to obtain the proper wage to put into the I-127. I will need to write a proposal and obtain documentation. I have begun this process in part in the interests of a sense of completion: I want to feel we have done everything in our power to help make your dreams come true. This application could be a back up to whatever plans you have to try to obtain a green card and working papers here in the US. Unless I can get a university to say they are hiring you, I will have to pay $1100 to make this application. In fact, Julia Pavone has invited me to be guest curator again this year for an art show for Petar Marinov and Zdravko and possibly Hene as well this October 5th- November 10th. So, this application is a legitimate application. If your tourist visa is extended for several months only, this may be a way continue to stay in the US if you wish. I will try to have all the information completed before we leave for Europe on June 15th and you can send it in or not as you wish. If you don't want me to pursue the application let me know. Here is our schedule, by the way:

May 11-13 Seattle area
15-25 San Diego area
June 1-15 Connecticut
16-25 Paris
26-July 1- Provence
July 2-11 Prague
12-31 Bulgaria
August in Connecticut except for:
7-11 Aspen
23-25 Bread Loaf Writer's Conference in Vt.

For the moment, I am going to keep the Lincoln here (parked in my sister's parking spot) until we see how your plans work out. If we should need to come here this summer for any reason, it will be good to have a back up car. I may give it to Ricardo at South Mobile along with the title for him to sell once we leave for Europe, however. If big rains come, or if they come back to their apartment - I think they will come for a short visit in June - please park it in our spot and put the Volvo on the street or in guest parking.

I would ask you to make a conscious effort to be in touch with us during the summer by email. The letters don't have to be long, but I would like to know that all is well with you and the apartment. I would ask you to be careful about the people you might invited into the house and to keep a low profile with the neighbors. You are not renting here, so you do not need to fill in any rental application. You are simply house sitting for the summer till our return. Our plan now is to return November 21st and then fly to San Diego on the 24th for a week. December 1st we will return for the winter.

Can't think of anything else for the moment. If you have any concerns or questions (I'd like to show you how to clean the filter to the air conditioner which should be done every month, by the way) just let me know. I will tip in the numbers for repair services should you need them.

I hope the use of the apartment and car will be help to you and that all your hopes for success this summer are met. We trust in your integrity and good will in accepting this gift to you and feel sure you will look after our affairs here as though they were your own. Let's try to have a dinner together Friday or Saturday before we leave to celebrate new beginnings. All best, Richard

26 Miles Across the Sea

Santa Catalina for William and me. Just me and William. Our host has gone back to San Diego and left us in charge of his fabulous house, the jet ski's, the motor bikes, the golf cart, the cd and video library, the birds of paradise and pink geraniums, purple bougainvillea cascading over his balconies like the hanging gardens of Babylon down to the little port and its sea glass waters. .

Last year, a nice looking guy about my age hung at the edge of the audience as we read our poems at an end of summer literary festival. William and I stood on the pier in

New London as the tall ships glided behind us, a perfect backdrop for William's sea poems. A magic day. I read some poems for William and seeing him there, grey hair blowing in the wind made me a little friable emotionally like the beautiful woman was crying and smiling at the same time as I read. I wondered if the guy who listened so intently might be gay, kind of hoped he was gay, but it turned out his daughter was a freshman at Connecticut College where he'd heard about our reading.

"What can I do for you guys," he asked at the end of the reading when he came up to meet us. "Poets ought to have people looking after them."

"Bring us to San Diego," I said, half joking. "My sister lives out there."

"Okay," he said. And a year later we have become fast friends, criss-crossing the country to visit each other, attend an art opening, give a poetry reading. Medici Michael. Our archangel friend. Every artist's dream. Pots of money from his legal practice, generous spirit and generous host, looking for projects, a little shell shocked and lonely as he contemplates divorce, like the brother I never had, confident, straight shooter, someone I can say anything to as he and I try to sort out the affairs of our middle aged hearts. His own paramour, (is that how I would describe Nick) is causing him as much grief. We are helping each move on, move out of our disastrous relationships, but not having much luck.

"I waited all winter to see if he would have sex with me again. It was a test. I mean, I don't want just a roommate. And would you believe on the very last day we left, we did."

"He just wanted to keep you hooked."

"No, I was the one pressing him. I told him I just wanted another look at him to remind me. And he said okay. He's been working so hard his right hand has begun to twitch like Dr. Stangelove. I was really worried, thought he might have a brain tumor, that that would explain his behavior. God, I hated leaving him like that. He was so beautiful. I've never seen a more beautiful guy. He dropped his shorts and I worshiped him so warm and ripe, kneeling right there on the kitchen floor, and then he let me take his gorgeous body and then we loaded the luggage and flew away."

"So, he's staying in your apartment..."

"Just until we get back next winter. Then he'll have to find his own place. I mean, I'll always love him, but he's definitely not building me into any part of his future. I've got to realize this is a dead end and move on. Its become almost a mantra, but why can't I let go? I mean they say out of sight out of mind, but it's just not working."

"Making the heart grow fonder?"

"Something like that."

"Well, we'll have a good time this summer," Michael says, big smile, squinty eyes as we sit on the sun-drenched terrace, a great flock of Birds of Paradise, firebird orange and purple tongues, erupting from a row of giant clay pots.

"I remember one Easter in my hippie days when I went around giving everyone I knew one of those flowers. The word in the commune was that Merton and the Dali Lama and Theilhard de Chardin were having a big spiritual confab in Asia (despite the fact that some of them were 'dead,') and that the world was about to change. I had this LSD vision demanding that I celebrate by giving out Birds of Paradise that weekend. God, how many years have I been looking for enlightenment. But I never seem to break though. I seem so stuck, so uncharitable. Why can't I break the mold and be a better person. Why am I so hard on people? Why do my nephews drive so me crazy with their pierced tongues and tattoos, their brainless surfer lives. My sister so bossy, so arriviste. I see myself like my father more and more each day. He was so unforgiving, so hard on people. Why can't I let it go?"

"Everybody has something you can hate them for," Michael says with his laid back, California simplicity. "You just can't focus on it."

He is a good guy, Michael. Doing good comes around in unexpected ways, he says in enlightened self interest. He is making progress. It's good to be around him. He can teach me. Friends teach each other, inspire each other to the good, this, this highest notion of friendship according to the ancient Greeks. But what will it be like this summer, I wonder as we travel in Europe together with his daughters. Will I learn to be more generous of spirit with two teenage girls who have been given every possible advantage and will no doubt expect a great deal from this trip.

This week in the village of Avalon there are 500 buffalos painted lavender, taxi cab checker black and yellow, the American flag, rainbow, transvestite. They celebrate the real buffalos who wander the interior of the island on the other side of the Wrigley Manson at the top of the mountains. Time to put your concerns on the back burner and shower William for a tour of the island. He wants to read Huck Finn which somehow I missed in my youth. We'll find the library, have a bowl of soup. We'll plant the flats of Sweet William that Michael has left for us as a kind of sweet entertainment. Maybe I'll give Sweet William a massage. He loves having his legs massaged with sweet oil when he's sat too long and they've swollen up. And maybe he'll massage me back, the way friends do when they are in love and on vacation.

Catalina 2

I shower, make the coffee, take a moment to dream of Josh, and install myself comfortably in front of the computer when I hear rip, rip, rip from the bedroom next door. William is readjusting the Velcro knee brace Dr. Miller fitted him with just before we began this vacation. Now a guy with a chain saw is buzzing off the limbs of a giant Eucalyptus tree hovering over the villa next door. Hard to sit at the blank page sometimes, just physically. A room of one's own, that's all it takes says Virginia Wolfe. In theory, writing is like jogging, a sport you can carry with you wherever you go - No need for jet skis, golf clubs, or lift fees. Just take a pencil and paper and "do it," as the Nike commercials command. But how to tease the blinking cursor along the line, ignore the sunshine pouring through the window and the men calling to each other like friendly monkeys in the Eucalyptus outside.

"I come second, you come first," William says, sleepy, tumbling back into bed for a while. And, guilty, I think "turn off the computer and go make breakfast for your friend. How many more brilliant mornings on such an island do you have with William. Go out and smell the roses, eat the lotus." And for the thousandth time, "does the world really need another book by me, me, me, even it's destined to go unpublished and remain nothing more than a kind of therapeutic exercise in sorting out my life."

"I'm just writing this for myself" the girls would protest in my creative writing classes when I started teaching at Mr. Vernon College for Women. And, of course, each of them secretly dreamed their words would one day out. Like Sylvia Plath or Emily Dickenson, their genius would surface one day long after their parents had divorced, their boy friend run off with their best friend last weekend at the Cape, the summer ruined.

"I told you I was sick," the tombstone of their journal would proclaim.

Ring, Ring. I rush to the bedroom next door where William is pretending to sleep for my sake and pick up the phone: a robot proclaiming, "This is Michelle, we are conducting a three minute survey...."

“Yeah, well, fuck you.” Click. Michelle could care less, as they say, and goes on her mechanical way to interrupt someone else’s day.

“I’m sorry, we do not approve of this use of the telephone,” Emmy Maxwell used to say before hanging up on some pushy solicitor trying to get his foot into her ear. But Michelle won’t even give me this satisfaction.

Crabby Richie. What’s up this morning? I guess it’s Josh, floating in the psychic background still, despite the coffee and sunshine. My little dream boy, calling to me from the quicksand of sleep still.

At the reggae festival last month, a forty-foot blue man caught William’s attention, hair streaming, swaying to the music as generators pumped air up into his balloon body. A boy stood watching William - transfixed boy, transfixed William, transfixed me. A perfect boy, trim, short blond hair, with one lovely flaw completing the perfection, a “slow” eye that turned his face into a question, a cocker spaniel tilting its head, the dear look of a child who might, in a minute, blink out of his concentration and return to his usual smile. The blue man hooked William whose face hooked Josh whose face hooked me, a little chain of delight that, goddam it, had me instantly in love again. And I pursued it, of course, and it only got worse.

Not yet 30, Dr. Josh it seems, boy captain and executive director of a foundation committed to saving whales. Just in Florida to fit an exploration vessel, then off to Papa New Guinea to talk the government into declaring their territorial waters a breeding ground. While in town, visiting - OF COURSE - his girlfriend. But like many young people these days, being gay for Josh, seems just a lifestyle and nothing that would stand in the way of a friendship. For a couple of weeks we shared our poetry, cooked dinners, went to concerts, our delight in each other growing tall as the blue man. Oddly, our schedules overlapped and he brought his mother to meet us at our reading on Mother's Day in Seattle. And it seems we are dreaming in simulcast as well. A little series of frustrating letters has muddied the waters in a curious way and landed me a kind of sweet pickle of affection.

I remember once when my mother, having despaired of having any blond-headed grandchildren out of me, took me aside and gave me the gay version of the birds and bees. Not overly happy about my choice of a lover twice my age, she told me there are many trees in the garden - I don't think she said fruit trees - that I might enjoy any number of them, that I should consider them all before deciding I wished to spend the rest of my life with

William. Pretty enlightened when you think of it. Loving. Loving of me, that is. Looking out for my happiness.

"Richard, Richard," William calls from the bedroom. And I guess it really is time to release him from prison. Breakfast has already slipped into lunch.

June 7, 2002

Just a week left till we fly to Bulgaria. Amazing. But the emails trickle in now confirming the details of our trip. The embassy can only host a reading and will not ask that we give workshops. Can they hear my sigh of relief in Sofia. The new ambassador will meet with us despite his "hectic" schedule. The Journalists Union has agreed to the dates I've requested for their rest house on the Black Sea. Stoimen calls from Vienna to ask that we stop by Vienna on the way home after our visit in Varna. I wake insomniac with details to be attended to, put on a pot of coffee and kiss William good bye for a few secret, precious hours at the computer. What does that new commercial say on TV, it doesn't matter how many good ideas you have unless they're realized. Pages of "to do" notes get longer and longer.

I have finally made some sense of this studio where

I work. What joy to be here among my book and art, looking out into the green forest that surrounds us here. William so clean and sweet and warm. How small he has become. My peanut poet. I can hardly bear the tenderness I feel for him. How lucky I have been in my life. I think of my dear mother now, husband gone, alone in her large apartment with no one but the game show hosts to talk with. How can she have let herself drift into a loneliness deep enough for her to give up the beautiful apartment and check herself into a nursing home, the one thing I have promised myself to never let happen to William, something I would almost die before doing. I see our dear old friend Josephine in her own nursing home, month after month, prisoner in her bed, always so shining and cordial when we visit. How can she bear it? No matter how many anti depressants, I could not take it. But perhaps when I am 80 or 90 I will understand it, as the octogenarians are always so quick to point out.

I have the beautiful portrait Dora Boneva did of mother her in 1995, tinted glasses, pensive, non-committal model. She will look out at me as long as I live, and how grateful I am to have that painting at least when I must be away from her. There will be no more visits to Florida. The

Vigil we kept for my father is over, my future role now still a mystery.

Vigil

A lone pelican
parks himself on the dock
guady as Lincoln stretch car.
A snowy egret begs for fish
at the back door of the clam shack.
He lifts his star-shaped foot slow
as Shiva dancing the world anew
but the door of Paradise
does not open.
A thin brilliance
washes the bay -
light transparent
for winter and distance
despite the afternoon intimacy.

We sit in the weak sun
mesmerized by a flock of sandpipers
scurrying at the wave's edge
pondering the doctor's auguries,
why the marble heart should

shatter just now as though
love were an accidental explosion,
buried ordinance, long thought dead.

Tonight like every night this week
she'll go to bed alone
with the sunset, afraid
after all these years
of the dark.

Across the river
he'll watch her
turn out her light
from his hospital room,
the silent television
blinking like a blue eye
blind to his fear,
his solitude.
I'll close her bedroom door
taking in the mystery
of that body from which I fell,
ponder what part I'm meant to play
in the lives which merged
to form mine, the soul whose

death portends my own,
dreaming on the terrace
waiting for the sun.

I write a dutiful letter to my brother and sisters in an effort to pull us together for what will be a difficult future I suppose. And as I write, the bird clock comes to 7:00. I approach the image of pretty pink and grey pigeon on the clock surface singing to me. “Mourning Dove” it reads. “Because it sings in the morning,” mother told me once when I asked her about the name. And, of course both are correct.

Dear Barbie,

William and I are back in Ct. now. It’s early, pouring rain, but the black of night will soon turn green with the jungle which has grown up around the place again this summer. It is very beautiful this time of the year here and I am filled with such joy to be back and in the middle of our plans for Europe.

Thank you so much for the effort you made to celebrate mother’s birthday. The cake was pretty spectacular, though we worried a little about the “red velvet” part: enough red dye to feed the Russian Army (ha and ha.) I have to say it was not an easy visit for me. The beautiful apartment mom and dad worked so hard to establish for themselves had become a kind of second home or base for me and William in York. We enjoyed visiting her there in her own home. She insisted (as a way of making the decision final?) that I take the pictures and things that we contributed and it was difficult. I can't imagine her wanting to give up the apartment, and I left her with the suggestion that she try to find some live in, or "full time" help in the month or so before she moves. If she found someone she really liked, it might change her mind. But suggestions such as this are not only seen as questioning her decision, but her ability to make a decision. I worry that her pride will have painted her into a corner and that if she doesn't like it (too hot, too small, too few interesting activities, too few interesting people) the ego invested will keep her from trying another option. The bottom line in all this is her happiness, of course. But she seems in far better shape than any of the folks I saw in that home. She drives a car, and arrangements could be made for something like a first alert pendant. That episode of not being able to get out of the tub seems to have really frightened her and triggered the whole decision. They seem to have new units which will be finished in October and perhaps she could be put in line for one of those (though she will not wait till October, having set all sorts of things in motion for the move.)

Part of what I was feeling was my own sadness at seeing her age and contemplating the inevitable end, of course, the way when we go to a funeral, our own mortality becomes painfully evident. It must be hard for her, despite the optimism she is trying to project. And who knows, if she were to become ill in the next year or so, it may prove to have been a clever decision after all. Maybe she will like the meals they cook and not having to cook her own. Free ice cream 24 hours a day, doesn't seem the right incentive for me, but I am not 80+ years old, I guess. "Be patient," my friend Josephine said, immobilized in her bed in a similar place in Cockysville when we visited this time. She will be 94 on August 19, the day after my birthday, and knows the "lesson of loss" that ageing brings.

Well, with British pluck (shall we say Johnnie Bull headedness?) she has made her decision and at this point it seems irrevocable. She has enough nice pieces to make the room comfortable and attractive. I hope she won't feel she has to hang around there all the time and will consider visits to Florida and California, maybe a cruise now and then. I plan to try to keep in closer touch with free cell phone minutes. And I plan to visit in mid-August when we get back from Europe. I have a friend in Alaska who has invited us to visit and will try to talk her into such a cruise later in the summer or next year. We'll just cross our fingers and hope she absolutely loves it. I know it means a great deal to her that you are close by and, believe me, it means a great deal to me too. Everyone knows how much you do for mother, what a large part you have played in her life, especially since dad's death, and we are extremely grateful. I wished I lived a little closer so it didn't mean putting William through an 8 hour drive to get there, but I'll continue to try to make regular visits. Till August then, we send love to you and George and hopes for a pleasant summer. Maybe this summer I can find someone in Bulgaria to teach me how to Salsa and we can dazzle them at Ben's wedding. Do they have any Arthur Murray's in York? Yours, R.

Very Dear Alva,

These are crazy days indeed as we prepare to leave for Europe this Sunday. I wake insomniac each morning with lists of things to do dancing in my head. A choir of starlings has taken up residence around the air conditioner in the guest apartment where we are living (a rock band, a goddamn blast of baby birds which sound like white noise amplified to freight train pitch as I slip out of dream and begin the day.) Last summer I bought some sticky stuff at the hardware which is designed to annoy their little feet as they make their way into the nest and discourage such homesteading, but I haven't had the courage to use it. Three more days of torture for me and then they can take over the house and live out their young lives all summer long until we get home: then it's war. But for the moment, William won't permit any infanticide. Did I ever show you the "poem" that came from such cavalier toying with life after a little experiment in France a couple of summers ago. I shall tip it in at the end where you may simply hit "delete" to save a few minutes in your day should you wish, once you have come to the end of the "body" of the letter as nuns used to call it when we were instructed on the formula for writing a personal letter (sic.)

I really hope we can drop in and see you before we leave and catch up a bit. Our travels include festivals in Paris, Avignon, Prague and travel in Bulgaria. We get back on July 31 and then are pretty much home all summer at which point we'll come in and divest you of what Bulgarian art may be clogging your storage. Are the shows for Nicky Marinov and Diana Stoilova down now? I see she is featured on your web page. We'll be able to visit with Stoimen in Varna at the end of July happily and plan to "talk turkey." He has somewhat mis-understood the idiom and translates "turkey" into "money." I wish I were able to offer him a veritable Thanksgiving feast this summer - I plan to meet the Prime Minister finally to see if I can coax some funding out of him or the government to present one of Stoimen's big paintings to the UN in Geneva. But things are tight everywhere. My old classmate Doug Casey has had me put my little nest egg into gold and this past month I gleefully watched it grow by a third. But in two days we seem to be back where we started a month ago. Easy come, easy gold. He seems to have lost the Midas touch.

We spoke of you last night at Jane Bredeson's. She'd arranged a dinner party, in part, for us to meet a Bulgarian student at Conn named Andrey Anev - nice alliteration, huh? He's something of a work of art himself with his variegated hair color and Raphaelite face - like some sort of sea creature, otter or seal, sticking his gold-striped head up amid the kelp: "What, sardines, did you say? A school of sardines? Where's that?" Charles and Bettie Chu may bring him to the opening on the 22nd - I've encouraged him to meet you and participate a little more in the cultural life of the city. Seems like a very nice guy. Is off to Turkey this summer to go wind surfing with his family. Bulgaria is such a mystery to me. I never know how people manage. Off to Turkey, wind surfing. You'll have to come sometime and see this wonderful place with us.

Well, William is clomping around upstairs, forced out of bed no doubt by the little devil infestation, ending whatever sort of fun I'd hoped for at the computer this morning. There will be other days for spilling ink. Love, R.

LES DJINNS

"This will not do," I said
tracing the black line
laid down like a living shoe lace
or a carpenter's level line
from garbage pail to pantry
across my kitchen floor.

Sugar ants or no, the little
darlings had to go, made no
good garnish to the olive bread

or pot au feu they meant to
carry off - so off went I to
the hardware store for something
appropriately genocidal.

Simple as sugar and strychnine
whatever the active agent and
by morning the black line was
still in place, but marching not.

Instead, Lord Buddha sat at my
kitchen table inviting me to tea:

"They were 12,345 lives, you see,"
he said. "And about that leg of
lamb in your stew. We need to talk."

And I, because I was in a bit of
a hurry and had no time to chat,
live now with almost 13,000 brats:
devil spirits who watch me burn
the toast, break the wine glass,
drip vinegar on a hangnail, or
accidentally fry my modem -

each one buzzing like a May fly
just before he buzzes off:
"What do you think of your
sugar water now, asshole?"
And off the wheel he flies,
Nirvana bound, leaving me
with 12,341 reasons
to think things over.

June 22, 2002 7:30 a.m. REPORT FROM PARIS

We've taken the train to Paris. It's chugging away on the desk now, while William saws small logs on our host's plush bedroom mattress, and I wait for the effect of a Valium to kick in. "Ça arrive," as they say here. No pain in the stomach, but I have turned the entire day into "l'heûre verte," the green hour, as dead poets in years past might call the time of day when aperitifs called for absinth. Les Absintheurs, as the little booklet describes them in a series of pamphlets on the subject of drinking absinth which one of the book sellers presented to me today after I presented him a glass of the pale, mouthwash-green drink I bought in duty free in Prague just before coming to Paris. So, train or no train, the manic effect of drinking absinth all evening has me a little insomniac. Paris has me a little insomniac. This crazy festival has me manic-insomniac.

Our little booth is number E8. 094 is that of a beautiful red-haired man who flirted with me on the street as we waited for Sooky to bring round the car this evening.

"You have beautiful eyes," I insisted.

"Everyone has beautiful eyes," he replied.

And as you enter the open air market, on the left there is a booth for Canadian, or rather, Quebec poets. There you'll find another angel, a Prince Valiant beauty named Pozier or some such who read a very moving poem dedicated to the young people of Afghanistan the other night when a hundred or so poets gathered upstairs for a reading connected with the market. Upper chamber. Sacred business. I sat on a guard rail on the window among the geraniums and on several occasions just about did tumble down into the street below as people pressed more and more into the room.

All day long we hang out at our little booth, while Marie and Sooky write furious letters to Ambassadors urging them to come to Avignon for our next "gig" at the festival there, arrange our books on the table, proffer

ECHOES, the art folio book Stoimen created for our poems last year, shmooze, and net work for all they're worth. And William and I get the chance to meet people. Some today:

Alexander. A Russian American living here in Paris the past 30 years, formerly of the Corso, Ginsberg crowd in San Francisco. Fabulous, Wallace-Stevens like work, fabulous Rasputin-like eyes, fabulous, stick-like body as though he might turn, at any minute, into a willow tree.

Puffy little Jan Max Tixier, gangster poet from Marseille, who has translated our work in years past during a stint at the Camargo foundation in Cassis. "Please, Jean Max, come over here to the booth for La Traductiere which took your translations of our work without payment or proper recognition and let me help you shoot the editor's knee caps off."

Jane and Jeffrey, an American couple from D.C. who have popped over for the weekend and have somehow managed to have their wallet stolen:

"Yeah, yeah, Jeffery. I've heard some pretty good excuses why not to buy my book but this one is pretty good," I joke with him. And poor Jane, on the edge of bursting into a very great smile or flood of tears. I give her a broadside. It turns out a smile. Imagine their pluck in coming out for a poetry book fair in the afternoon of a morning which must have been hellish. Nice. I love my countrymen so, sometimes.

It seems like if I had a dollar for every book of mine I've given away in my lifetime I would be a very rich man. What to do? Not only do I have to write the damn things, I have to lug them around Europe to give away as gifts. But people like Alexander and Jane make it all worthwhile, I guess.

Left my bed in part because I can't stop touching William on the face, shoulder head. He too wakes up from time to time to say, "I love you so much." What an angel he was today, each of us in our candy striped, seersucker jackets reading our poems under the trees at the café with elegant Nimrod (purple black, dagier -like poet from Chad) who we met at the translation festival some years back, reading translations of our poems along with Claude Munier, Falstaff-like poet, translator lady joining him on the dais. How kind and able they were, how neat to hear your words transformed into another language, liquid gold.

At one point I couldn't resist the music blasting away in front of a Cathedral size church from which our square takes it's name and wheeled William over there to listen to the music. The solstice today, longest day of summer, and we listened to fantastic group of young Algerians (Kabyle), or some such, Sooky informed me. Blue eyes, light skinned, their own race and with their own language apparently - how can I not have known this? Never heard of them in the days when I was part of the Royal Moroccan Air Force and we were helping the King clean up the southern part of his kingdom in a war with the Polisario. Chad or Algeria or both, I forget which nations borders were in dispute exactly. Bedouins I remember, and the Blue People, but Kabyle?) Wonderful music - Very good James Brown with sax and trumpets and all, and shifting then into electronic Oud, and a sing song rhythmic dialog between two boys calling to each other from opposite sides of the stage. I could just see them under the stars and high atlas, about a campfire, eyes shining, trying to outdo each other.

Apropos of nothing whatsoever, I recall a lovely expression Sooky taught me today: "On ne s'est pas reveillé pour les prunes." Which translated roughly means,

"You don't drag your ass out of bed to eat prunes," or, it will take a hell of a lot more than that to get me to do the sort of work you're expecting of me. You could use it any number of ways, I suppose. I'll have to tell her this the next time she insists I do something she wants me to do because she wants it for some political or aesthetic reason of her own, and the only justification she can offer is that I am in France and the French do it this way. Remarkable, that we can have encounters that genuinely threaten to end our friendship, and later in the evening be sitting, just we three, me William and Sooky at yet another sensational café having dinner, while a chorus of 60 sings Broadway tunes across the street on the steps of yet another baby cathedral - in love again.

On June 21st Paris celebrates the longest day of the year with free musical concerts at street corners across the city. I sure as hell hate to admit it, but these damn French sure know how to live. They can be snotty as hell, of course: I go to a pharmacie and ask the svelte, cat-like boy for vitamins which turn out to cost about $.50 each. Amazed, I let myself in for a classic line, a line I knew is coming even before I open my mouth:

"Man, I can't believe it. In America they'd be about

$.05 each."

"Then why don't you go home and buy your vitamins there, Monsieur?"

To my credit, I think, all I replied was, "no, I think I'll find another pharmacie down the street," even though he let me have the coup de grace with a cheery little, smug-assed, "Au revoir, Monsieur!" The sort of parting shot bureaucrats in America have been trained to deliver to let you know you're fucked, there isn't a thing you can do about it, and they enjoy enormously having the power to let you know as much.

Well, we all have it in us, I suppose. William's snoring begins to augment the hypnotic of effect of the sleep machine chugging away and the valium superseding the mouthwash which earlier washed my brain, and perhaps I'd best drift back, or finally into dream or give it a try at least. I wish I had dear Josephine's poem about the Chinese insomniacs here with me or in my head.....

Wednesday, the 27th. Avignon. At the hospital.

Sitting in the ER at a French Hospital. I hope Sooky has gone home. She was kind enough to bring us, after the bizarre story I put us through at the Police Station. I was sure the key to the car was stolen when I had only forgotten that it folds into the plastic carrier that the Citroen luxury car we've rented. I feel a terrible stress these past few days, real culture shock, or poetry shock. Hanging out with three sweet, intelligent, crazy, forceful women has taken a kind of toll on me. This can be the only excuse, except, perhaps, that I drink each evening. Well, what to do. William has had trouble for the past few days with his intestines and I fear a partial blockage. Also, he has what I think must be genital herpes, though how he may have contracted this, I don't know. I suppose it IS possible to get them off toilet seats and god knows we have been sitting on enough of these these past few days.

I would love most to have about 24 hours rest, non-stop. But I'm afraid it is not going to be possible. Now, across from me there is a poor, unfortunate, crazy young man who would continues to speak non-stop with crazy paranoid rantings, low voice enough, but, God I don't want to be engaged in French for a while.

I really do think it will be me that dies before William does. We joke of it all the time, but the stress I put myself though daily is becoming a little too much. I guess I should slow down a bit.

Here in Avignon, most of the morning was very pleasant, sitting in Marie's wonderful garden. Sooky came and we worked on the program for several hours until William began to complain again about his stomach and being blocked. Have I sensitized him too much to the idea of this danger? Finally, it is my paranoia that has saved him I firmly believe on several occasions: squeaky wheel gets the grease, etc. But at what expense to my nervous system?

Nick writes that he has moved in with Ginger - closer to his work and so he won't have to be alone. Why would I hold it against him? I love him and anything that will make his time in Florida easier is what I want. The nostalgia for some idea of love that always kept dragging me forward still stings me though. I wrote him a snotty reply to his letter, but I will write another to let him know I want only the best for him. And if he and Ginger have sex, or marry, or anything else at all, what should I do but wish them all the happiness, or him at least. But it was never a question of some future with him these past years. What button am I in the process of pushing now as I write this? Am I about to set off another obsessive rumination. No.

So, I have looked at our letters and it seems that I wasn't so snotty after all. Cordial. This the right tone to take:

Dear Nick,

Glad you're doing fine. Please be sure the Lincoln in parked in our parking spot when you are not at 3915. I'll tip in a letter I wrote recently to give you an idea of our time here in Paris. Keep it clean, as my father used to say, and please do keep us informed of how things are going with you. Best to you and Ginger both. R. and W.

p.s. Don't forget your promise to paint the apartment at some point, though if you now reside chez Ginger I suppose it will be more difficult and less of a concern for you. Still, there are four months or so before our return....

So now, one solution to my stress is to sleep, like William who is snoring softly on his bed while the sweet crazy guy holds his peace a minute.....

June 30

Woken this morning by a chorus of bells here in Avignon, like the dogs calling to each other along the river, passing along the guard as the ice breaker carves its slow green “s” in William’s poem about the Thames. Can’t decide what to do this morning and filled with guilt that I have to ask William to stay abed while I figure it out: jog, go to the secret garden sex shop tucked back in the side streets off the Ave. de la Republic, or sit in my own secret garden here at Marie’s to flesh out this trip and get eaten by the little bugs that have proliferated with the summer’s growth.

Last night William says in his serious, ominous tone that we must talk. I press him and he confesses he is afraid of losing me. The poor sweetie. I wonder what he means. I tell him I am with him forever, but I wonder if he means that it is likely that, indeed, I will be the first one to die in this friendship. I haven’t kept the promise to my father here in this town, the promise to be happy, and the promise to love him and make him as happy as possible in these final, important years. He’s lonely he says. I transfer him from one thing to another, in the process I sometimes have to change his trousers because he has peed himself - I forget to remind him to pee, he forgets to let me know he needs to pee. And then I am angry and shout at him as I wash him up or change his clothes. My eyes fill a little now as I think of it: for him and his little humiliation, for me, for the work involved.

We have worked so hard on this trip. He has been extraordinary in the efforts he makes to keep to the schedule these banshees have designed for us. For four days we manned the booth in Paris for the "Marche de Poesie," holding down the fort while Marie zoomed around making connections, schmoozing. Sweet troubled woman, beautiful still, neurotic passive aggressive, trying to run a poetry center on a shoe string, constantly hawking her wares and poetry - like me. The worst aspect of being a writer, the necessary promotion, yes, self-promotion. Poe Bus, as Maxine Kumin calls it. Still, it was the chance to meet some very lovely people, new friends. And that perhaps made it worthwhile.

This time a woman named Katherine who delivered a lecture before our reading. Bright, tough, very knowledgeable about American literature and our work. And her boyfriend, a poet too, who read the poems in French. A shy woman who made accurate translations but with the impressive ability to carry over the rhyme scheme in poems such as "Winter He Shapes Up" which are so crucial in William's work particularly. And Francoise, Sooky's "press secretary." A real comedian this, batty as Gracie Allen, or Lucille Ball. rolling her eyes in bourgeoisie indignation at the school system in France, how hot the summer has become, the price of peas. Her lovely hands fly about like pheasants startled by a hunter. Whit Cook said once of Josephine Jacobsen that "she could live on the chit chat of her chit chat." Francoise has her beat by a factor of ten.

I feel a little like Orpheus at the hands of the Maeneds each one tearing at a corner, pulling in her own direction to get the boy precisely where she wants him. Still, there have been moments in the garden explaining the poetry to Sooky, a dinner in front of the Pope's Palace with two charming American tourists wowed by William's poetry, the fading yellow pink light setting the castle aglow as we ate daude, drank our wine, and came to know each other a bit. And some nice expressions have entered into the bright lexicon of my French: "Lache moi les basket," ("Let go of my tennis shoes!") for example, something a child say to his mother when she tells him to sit up straight, of finish his broccoli. "Lay off me!" roughly the translation. A little more polite that "fiche le con" or "get the fuck out" as it were.

One day we did have a rather spectacular day, though. Sooky's house in Bannieux that she bought in the early 50's had been robbed and she needed to drive to file a claim with the insurance. In the old days, there were no roads and she had to carry her own water in. Locals would deliver fruit or other gifts. She never locked her door, could leave for a couple of years if she wished and not worry. A kind of Paradise for one who fled Viet Nam to New Caledonia only to be caught up in a revolution there too. At last, a place where she had solid peace of mind. And now, robbed, violated, the snake has entered the garden once again.

Her husband died several years ago and she felt like snow white awaiting the kiss of the Prince. Instead, it seems the dwarfs have made off with all the furniture and carried it back to the wicked witch. Still, they left the house, her kiln, and three borie the little bastards couldn't cope with.

William stood in front of one of thc bories transfixed like a child in front of a miniature train set. The ancient stone structures are formed by a primitive, but effective architecture, stone laid on stone edging out like a Roman arch until a perfect bee hive is achieved. It's not known where they come from, perhaps as early as the first or second century, created by the early Galls here in France, or possibly by religious groups in flight during the wars of the 17th and 18th century. Remarkable in any case.

But now the bells take up the call once again, an hour has passed, and I must release William from the prison of his bed. They must have been Marie's children's beds. They are in any case a cradle from which he has no power to rise and Marie, from which, Marie, still abed, could not help him rise.

Serafamivo

At long last at the computer again, hiding here in the little closet/ studio in the William Meredith "museum." Here is William: in a flight suit standing on the deck of a carrier waiting for his plane, Flying Tiger at Princeton, pulling on a prop to rev up his plane, standing in his bathrobe beside me in my jogging outfit feeding the swans in Connecticut, some actual feathers gathered by Lyubomir during a visit lying like magical talisman on the bookshelves. A calendar of Dora's paintings of New London from the time of her residency at the art center. A large American flag beside a photo of me and William and the President the year we were made citizens of Bulgaria.

In years past, I would wake up and knock on the door beside our room and find Nick sprawled on his bed like a sweet Endymion. We might make love, go for a run along the alpine roads, fire up the coffee, herd the goats out of the front yard, flirt with the neighbor lady who would come each morning with warm milk she had just coaxed out of her beautiful cow. Now, I find sleepy-eyed Boiko instead, having a smoke, hanging out so he doesn't have to do the dishes or take down the wash from the line out back. Two silver cups and a candle stick sit in elegant formality on the mantle of the little fireplace, Nick's birthday gift from a previous summer. I left them in a gesture of finality some other year when I was certain our friendship was over. And throughout the winters they have stood in the emptiness of this room. Now they are a kind of torture for me, reminding me how things have not worked out. I have had to struggle to be happy as we travel the same roads that we covered in Nick's little yellow Skoda. Driving by acres of sunflowers, old babushkas gleaning the fields and storks gleaning after them. How he interpreted the beauty of this country to me. Sharing it with him and William as we traveled made it beautiful, the joy of seeing a sunset with someone you love.

Well, I have old William still. I killed the flies

bothering his sleep early in the morning and later hustled him down for a hot shower before the electricity cut off in the village. Yesterday, I left my little military style cot and climbed into his. We lay laced up in each other, I covered his face with my hands to keep out the sun, his dear old head on my chest. "Anticipatory grief" is never far in the background when your lover is as old as William and has had such a troubled medical history. But yesterday morning I made some progress in seizing the day, my mission on this trip to share my happiness for perhaps a final time here in Bulgaria.

These fabulous mountains - the sun playing over little valleys dotted with barns and peasant cottages like a scene from a Swiss calendar. Today we will wend our way down to Plovdiv, a two hour drive along crashing trout streams, the purple waves of mountains drifting back into an ancient sleep. Orpheus will sing alone .

Plovdiv - Saturday, July 20, 2002

Something nice about this date for me. All the two's and the zeroes. William and I are two. Can it be 2002? How to fill in the zeroes in the middle of the year. The emptiness of this trip without Nick. So, I'm sitting in perhaps the very chair Lamartine sat in when he traveled in Bulgaria and wrote his Voyage to the Orient. The museum room in this house has wonderful old photos of the poet, his travels outlined in little red dots from Italy to Beirut. Along the way he has documented the "Ottoman yoke," as it is called here: Bulgarian peasants working the fields like slaves, forced to adopt Islam, bear their children. But for 500 years it was the only game in town, an empire that brought commerce, wealth, law and order to what had been a feudal system. Many Bulgarian words are of Turkish origin, the conquerors have entered into the history and blood of this people as profoundly as the moors in Spain or Greece. But it's not an observation one can make casually here in Bulgaria where such historical grievances have become part of the national collective identity or consciousness.

To be Bulgarian is be aggrieved at the Turkish yoke and the territories such as Macedonia which were part of a greater Bulgaria under different czars in the past. It seems every country in middle Europe once was a kingdom that included all the rest, and nostalgia for days of former glory continues to fuel the wars and ethnic cleansing that always seem on the verge of erupting in this part of the world. Easy for me to say, I guess, the virginal American with very little history to burden my soul and identity.

My desk hangs over ancient cobblestone streets on the way to the Roman theatre at the top of the hill. The old quarter on this ancient hill is a labyrinth of such streets that tourists wander by day. Many of the houses here have these beautiful enclosed porches projecting from the houses on the upper levels, supported by graceful wooden buttresses. The rooms are painted in gay 19th century blues, yellows, rose, and graced with intricate wooden filigree detail. A sweet breeze blows through the windows. The street is deserted except for the occasional black white and orange tabby out for a stroll. Now, in a graceful leap she scales the neighbor's garden wall and sits perched on the red tilled roof.

I've forced myself to get up and write about it after a late night dinner and spontaneous art show. The long haired hippie boy selling souvenirs I've met in years past is still at the same corner, the unofficial mayor of the town. Soon he will come and bring the extraordinary artist who opened his gallery for us last night after dinner. Sensational work, electric Van Gogh. But can I take on another project, yet another artist to bring to America?

The tensions of too much togetherness dissipated

last night at dinner, a wonderful restaurant which incorporates Roman ruins and contemporary murals into the structure of the building and outer walls of the garden. The star sisters stood under a tree in the elegant black dresses and bare shoulders and sang for the clients. Their father was crying slightly when they came back to the table - pride and too much gin. I tried to explain his emotional fragility to him - a high powered lawyer with a forceful personality suddenly is in a country whose language he doesn't understand, at the mercy of cultural vagaries, no longer in control of his situation. And his divorce, and his break up with "the other woman" and trying to keep his daughters' love in the middle of the slight mess he has made of his life. Too much fuel feeding the depression. Too much booze. But he is strong, and attractive, and rich and successful in his work and this will all burn off like the fog that shrouded these cobblestone streets when I first woke this morning.

It has been a great deal more work than I would have thought so far this trip. But, I have managed connect all the dots of the complex constellation I've designed for our summer travel. Michael managed to meet us in Prague with his eldest daughter, Lauren, we spent a week of tourism after our work was done at the conference. Sometimes our readings do not go well - the stroke affecting William's control of the drooling and my evident discomfort, insufficient rehearsal time, or not enough rest before going on stage. But this time the poems wove together seamlessly, the tone friendly, comfortable, the rapport with the audience palpable. A wave of applause as we left the stage, a long line of students book in hand waiting for an autograph. We earned the substantial honorarium and did not disappoint leading me to hope for a return engagement one day perhaps.

Prague proved to be the miraculous town people are beginning to call the new Paris. Heroic squares, castles, churches all untouched by allied bombing in the war and so, a remarkable window into the past. We sat in the jewel box opera house listening to Don Giovanni as though in a time warp and only hearing the news. We jumped on the bus with a group of students and drove a couple of hours out into the country side to Karlovy Vary for the film festival. Karlsbad is the name in German I suppose for the resort established by the emperor when a stag led him to the spot one day while hunting. One of the great spa towns in Europe, patrons from Goethe to Frans Joseph came to take drink from 14 mineral fountains along the colonnades and take a glass of Becherovaka, an herbal liqueur considered to be the 15th fountain of health.

The reading in Sofia proved less successful, not for our work, but that of the embassy. They have paid us a thousand dollars and almost as much in hotel costs and only managed to stir up 20 people for our reading. Lyubomir was shocked that they didn't at least have a poster for us, but who knows what they did. The Ambassador made a courtly introduction and then split. Seems as though the Bulgarians were balking on their promise to destroy Soviet missiles in exchange for a chance to enter NATO. Apparently our government is insisting that a US firm do the work, that Bulgarian inspectors not be permitted to be included, and that no guarantee is to be offered for the health of the surrounding population. Millions will be spent on the project and you can hardly blame the Bulgarians for wanting to do the work themselves. I can't imagine why we wouldn't underwrite some sort of insurance, the way we do for nuclear power stations. Michael would be very good here, but Levchev tells us at dinner not to try to give advice to our embassy. "They work for us," Michael declares with the cheekiness any American feels free to exhibit. But Levchev is a master politician and is probably right in thinking all we'd get for effort is a black mark in our dossier and a guarantee never to be invited again.

Anyhow, our reading was fine, and the actor was fine too. Tall, gazelle-like boy with very fine dark eyes and features. He said it was an honor to work with us. I got his phone number. How many phone numbers do I have? Will I someday begin to call these beautiful boys I meet along the way?

I remember the German boy from Munich with whom I had terrific sport one late afternoon in Prague. Thirty different pornographic movies going at once, a room with a bed and a window in case you liked to show off, a loft with a bed, glory holes. Even forgotten his name now, but not the eyes. Tight brown body. 43. We stripped right away and were all over each other . "He wants money," he said of the guy in the next booth that he was trying to interest in joining us. "I don't pay money," he said. Nice sport. Mutual gratification. Friendly, bacchanal, healthy, finally, I am sure. "I am a good sucker!" he announced and gave me his address. "There is a big gay parade in Berlin," he said. "You come." If only occasionally, such encounters are so restorative, can feed the imagination for months to come.

So, now we are on our way to Bourgass. Bye bye

Plovdiv. I'm sitting in the back seat while able Boiko drives us. Not as beautiful as Nick, not the same at all, but friendly, good company. Before we left, we sat in the garden under lush roses and bunches of green grapes that will turn purple by summer's end drinking rakia with Sasho and Vera, the old guardians of the house. Sasho has a hand gnarled too by contractures from the stroke. He has William's same sweet smile, smooth skin, disposition. Like children with Down's Syndrome, or the blind, their sweetness a kind of natural defense mechanism? We signed the ancient guest book and looked at old inscriptions from years in the past.

Across the plains in the distance, white bolts of lightening shoot up from the earth, tearing the sky apart. A single white horse grazes. I remember the night Nick and I first stood on the balcony of his apartment in Sopot as a terrific summer storm ravaged the sky and we slowly and deliberately ravaged each other. I loved him so dearly; The scene would have been too purple even for the most rabid romance novel. And now, more fields of sunflowers, forest of yellow recrimination. Love lost, love unfulfilled. How did it come to this.

Ahead, a gypsy girl sitting amid a load of watermelons on an old Russian truck, talking on a cell phone. How I love this country, Nick or no Nick.

July 25th - Full moon, Black Sea

Will the sweet waiter who has flirted with me today come to see me tonight at midnight as I hope. Am I well enough to visit with him if he does. The days here get worse and worse and I try to overcome this terrible flu that has gone around, first Lauren, then me, now William. All evening I have changed his sheets with fresh towels as he erupts in profuse diarrhea and vomiting. It begins today just as we are leaving from our visit to Karin Dom and lunch at the founder's house.

Ivan Stancioff is a remarkable American who gave up his American citizenship to become this country's first foreign minister after the end of Communism (the polite euphemism for the fall of Communism in a country where the party still has power and may yet take over the state once again.) The King has failed his job, apparently, and the papers count the days till his deadline for change arrives. This is why Stancioff did not vote for him apparently, the stupid mistake of saying that everything would be put in order if he had 800 days to fix Bulgaria's problems. The people believed him: the King would return, wave his scepter, and fairies would fly once again over the Magic Kingdom. 50 years of communist rule has been pretty successful in turning a large part of the national psyche into that of a child it seems.

I made the mistake at lunch of recounting the little analogy I cooked up last night drinking Bekerovka on the terrace under the moon - I slipped into the Keroac hour where everything I thought I wrote and everything I wrote I thought magnificent.

It seems the eternal flame at the heroic memorial to the Russian soldiers who died "liberating" Bulgaria has gone out. No one any longer lights the nightly fire in their honor over the hills of Varna since the demise of Communism. I imagined some old Russians from WWII, perhaps having lost someone in the war, coming to Bulgaria and finding the general hatred for Russia that predominates here. I thought of how American to be liked, how in parts of northern France especially we are still loved for saving France in the war, though lately, particularly among the young, how the French hold us in disdain.

"But you didn't stay in France for 50 years and set up a totalitarian state," the Executive Director shot out at me, as the melon went round the table, and proceeded to launch a diatribe against my logic which spoiled the affection which built in me all morning as we toured the rehabilitation center for children that Stancioff had turned his familial estate into once the government returned it to him in the late 90's. Heartbreaking children, beautiful the way such damaged creatures always are. Autism, cerebral palsy, birth defects, all are treated with kindness and the latest technology. They presented us with paintings they'd done for us, we toured the Montessori classes established there, the special therapy rooms. The center is open to everyone and no one pays anything according to the director, though I had heard the predictable Bulgarian cynicism that it was for the well to do. Whoever is chosen and however, love is the engine driving the place, and Stancioff's efforts are genuine philanthropy of the noblest kind is seems to me, exactly the sort of generosity of spirit the country needs at present.

According to Levchev, there is no longer a middle class and the inequities make the difficult economic situation more and more intolerable. In Plovdiv, the house keeper makes $15 a month it seems and the prices here are pretty much what you would find in the US. One was trained not to complain in the old days, but now people are free to complain about the BMW's crowding the streets while the price of electricity doubles in a year.

Well, we gave our books and thanked him for the extraordinary reading he arranged at the auditorium in the Karin Dom last night and at the final stop at the toilet before his car took us home to the Journalists House, William lost control and I spent 20 minutes trying to wash his underwear and trousers in the terribly hot and cramped toilet. I was very severe with him for not monitoring these functions more closely and giving me enough time to head off such disasters and I regretted it terribly when we got home and Niagara Falls began making it clear he was acutely sick. Guilt and my memory of how sick I've been in the past couple of days sent me out to buy laundry detergent, Kleenex, soda water and other necessary items to look after him. Throwing up his medicine, his fever, the risk of dehydration all can be serious and I find myself praying once again that God will let us get through this again, so I can have time to be nice to him. How often do I forget that he is sick, just sick.

Waves of nausea flow though me like the waves crashing below this terrace on the Black Sea. I guess my daydream of a little company from cute Krassin is not to be, that I must shut down this dam computer which has failed me so during this trip. Why can I not connect to the Internet and why doesn't CompuServe recognize my account. What important information am I missing? I broke down and called Nick tonight to see if he was having any problems with INS, to tell him I miss him here in the hotel where we met and spent so many summers in love, and hating each other. The answering machine was all I got for my money. I shall sit on the terrace for a bit, in the dark, but with the moon spreading a golden carpet to the horizon, a ladder I would climb if I only could to take me away.

Next day

Waning moon, and I must give account. A kind of prayer back to say William got over that horrendous flow of shit and pain to the extent that we had a fine dinner with our friend Dimitrina tonight, just the three of us. Several years ago I got her fired by ego, i.e. I said, "Tell the commie bastard you aren't coming in if you don't want to, or that your friends are welcome here or whatever the issue was. Now she is managing a fancy hotel and has the same dignity and intelligence. The best Bulgaria has to offer. I think William will be well enough to go to Gotze Delchev to receive the reception the mayor has prepared for us. Agonized all day over it. But William seems fine now. And I must fulfill my commitment to love him and take better care.

July 26, 2002 - on the road again

Well, William has pulled thorough again, praise be. The really awful diarrhea he suffered which seemed almost fatal, has gone and he is more or less his old self again. So, we have followed the advice of the nice woman from Seattle who came to our reading that I met on the beach jogging yesterday, and have decided to continue on to Gotze Delchev and the reading Nicky Marinov has set up for us there. Guests of the mayor and a party beforehand in Blagoevgrad with the river people. Today, Stoimen came with Margarita and his daughter as well as Stoyan Tasanev and his mistress- exquisite woman, tall, thin, with a dress in black with large red roses at the bottom and a red top covered by a black lace jacket. Topped with her black hair tinted red, swept up into a French twist with a few strands falling across her cheeks. Exquisite and cold. A real model. You look at her and a ravishing smile. But I hated being introduced to her in years past knowing she was the other woman and that I was being asked to accept her as an equal in the little social group we had formed. Well, pleasant enough. And Stoimen so sweet, so solicitous. Here on the Black Sea is where we met twenty years ago or so. His beautiful daughter is the spitting image of the wife he took to Vienna to cure a brain cancer and when it did not work, he stayed on with the daughter to make a life. Lovely to swim with him in the Black Sea again, just the two of us in our underwear after a lunch and then coffee at the small café down at the edge of the water. He wants to continue to work with me to try to sell the large paintings. Perhaps I will finally meet the Prime Minister the day before we leave. I hope so. We've heard so much about him and his failed performance. Perhaps he will perform for us.

I spoke of Natalie as we bobbed in aquamarine waters made fresh by last night's terrific storm. Pity any poor creature that was on the water last night. This is why they call it the Black Sea. I've never see such storms blowing up in no time, turning the sea pitch black covered with crashing waves. The rains like a monsoon. And then the following night, the moon again holds her lantern steady flooding the sea. I guess some summer I could come here, calm, and just use this place as a retreat.

When he first came to American and Natalie was with us for the "project" I had to say to him right off what I had in mind so he did not make a play for her and spoil everything between us. He took on an avuncular role and respected my wishes for which I will always be grateful. I told him what a disaster it proved to be, how we fought over everything, her need to make money, how unkind she was to us. I will never know till the day I die I guess, if she was only using me. But the situation was horrendous and I guess I should thank God no child came. Why can't I be content like so many people in life not to have children? People like B.J. and even Stoimen's present "wife" Sylvie.

Nick's shadow has fallen over this entire trip. Boiko said we should not make an effort to see his family, that it would only hurt me. Perhaps calling will have the same effect. This trip is taught me how to let go of Nick. Is this to be his role in my life, to teach me how to give up the sweet world as we must all one day do, or ever do daily, if we are to achieve peace. I still have not been able to incorporate these eastern ideas into my life - but I have never seriously tried: no meditation, no serious reading on the subject. This fall in Connecticut when all this travel is over I must return to this speculation and finish this journal. Vania Lipke, the french/Bulgarian poet who is part of our summer scene here said to me on the phone tonight that I must make myself as happy as possible and that way William and I will both be happy. Friendly words, and probably true.

Well, early morning wake up call placed, will pack in the morning and hope we get our butts home without further incident.

July 28, 2002

On the road to Gotze Delchev with some of the river people. We are driving by a river where there are catfish two meters long in the very deep waters, a little like Loch Ness, but true apparently. We will drive by Rupite I guess where the soothsayer Vanga lived and gave succor. We've had a lovely lunch with Eli and Lucien who gave us three rugs made by his grandmother. Boiko took us to the church and showed us a series of 14 icons at the base of the icons with Adam and Eve - they must be at the base apparently. William has given one to the Meredith house while I was at the toilet, of course, and I had a lot to do to explain that we would always get them back if the house failed for some reason. We've spoken of a possible exhibit at Carnegie Mellon where William got one of his honorary Ph.D.'s this time to bring Lucien's wife and children. Crazy to take on another visit by the river people, but the President did say that he would be willing to help us in any of our projects and perhaps he can get Austrian Airlines to spring for tickets for them all the way they did for the Vice President and his party two years ago.

Boiko has given me photos from the last vist and there is Nicky, looking so beautiful in his green jacket. Too much rakia at lunch and I let myself dissolve in some silent tears for him. "After William," this was the love of my life," I explain to Boiko in the back seat with me. We try to call his sister, but no luck. I'm better now, curving up these dry hills on our way to the Green Border. We had hoped to visit Lucien's studio and to take William to the church where Boiko is doing his icons. But when we call, we are informed that there is a formal dinner at 8:00 hosted by the mayor. Well, thanks a lot for the notice. Maybe we wanted to sleep a little after our journey, relax a little on a Sunday? So, Nicky Marinov is "nervous" i.e the Bulgarian word for pissed off, fucking blue angry that we threaten to be late. It might have been nice to inform someone that we had this invitation?

July 30, 2002

So, on the road again after our visit to Gotze Delchev. Throughout the day we have had rain and bright sunshine as we followed the Mesta River out of Gotze Delchev and then the river along the road to Blagoevgrad which runs very deep and has cat fish in it six feet long. Never heard of such fish, but Boiko assures me it is true. Surprising Bulgaria. You never know what you will find.

Yesterday I stood on the balcony of the hotel a mile outside the town and looked down to see 26 turtles in some sort of garden pen they had been put into. They even had eggs in the pen. Raised for eggs? Turtle soup? Who knows.

Nicky Marinov had arranged his typical dramatic presentation for the reading. Large green leaves were spread on the floor like footprints leading to the table where we were to read. The table was encircled by candles and copies of our poems lay spread inside the circle with more of the beautiful green leaves. Taking his artistic cue from Whitman, I wonder. The exquisite young Kate let me down a bit, reading the poems like prose and throwing away the endings. She was unfamiliar with microphones and read alternately too loud and not loud enough. At one point she knelt in the center of the circle and in a very dramatic, and I suppose effective way, read William's poem "Crossing

Over," one of her favorites.

After dinner we wound our way out of town to a mountain hideaway for yet another banquet sponsored by the mayor. William and I were parked like icons at the head of the table, left to our salads while the rest chain smoked, chatted away in Bulgarian and drank rakia. After a while, though, everyone was fuelled to the max and we began singing and dancing wild lines of Greek style dancing. Tatania danced with me, a blond lawyer with enormous eyes (and breasts) and later was part of a group of women from the table dancing wild complex steps. At about 1:30 William protested his desire to go to bed and Pancho took us home. Why did I not catherize him and go back and join the rest who stayed up till 4:00 dancing and drinking. I woke, sad again for the lost opportunity. Why do I not enjoy myself more. I was the guest of honor, could have had any of a number of the women there., but I went home and went to bed. Worse, I said that anyone who wished to say goodbye, would need to come to us at 11:00. In fact, I did change my mind and we had a lovely lunch around the Olympic size swimming pool painted an odd emerald green as though the bottom were covered in moss. In fact the water was quite fresh, but an odd color to paint a swimming pool - but beautiful.

So, I must make more resolutions to enjoy myself in the future. Why or why did I not return to the party where all my friends were. My great concern was William, and I lay praying that he was not developing a blockage once again. It had been about 4-5 days since he had a bowl movement, and I envisioned checking into a hotel here in Sofia. But finally, this morning, he had some success and gave me an equal relief. These river people, such beautiful friends. We all kissed goodbye, men on the mouth too, and headed back to Sofia. Now we drive the high road above the city, under the Vitusha mountain which attracts clouds and weather and makes the winter severe sometimes. Sad to be leaving this country. But it has been very hard work, and it will be a joy to see Daisy baby again and rest a little at last on the river.

August 2, 2002

Summer on the river. Torrential downpours all last night then cool, and bright this morning. The day sure to push into the 90's later and build perhaps to another summer storm. Daisy has come to our bed to play after an early morning run. On her back, paws in the air, kissing William's sleeping face. A little like the joy parents must have, having a toddler come to their bed.

The night was heavy though. Sweating, chills. Time for another AIDS test. What would I ever do if the unthinkable happened? And I know the unthinkable will happen one day, William will die and I shall be left with the enormous bills we have run up again, no retirement, alone and lonely, regretting the loss of my love and my lover, Nick as well. Unless I begin to work hard now, this summer, to change my life. Who was it of my friends who said that people don't change. Well, I must. This bright morning fills me with hope again. We are back from Europe. We met the rigorous schedule I set for us. I was often a tyrant, but we got through it. Now I must economize, loose weight, and become a better person - in two months. I have to apply myself, as Josephine suggests. Get up early like this and get some work done each morning before William is up. Find someone to help me in his care so he doesn't sit in front of the TV all day while I work. Fiddle through the summer like the cricket of legend though. Enjoy yourself with William. I've started the day with the "cake of the week" from the grocery store and a session with MEN magazine and the old palm pilot - shower and resolve to begin the diet when the fridge is empty of the fattening left overs the Italian and Chinese restaurants have delivered until we got our car fixed.

Tuesday we leave for the ERIS conference in Aspen and perhaps I'll begin the salad trail then. My old classmate Doug Casey set up this society twenty years ago for contrarians and libertarians. Perhaps I should write about it too. Last year we met some very strange birds there, people who have all made a fortune by doing the opposite of conventional wisdom. Douglas has agreed to be my counselor so I don't wind up selling roses into my 70's and 80's. He's made himself $40 million or so over the past decades by telling the world the sky is falling. Books like Crisis Investing in the 90's and The Coming Economic Crisis. But it looks like this time he might be right.

I have perhaps shot myself in the foot once again in dismissing the tenant who looked after Daisy while we were away. I hoped she would live in the guest apartment this summer until we returned to Florida this winter. But when we got home I found a ton of sand in the driveway she had put in for her child to play in. She'd gotten into the storage without permission to get a lawnmower - a good thing I guess since she wanted to mow the lawn. But the house is dirty and there are bags of empty beer cans from a 4th of July party I suppose. A handsome woman with plenty of beaus from the Navy base. I shouldn't go on gossip, but she comes with lots of caveats from people in the community. Better to take back the house and find a serious renter I have decided. But it could have been the answer to my prayers to have a capable person here to look after our affairs while we traveled this summer.

124 emails await me when we get back, one, inviting us to Bosnia for a poetry festival at the end of October. I've written the embassy and asked for support for our travel and if they come through, I think we will go over for a couple of weeks. Josephine will not be pleased, but this is a town I've never seen and perhaps I can write some articles on Sarajevo and the festival and possibly attend Stoimen's book fair in Frankfurt. I'll try to justify this gypsy maneuver once again with work, but I guess in a way I am fleeing boredom. But why not. Our life is short. And travel involves us with others. It was sweet to have Boiko and Pancho carrying us around Bulgaria this summer. I loved Bulgaria, despite the nostalgia for Nick. Perhaps I'll put a real effort into a fall trip to Blagoevgrad to exhibit the art folio book Stoimen did, ECHOES. The Book Fair and then poetry festival in Bosnia. Get to work Richard. Save the winter for writing and sunshine. I am a lucky man finally. God I love you for the gifts you have given me. Let

me make something of them now while I have my energy.

August 7, 2002 En route to Denver

The clouds drift by below, fields of brilliant white mushrooms, white fields, a sea of white and a far off blue horizon. A flat tire on the way to Providence nearly meant a missed plane, but with much sweat and energy and crashing lines - flying through the airport like O.J. in a wheel chair, we made it. A mild depression from last night's terrible dream. I have trained some sort of Gila monster to bite my mother, but instead he bites me and handling his skin has turned my forearms into black rot. The aggression toward my mother is the most disturbing thing. Can it be I am trying to work out the fact that we both seem destined for another round of bladder cancer, am I blaming her subconsciously. She gave me life, has she also planted the seeds of my death in our common gene pool? I watched Dr. Quinn's face grow concerned as I talked on my cell phone and he did his cystoscopy. It has become so routine, I never expected him to say he found something worrisome.

"I'm sure it's nothing," he says. "But I'd like to check you again before you go to Florida. The urine test will be ready in a couple of weeks and will help us see if anything's going on."

I pick up a pamphlet from his office which describes bladder cancer - the stages, the prospect of chemotherapy, metastasis. Clearly it can kill, but the urologists have said it was unlikely to be the thing that did me in. Mother is resigned to its being a chronic problem. At 80, this is one thing, at 55, such chronic illness takes on a different character. So, it is hard to be happy now, to carry out my plan of getting in shape again, reforming my character, being absolutely kind to William, helping him to enjoy his final years in a way I have not done in the past. Lyubomir's plans for a big 85th birthday celebration year with events at the Library of Congress, The Academy of American Poetry, Connecticut College and events in England, France and Bulgaria will take a lot of work, but it can be a spectacular year to look forward to. The calendar with his poems and photos from WWII could be part of year. Participation at the Frankfurt Book Fair, the exhibition of Sooky's new book in French, perhaps something from Stoimen in German. Events in Serafamivo, the Black Sea, Sofia. Exhibitions at the Von Schlippe?

The big decision now is whether or not to take the job I have been offered at Three Rivers College this semester. An honor that they would call be back. I worked so hard last year to get the job and do a good job at it, it seems silly not to do it. I worry that I will have to abandon William to the TV and to nurses and friends while I work, this just when I have highest hopes of truly living a full, loving life with him. It will get me out though, force me to meet others. It will give me some status as a worker and help toward my Social Security if ever so little. Time magazine has a cover article of how boomers will be forced to work far into the time they would normally retire. This sure to be my fate, and if I have to go to work again (when, no doubt, not if) I don't think teaching will be the way I will go. Too little money, and the fact that I don't really like teaching composition. But I can consider it a kind of hobby for now, and perhaps it will be easier having taught the course last year. Since it's scheduled for the evening, I won't have to get up so early and co-ordinate nursing care before I leave. Given the job market now, I guess it would be foolhardy of me not to accept this work. We'll still be able to go to Bosnia if the embassy comes through with funding. And perhaps we might even be able to go to California for William's therapy.

He's so sweet. His first reaction is to "bag it." But when I explain that I might like to consider it, he agrees.

This sweet old guy is really such a wonderful man. He is a kind of saint. So sweet, so dignified. This fall, I will try to emulate him in my dealings with others to avoid being the sort of embittered, angry man my poor father was at the end of his life. Who was it among my friends that said, "people don't change?" I've go to disprove this axioim.

August 11, 2002 - On the plane home again.

We've spent four days with a strange mixture of Libertarians, anarchists, and health quacks - mostly rich old guys who make their money setting up off shore bank accounts to help clients avoid taxes, or pushing gold stocks to hedge against the "greater depression" which is soon to descend on us when the dollar crashes. Douglas set up the conference about twenty years ago and dedicated it to Eris, the goddess of discord. It has become a kind of club for characters who have made a fortune doing the exact opposite of conventional wisdom. At one point I go so fed up with tirades against the federal government, and injunctions to arm yourself for the coming of mob rule, I thought we'd have to leave. It was like living in a scene from the Boys from Brazil. Every chance they got to flaunt the non smoking laws, out came the cigars and the outrageous arguments. Speakers ranted against multiculturalism and the influx of non whites sapping our pure, white Arian heritage. Speakers ranted against the AMA and promoted various coactions of herbs and god knows what to stimulate the brain and reverse the ageing process.

And yet when you met them individually, they proved to be extremely kind and interested in what you were about. Jim Gibbons is a prime example of a really considerate fellow, who despite his penchant for Ayn Rand, is one of the most decent people I've ever met. Someone I can learn from. His wife is a doctor in Olympia with hair down to her knees - brilliant and eccentric, with three beautiful little children that she watches over fiercely. Jim has given up on a career as a screenplay writer, and has established a shell fish company specializing in Goey duck, an absolutely obscene long neck clam that exactly resembles a flacid, Arnold Schwartzenager size penis. The Chinese consider them an aphrodisiac and Jim has fifteen million dollars worth of stock maturing in PVC tubes planted in the Puget Sound. Last fall he took us out to inspect the nursery, and even let us buy into the operation a little, just to keep us in touch as friends. So cute, William sitting aft as we lowered Jim's speedboat into the water.

Chasing a flock of water birds as we made our way out to the gooey duck fields.

A handsome guy. Sensitive. How charming to watch him play with his three little babies. A guy's guy. Strong and silent with a lovely, dry cheekiness. After a year's separation some time ago, he and his wife have gone to counseling over the years to tune up, and it seems to have done wonderful things for his character: At the conference, one Erisian was particularly obnoxious. Big black beard, enormous pot gut, cigar smoking, loud, with a voice three times as loud as it would need to be in conversation. He wore his company's tee shirt on all occasions announcing e-gold.com and bragged incessantly about his ability to buy and ship guns, his connections with the war lords of Mogadishu. Jim sat in the Jacusi with him one afternoon patiently asking him questions about his business which this character shouted out answers to, annoying the shit out of the rest of us sitting in the sun.

"How's the water?" a nifty little Canadian groupie shouted to me full force as I got out of the pool.

"Government has too damn much chlorine in there," I shouted back.

"Eh, Eh?" William shouted to me. But no amount of

hinting or teasing could shut this guy up and people began leaving the pool in self defense. I am absolutely positive Jim was engaging this guy because he knew how lonely this creep must have been. If nothing else, these Erisians are all very bright, despite their eccentricities or downright personality disorders. I am sure Jim was trying to include him in the group, to diffuse his toxic effect a little out of kindness, the kind of kindness he extends to William so often.

"Wait, I just want to finish this," he said of his conversation with William when I came out of the grocery store with snack for our cocktail party and indicated I was ready to push on. And he carefully probed William's thought with patient questions until he understood what William was saying. This morning I was up early packing and checking out and didn't have time to say goodbye to some of the friends from the conference. At the airport, just as I was going through security, someone poked me hard from behind and there was Jim, who had taken the hotel shuttle to the airport just to say goodbye to us.

"I love you," I said as we hugged, the emotion pushing me a little over our normal form of discourse. Jim just smiled back at me with those black eyes of his, little fires igniting under the bushy eyebrows.

Last year, we were invited to read our poetry and they scheduled us to sing for supper just after the final banquet at a cowboy bar. I was very dubious about how this would work out and when the band shut down its crescendo of rock and roll tunes from the 50's and the other half of the conferees pressed in from the adjoining dining room to hear us read, I took the microphone with as though it were a viper. I could barely catch my breath and it had little to do with the thin atmosphere. The room so quiet after the riotous rock and roll I just wanted to turn around and run out. But William did a great job, and the audience listened more intently that any I've ever read to. They obviously didn't go to poetry readings often, because after each poem they gave a rousing, cowboy round of applause some with whoops and hollers which I feared at first might be a kind of ironic mockery until their faces, glowing and genuine, began to bloom in front of me. Just remarkable. I still can't figure these people out. It's like a bunch of sophomore nerds, the brainy anti social ones, who might create a new computer virus to disrupt global communication but who melt at the touch of a hand from some pimply girl sitting across the desk at the library.

Now a nice guy from first class winks at me as I stand waiting for William in the john.

"You might want to use the lavatory on the other side," I say to him. "He might take a little while."

"A couple of years ago, I told my father that we couldn't travel anymore. But he seems to be doing okay. Just a little slow, huh?"

I usually cringe a bit when people automatically assume William is my father. But this guy seemed just to be bonding, one boomer to another, looking after the elderly. And it helped me a little, my annoyance at being interrupted in the middle of my writing to have to stagger up to the rest rooms. It's just this sort of annoyance, or impatience that I have to begin to work on. None of William's problems, his drooling, his slowness, the coughing, the constant help in and out of the wheel chair - none of these things are his fault, How do I handle it? Do I accept, embrace my feelings of frustration, or work on trying not to mind so much. Or both. Yes, the little self help guide would probably say both, but how to do that exactly?

Several of the Erisians took us under their wing, and one couple in particular seemed a little more reasonable than the others we met at the conference. Jon and Kristen packed William's chair into the trunk of their new Lexus as well the portable oxygen I ordered to fend off the mountain sickness that took us to the emergency room last year.

Kristen had won the car last month for taking the lead in building clients and distributors for the health care products Jon invents to purify the blood and organs, to stimulate the brain and immune system. She had her choice apparently of any car she wanted, but passed on the fancy Mercedes and BMW's she was offered - too pretentious and not really necessary for their lifestyle she explained to the astonishment of the CEO who established the incentive program. A sweet, sweet, eccentric boomer couple, each in a second marriage living a very careful life of love and dedication to each other - no children, just each other and their joint career.

We drove miles up into the mountains along crashing trout streams to a polo field spread like a velvet quilt under the Rockies. As Doug and friends sported around the field we ate a gourmet barbeque with tables of the best wines and iced tubs with designers beers, Red Dog and Schmartz brain drink as well as ten kinds of spring and mineral water. Another outing had us at the Benedictine Monastery where Fr. Theophane gave us a tour.

August 20, 2002

Daisy has me up early and now, little whimpers to

go out, sitting there in her crate, head cocked to the side, little tear in her eye perhaps? Mum is up too. Children thumping around upstairs. No chance of sleeping, a moment with the computer before we load up the old Volvo and head back home to Connecticut. What will the crazy tenant have in store for us when we arrive, I wonder. Last time we arrived to find a ton of sand dumped at the head of the driveway to make a sand box for the two children who are not supposed to be living with her, house trashed. What will the eviction process be like if we need to go that way? She can drag her feet for weeks in the court.

Is this why I continue to get up with a wrenching pain in my "right lower quadrant" as we were trained to say in PA school? McBurney's point, just where the ligament, what was the name of that ligament, defined the upper limits of the thigh. Can it all just be nerves, or is there some other surprise waiting for me as I enter my 56th year? My old football coach, just a few years older than me, has survived colon cancer, but seems to have had every complication possible in the process. "We all have to face it at some point," I said at my birthday party at Barbie's last night. "And it's going to be tough. These days I am big time into carpe diem. We have to take our pleasure, intellectual, physical where and when we can."

Last weekend in a pre-party party our friend Nancy gave me, I put theory into practice in a lovely way. Sex with Nancy. Imagine. She pushing 70 if a day, but figure in tact, and sweet and willing and talented in bed. We made love in the evening and morning and it felt so natural, so wonderful to be gliding inside her, taking our time. And in the morning she on top, holding me firm as she had her orgasm. What was in the food, I wonder? How did I maintain such erections throughout the night and morning? I guess I thought of myself as Nick, remembering how courteous he is with women, how clean and natural his sexual treatment of the opposite sex. It just seemed so friendly and sure left me feeling set up. I remember Lou Paget who gave her talk on the sex at last year's Eris Conference saying that women tend to forget an important gift that they give to men: they give a man his sense of his own manhood. An astounding power when you think of it. Far more important than the sex itself really. A woman, in loving a man and giving herself to him sexually really defines who a man is. I remember the glow that I felt after our sex for a couple of days. I felt trimmer, more capable, kinder to people. On occasion I'd remember my balls all wet from her, my filling her, her body a hood to my own sex, our nakedness - and this cheered me throughout the day. I found myself anxious or more willing to do the things a "man" does like taking out the garbage, packing up the car, helping William, like my child, into and out of the shower or dressing him. This is precisely the sort of feeling I want to cultivate as I age, in these years in my 50's and 60's. A kind of easy glide, gentility, elegance. There will be millions of boomers who will be around for these years. We will continue to define the culture as we age and if it could be in this positive vein, if we aged gracefully as a generation, a tremendous good could occur in our country. Like the sweet people at Eris who were so good personally, and so wacky in their political and economic beliefs however, just as much bad could accrue as well. Think of George Bush Junior, the beady eyes, the lack of intelligence, the transparent hypocrisy of his altruism. But think of Bill Clinton too, I guess. Clinton was smarter, but I wonder if he was any more sincere when he would give his political speeches outlining moral goals for the country while he was doing Monica in the corridors of the White House. None of his fellow boomers cared I guess, what he really thought, as long as the right principles were in place, the right rhetoric flowing from the President.

After the weekend with Nancy, an ease came over me too about Nick. That there are others out there for me, that heterosex could be as good as gay sex, that I might not need to be so driven about him, so obsessive, that I might be able finally to just let him drift off, or become friends from a distance as he makes his way in the world, seeks his independence, seeks his own way and new loves. Nice to realize how much I enjoyed sex with Nancy, to think I might one day just live a straight life with some good woman. How so often sex with a man involved darker fantasies for me. Rape, power, seduction, submission, pain and pleasure, danger, going to the edge. And playing them out turned them from fantasy to reality with T, for example. Chained to T's wall, blindfolded, while T. and company had their way with me. Or having my way with T. and his friends, me in black leather, me with whip and ropes. T. dead now, mysteriously. Playing too hard, I wonder. Sweet T. A former seminarian who needed to play out his Catholic neurosis till the point of death. Like Saint Genet and the fraternity of the black rose.

Last night we visited my old high school friend Danny. Charming guy, a good football player in high school though diminutive in stature. Like a little pony, small ankles, strong. I remember how awkward his goofy spikes seemed in flopping below his small ankles. I remember his sleek white butt in the showers, alabaster, the way only a teenage boy's can be. Danny was two years older and feisty. He scandalized me by telling me you didn't have to go to church on Sunday when you were traveling. I fought him on this heresy as fiercely as Torquemada. I couldn't imagine contradicting the church. He took my sister to the senior prom, but married someone else, had children and drifted into the past. Strange to have a crush on my sister's date - Analyze this, Richard. And now to find they are just cool social friends at the country clubs they belong to. Danny living in his little mansion with his gay lover, working for Peace and Justice, a kind of half way house for dying AIDS patients, fighting the military camps we support in Latin America, organizing the gay community in Pennsylvania to bring about change in the church's position on homosexuality. His professor at Villanova had calculated from the bible apparently that if you ate 3.2 ounces of meat on Friday it was a mortal sin. Anything less was a venial sin. Apparently, that stuck in Danny's claw. It got so even his wife noticed how he took in the men rather than the women at the beach. And one day Danny blinked and saw the world anew it seems, and changed his entire life. And he is still taking issue with the church and trying to bring some sense to his life. He seems fine: moral, happy, successful. He even seems to have worked it out with his wife.

Will I ever flip from my adult life as a gay man into the other camp, just the opposite of Danny I wondered last night as we sat in his mountain top living room, the whole town winking and blinking below in the valley. Will it be too neurotic to keep my life open to anything in life which comes my way? I think with my last letter to Nick, I have finally made a step at independence. He's moved out of the Florida apartment and is living with Ginger. "They're doing it," my friend Michael assures me. And at first that broke my heart when I thought it must be true. I'd call and he would not have the time for me. Ginger calling him to supper, they just walking out the door to go to a baseball game together. So, I closed up the apartment and we will see this winter where things stand. But this is perhaps a good moment.

Dear Nick,

It was good to talk with you last night. I will send along the phone bill I spoke of. It seems that you made three calls through the internet to an adult entertainment website that bills the phone you are calling from. Perhaps it was to use a chat room? The bills are for June and July. The call actually goes to West Africa when you make such visits on the web. The total comes to about $300 and I want you to pay this back, please. When I first found out that such calls were made I immediately changed my password until I could find out what was going on, i.e. if someone was stealing my identity for example as sometimes happens on the internet. I guess this will mean you won't be able to use the computer I lent you until the new password is put in, but you seemed to indicate that you don't use the computer much anyway. If you want to use it in the future, let me know and I'll give you the password over the phone.

Since you have moved out, I've asked Bob Deacy to close the apartment, move the cars and send me the titles needed to sell the Lincoln. You can send the keys to the car and house to him at the Claremore Drive address.

If you need to get into the apartment or if your situation chances in the next few months, just let me know. As I mentioned, we won't be returning to West Palm until mid-December at the earliest. We look forward to seeing you when we get back down and hope you will drop a line from time to time, or call to let us know how you are doing.

I'm glad you had a good time at the ball game. It's a great thing to do, isn't it? And I am pleased you are making your way in West Palm. Your motivation and ability to make the visas work are impressive. I wish you all the best as you continue to look at opportunities. I have decided to take a teaching job again this winter as I did last year. They called me to offer the job and I felt good about that. My student evaluations were very good and that made it seem worth all the effort last year. I may do some teaching in Florida as well this winter with William. I need to start putting some money into Social Security so I'll have some pension when I retire. I hate to be away from William when I do this work, but he understands and is supportive. These are precious years for us though, and I am always saddened when I think that he is at the end of his life. All the more reason to try to live fully now. Well, please keep in touch, keep well and say hi to Ms. Ginger. R.

August 29, 2002

Classes approach and I still have not paid the bills from when we returned from Europe or prepared my syllabus. The stack of notebooks filled with "Things to do" stands five inches high on the desk in recrimination. The tenant makes no sign of moving and it looks like we'll have to evict. Cannot find my glasses. The pain in my right lower gut is still worming away. But, there has come a gentle rain in the middle of this awful drought. The purple lesions on the back of William's legs prove not to be melanoma according to Dr. Miller. Daisy's allergies are resolving and William knee seems not to be seriously wounded from his fall at Bread Loaf. All is not right with the world, but I am hopeful that this fall I will begin to change my life, get things in order, loose weight, resolve our financial difficulties, come finally to a resolution on my feelings for Nick.

In the shower in the guest house now, I remember how his smell would linger, how his broad brown shoulders floated above the waist bound up in a thick white towel after his shower. Him shaving, private, as I knocked to use the bathroom and spy on him a bit. Now through all the windows I see stains from the sloppy job he did last summer painting the house. I'd asked him to pay particular attention to the windows, and, very Bulgarian, a year later they remain a splattered reminder of how often things went wrong with him. No word since my birthday call, no money from the calls he made unknowingly to west Africa when he visited some pornographic website. Goofy Bulgarian kid. Always something going wrong. And yet, the love burns on. I'll never really get over him I guess.

I thought this morning how wonderful I felt after my lovemaking to Nancy on my birthday weekend, how complete, and realized that Nick must feel this too, this affirmation of his manhood. Could I deny him that if this is why he has rejected me these past couple of years. I wonder if he and Ginger are sleeping together, they must be. And I think of how voyeuristic this seems on my part. Better to live my life this fall and see how things look in the winter. But it is not easy to forget.

At Bread Loaf, things were not any easier this year than the year we brought him along - he, the mysterious Adonis everyone wanted to know, he loving every minute, refusing sex with me. William and I have become such an institution there, each year are held up by Michael as a model of fidelity, the legendary couple that met there three decades ago. And the extremely young writers flock round us after our reading, reverentially almost. And William goes to bed and I go to the barn for the last dance and stand like a wall flower as the whole room thumps in unison and the very dance floor bounces in their single passionate leap.

I can not bring myself to go to bed with the Indian woman who has sat next to me through dinner and seems interested. Too much gin and I tell Michael I am getting so tired. And I begin to cry and I go to bed. No, next year we will go to Bulgaria and live in the mountains and will not return to Bread Loaf.

On the way home, dinner with Maxine Kumin who told William to go check out the hippie with the long hair and tie dyed bib shorts all those years ago when we first me at Bread Loaf, and has taken it on herself to be my Dutch Aunt ever since. She's gotten even more severe in her old age, the riding accident that nearly killed her turning her rigid physically and mentally it seems. "I don't approve of pedigree dogs," she says when I introduce her to Daisy, her political correctness extending right down to the SPCA. "You seem to take pride in the breeding of your horses," I remind her. "Got you there Maxine."

"These were adopted horses," she replies, and hands me a bag of corn from her superior garden to shuck for dinner as we sit in Mary's courtyard over drinks.

Who needs it? "May she be loved/ and beautiful without wrinkles until it takes/ carbon dating to determine her age," as William says of Simone de Beauvoir in a poem. I have to move into a future without such negative influences, and pull myself out of the depression that threatens to consume the last final years with my friend William who I truly love. This journal seems to have become a kind of therapy for me the way Bill Soroyan tried to do (is he the guy who wrote Sophie's Choice and a book about his depression?)

"I really do think you could win the Pulitzer if you set your mind to it," my friend Jim Gibbons writes from Seattle and I think, "not with this book, you won't." I'll have to start again on India if I want a book on India. This book is far too personal to ever publish. And if a reader wants really good, neurotic self-deprecation they can pick up "The Death of Ivan Ilych," or some such.

One good thing about Bread Loaf was hearing two gay writers read their work and the incredible risks they took in the writing. One story about a boy whose parents have died and who falls into a sadomasochistic relationship with the town bully was staggering for the violence and exploration of this dark sex. The bully cries at the end of his torture sessions for the dead boy's parents, locked in his own sadism as much as his victim in his masochism. Another author ruminates on every sexual detail that turns him on when "computer boy" comes to the office to fix his machine, a story which would read as pure pornography save for the super-bitch wit in the narrative. Not the well-crafted and humane stories John Irving or William Maxwell would spin at the podium all those years ago. The audience roared its approval.

So, "back to my spuds," as Mrs. Lemington says of her garden in William's poem. Maybe the rain has turned my thoughts dark this morning, kept me from the course I had hoped to set. William will be up soon and need breakfast. I must find people to come stay with him while I do my work today. I am filled with high hopes this fall. The season always re-invigorates me. I called Bosnia yesterday and the secretary assures me that I too am to be invited officially to the 41st annual poetry festival in Sarajevo. I'll write good articles on this festival. It will add to my life as a writer and be fun with William too. Our dear Bulgarian friend Krassin who has arranged this invitation will not be there for some reason. I guess his contract as a UN elections monitor is over there. I had counted on picking his brain, but we will have to visit in Sofia after the conference. Now a fax comes in from Josephine Jacobsen who has agreed to second William's nomination of Lyubomir Levchev for Foreign Honorary Membership in the American Academy of Arts and Letters along with William Jay Smith. Her dear signature is barely legible now. Ninety Four years old. And yet a new poem has just been accepted for the New Yorker. She says she is not interested in living to be 100. But what a model of civility and courage she is. This is the sort of model I must take. And get to work.

September 15, 2002

How the days drag on, what a fog I have been in. I call Bettie Chu this morning again to see if we might visit after her stroke and find she is about to be discharged. How can I have missed seeing her, this woman who has been such a loyal friend to us over the years, who has come each week to read with William after his stroke, who has stuck up for me in the community. Monstrous. I meant to visit several times but got caught up in my work. If I had paid attention I would have stopped by the hospital last week in the initial days when she must have been anxious for friends. We could have gone after our reading at the festival in New London, or on the way home from drinks with Jules Hallum as I had meant. Why didn't I just turn the car around when I realized I had forgotten our plan for the day? And now it is a decision I can never reverse. Many bad decisions these days - cutting Nick off from the apartment now that he has moved in with Ginger. If I had let him stay there, he would have been connected to us through the apartment, might have at least kept the mice out of our things and protected the paintings we've left there. My thought was to show him how much he had been given by us, so he didn't take us for granted. I guess it was a bit vindictive when he didn't have the time to take the car registration to the garage to sell the car, when he balked at staying at the apartment while house painters did the work he seemed unwilling to do. But if I had been more generous, let him have it as a back up pad, what would I have lost? Have I pushed him into Ginger's arms by cutting off his resources this way? Well, there was no point in keeping the phone going, and the car and the tv if he had moved out. It was costing us $100 a month just to keep the apartment working. But we waste that much at least each month. No, better to keep friends, and see again in the winter how things look. I must start again, pick up the pieces and try to continue on the road of what, spiritual enlightenment? Continue to do my work, look after William, finish my projects, get in shape and keep my eyes open, pay attention to my life and people like Bettie Chu. I am buoyed by the pornographic poems William and I wrote each other years ago and tried to published anonymously. Very erotic and a beautiful view of me as a lover then and what I brought to William. I can return to that person who William loved.

And when I make a mistake, try to correct it and move on. My letter to Bettie may help me in this today. My idea to her that we can control what me make of our disasters I should apply to myself. Mail the letter, go give William his medications and take my own, and share some time with him this Sunday afternoon.

Dear Bettie,

We were very surprised but delighted to find out that you were going home when I called this morning to see if we might visit you. When I first called, it seemed too early. When I called again you were about to have surgery. And today, off you go. It looks like Goldylocks didn't get it "just right," and I am extremely sad that we didn't get a chance to wish you well in person in what must have been difficult days for you. The fact that your hospitalization was so relatively brief is a good sign I think. You have been constantly in our thoughts, believe me, trite as that expression might seem. Well, I have learned a lesson from this and the only consolation is that you are on the mend and we will have the chance to see you just as soon as you wish it. Not on your first day home, but perhaps you might like to see us early this coming week? I'll call tomorrow to see when that might be. When we come, perhaps you would like to see some of the materials in speech therapy that you have so dutifully worked with William in years past. I'd be happy to read with you and him a bit if you'd like. One thing we learned from William's stroke and the therapy that was so effective when we went to the program in England is that the more therapy, the better. I'd be pleased to do it if only to thank you for the years of friendship and support you have show me and William.

I am consoled by one other thing as I write you, and that is our appreciation of your deep spirituality and how it must sustain you now. I forget where I heard the notion that we can not control the bad luck that sometimes comes our way in life, but we can control our attitude towards it, what we make of it. Hearing your laughter on the phone is another remarkable sign from you.

A final note, and you may make of this what you wish, but last week I contacted a fellow I met this summer in Colorado at the Eris conference who is a healer. Perhaps you aware of the sort of people who seem to have this gift who work in England and are actually re-imbursed by the state health care system. He is a successful movie producer as well, so I am a little re-assured that he is not a charlatan. In any case, I've had some symptoms lately which I ascribed to the possibility of my bladder cancer's return (my doctor found something suspicious on my last visit and we'll check it out again at the end of October). I spent an hour in a meditative state while this fellow, Kevin Carlisle, did whatever he does out there in Los Angeles for me. It can be done long distance, like Reike, is that the name of the oriental healing practice? In any case, I have to tell you, I have been pain free ever since. As you know I have been trained in western scientific medicine and don't normally make much of this sort of alternate care, but I'm not adverse to trying anything. I'd be happy to engage him for an hour's session with you at some point if you'd like to give it a try. Sounds crazy, but you never know.

And a final final note, a poem that came to me on September 11th. It comes with love. Bye for now.

911 - A Year Later

I lace my jogging shoes
a private protest, to stop
time, to run the exact

three miles I ran last year
as the brilliant sun
stung my eyes and
news of the terror
flooded my headphones.

Some clutched briefcases
or took a friend's hand then
to try the sky, like Icarus,
burned by the sun, shedding
his sad feathers to the white sea.
A thousand Roman paces,
each of my three miles will
sing a thousand lives
blown to the winds that day
as the winds now stir
the crowns of oak trees -
trees stirred by ghosting,
or the winds of war along
the Thames running silver
beside me down to the
nuclear submarines waiting
like patient sharks, silent
at the mouth of the sound.

And in the home stretch
up the last difficult hill
past the country cemetery
where I always pray three times
for the farming family laid to rest
and all the dear and lately dead
I am dumb, without a prayer,
marking each life, yard by yard,
as I listen to the winds
howling above.

September 20, 2002

Up all night with old William, first snoring, then a threatened seizure, and now insomniac with thoughts - "Baawee, keep your thaughts to yourself," the nun from Brooklyn used to tell Barry Chambers in high school when he would cut up in class. Perhaps I am the only one who will ever read this journal, a journal that has become pedestrian I guess, so private. So, it will have to be something for me in my old age I guess, or something I can use to keep heart, as the poet says.

A little yoghurt and orange marmalade has rescued

William once again from the seizure. “Bring on Nurse Daisy, and a little physical culture,” I joke with him to bring laughter into the picture. It seems to drive the aura away a bit too, distracts him from the odd feeling that overcomes him. Sometimes too, I think it may be a physical reaction, a kind of acting out, a self defense when I am mean to him as I was this evening.

The neighbor Chuck comes, the strange, silent fellow who works as a guard at the prison who has been helping us with odd jobs around the house. Interested in this old place, and us. A hunter who shoots deer out his back window or coyotes. Strange how wild this place has become, and wonderful. Foxes, deer. Chuck says he sometimes has 30-40 wild turkeys in his backyard, takes them as he wishes. Delicious, better than domesticated turkeys, but the legs are too tough. I tried to get him to take me hunting and old William kept interrupting our discussion, kept bringing it back to William. Boring. Was he jealous of what I was setting up? Perhaps. Well, love returns, and I worry and pray that he’ll be all right and he is. Talking him down, as it were. I keep forgetting he is sick. “ I am sick, Richard,” he tells me once. And my guilt floods over me.

Soon, I will keep my appointment with Dr.

Greenwald. Will he find a cancer in my gut, some explanation for the pain that is usually there these days. Just Irritable bowel syndrome, just nerves wrenching my gut? It's been better this week after my session with Kevin Carlisle, the movie producer, Reike master. I dutifully called him and got instructions on how to meditate and rest in a quite place with music which he did his psychic thing on me. Remarkably, the pain went away and didn't come back for several days. I could feel it ease up. Just relaxation? The fact that someone cared for me. He says he works with me in my alpha state or some such, so that when I fell asleep, he was best able to work with me. Strange. Why not believe. It worked. Almost as mysterious to believe in him as to say my own mind was responsible for relieving the pain. What a mystery we are, how difficult to know what we are, this fusion of body and soul, flesh and personality see my own grow flabby, both, but I can "still move all the parts" as William says of Hazard reflecting on his ageing process.

Chuck, the neighbor guy is just my age when I did the N.Y. Marathon and wrote the book on my training and my life with William. Hard to believe that was 15 years ago, that I am now 56. "Much too young to be this damn old," as the song goes. Very strange to think I am as old now as William was when we met, older, in fact. I found the extraordinary erotic poems we wrote to each other in the 70's and 80's and put together in a book. William disavows them now since he is "spade." But the joy they gave to me the other day. To see how much William loved me, how much physical pleasure we took in each other. I must never forget that part of our lives.

Well, the full moon has gone to bed and now the sun begins to rise. The frost covers the sacks of purple grapes hanging off the deck. And sleep begins to finally come to me. No time to read European Security tonight. The spring edition of 2000 has my interview with the President of Macedonia that I did when we went to Struga for the poetry festival. Soon, William and I will head east again for another festival. Our friend Krassin has arranged an invitation for us and our embassy is sponsoring our travel. Sarajevo is a town of legend that I have never seen and it will be great to go there, a fall project, meeting other poets, checking out the state of Bosnia after the war. I'd forgotten all the news about Dayton, the peace keepers. My old class mate Bill Clinton who made such political hay of our role in Bosnia. A courageous position, he showed some political spine then with a view toward supporting NATO and the new Europe. All old news for America and way on the back burner with war in Iraq about to break out. But our troops are still there years later and Bush threatens to pull them out. I must check out our embassy's website to see where we are. Perhaps Peter Liota can help me out too at the Naval War College in Providence. He's an old East European hand. I wonder what has become of him? The terrorist groun, November 17 tried to assassinate him when he was our air attaché in Greece. He keeps a low profile these days. I wonder if Greece really did wipe out November 17th in this recent raid?

I told Three Rivers College that I would need to go to Bosnia if I took this teaching job this fall, and they agreed. I'll only have to miss one class for this ten day trip to Bulgaria and Bosnia and have arranged for a workshop in resume writing and letter writing from career placement. I am pleased with myself that I have made this Bosnia trip a reality. I wish old Krassin were joining us though. It makes such a conference far more interesting when you have someone to translate the language and culture around you. If I were to ask the embassy for such a person, it might seem to compromise us, we might be seen as US agents, or some such. I'll need to be a little careful about my Arab bias there - I did not send the Burning of Port St. Lucie for translation because it blasts Milosovich and Serbia on

Kosovo. Here they have had a real, recent war based on ethnic and religious differences. I don't know enough about it to have a strong opinion. The Iranians supplying the Muslims in Bosnia can't be a good thing. But our congress supported such arms as I recall so they could fight their own war. Well, a note to Peter perhaps to see if he will come this weekend to visit and fill me in:

Dear Peter,

"A long orange knife slits the throat of morning," or some such image as I recall in William's poem, "Winter on the River." Anyhow, the blade comes beautiful and clean on the Thames this morning as I sit here, insomniac, and drop a line. I often think of you Peter and have tried to call. But your phone numbers never seem to work for me. Perhaps I'll try to call you at the college if you have not retired from that position by now. Weren't you planning to move on? How have you been? We really would like to see you. It would be great to catch up personally. But I've been reading the issue European Security and your article lately and would love to pick your brain a bit too as William and I plan to leave for Bosnia in October. We've been invited to a poetry festival there and I'd like to get your take on that

part of the world before we leave. I also have a bit of cabin fever as September ends. I've been working hard at a class I am teaching at a local college and the glamor of our travels this summer has faded. We were in Paris, Avignon, Prague and Bulgaria for 6 weeks this summer at a number of poetry festivals, book fairs, and writers conferences. Lots of work. But our poetry is making its way into French, and it was well worth the effort.

Listen, two crumpets with orange marmalade have enabled sleep to return and so I will close for now and try to call later in the day. William is fine, but from time to time threatens a seizure and when he is up I can no longer sleep. But I hope you are well and your family. Let's reconnect Peter. It's been too long.

Affectionately,
Richard and William

Sting

Sting is in Tuscany. Is it the title of a new cd? Where did I see it. I love the image. Sunday night on the stupid Emmy awards, Sting was in Europe and couldn't be there. I'm reminded of Alice McDermott's notion once when she was our neighbor in Bethesda and I stopped on the road to chat. "People never think about those years when they don't see you between novels." When a book comes out, I guess they think it just fell off the shelf.

Well, Rich is in Uncasville. Not quite as elegant as Tuscany. But Michael Fox's moral rubric for leading a good life, "Do the next right thing" works too on the career level: Just do the next thing. Just keep chipping away at your projects, day by day, make the pot of coffee, do the laundry and the dishes from last night's dinner, plan your classes, answer your email, and try to get to your desk as often as possible to write.

I slept well last night for the first time since last Wednesday - why does the preparation take such a toll on my gut. But I am relieved too to think that it does seem to be tied to my mental state. It means all I have to do is fix my mental state. I think of the cliché that you can't control what life hands you but you can control what you make of that, how you take it. Michael Collier writes that he is sure I will fight down the dragon as I have done in the past if this pain is indeed some sort of cancer.

Meanwhile little pieces of the puzzle have fallen into place:

Grant letter from our embassy paying for our ticket.

Mystic Seaport calls saying that our calendar project or day book look promising with the board. It will be the lynch pin for a William Meredith year with readings and events across the country and in France, England, and Bulgaria.

Mary Haddar calls from the Washington Post with ideas about an article for them which I must pursue.

The Day grudgingly accepts an article on the Bosnia festival.

Stoimen's paintings are accepted for the October 4th exhibit at Von Schlippe Gallery.

My classes are going well enough, I'm liking them more and liking the students, particularly the three angels I wake dreaming of from time to time. The two Aarons and Mike. Beautiful young men. But I've long since learned about the dangers of sexual harassment and the toll it can take. So, these boys must remain dream companions.

I call Nick from time to time and hear his sweet voice. I want to keep the channel open and come to Florida a changed person. Perhaps he will have changed too in his efforts to be independent. Perhaps he'll see what we given him, play less the spoiled teenager. Or perhaps he'll be married to Ginger. For sure I can't be hounding him by phone here. We'll have to see if absence makes the heart grown fonder. And meanwhile, I will try to give my sweet William a wonderful fall.

October 10th

Up playing with my digital camera far too early the way last night, I stayed up far too late. It's like learning the computer for the first time. You walk round and round the hellish labyrinth until you finally find an open passageway and make one more step to freedom. But the cd burner I bought seems to be an internal cd burner and I need an external cd burn
er. The bald-headed, hunky cop I flirted with last night (I'll buy you a hamburger if you sit down with me and show me how to use the software) gave me the wrong poop, and now I must go back to Wall Mart to get the right equipment. I'm at the point where I don't have any more memory and could foul up this computer and loose all the work on this book. Maybe not such a bad idea?

The new camera was wonderful at Ben's wedding, but Maureen says people always show the images on the camera and then you never see them again in actual pictures. I'm beginning to see why. "Take up knitting" Nancy joked with me when I told her how long it took to download individual images. I took a picture of my private parts like the back of a porno singles section and flashed it to her when she was on the phone. Wide-eyed, but didn't miss a step in her conversation. I must remember to delete the naked Richie shots when I send Ben his wedding album. "I don't like that trash," William said, impressively.

Glenn Morazinni says when he visits and I describe the book a bit, that it has to be more than just ego. And I wonder what he would make of this journal. He's such a lovely guy, suffering from some neurological disorder like MS that keeps him at about 25% speed. But he continues his therapy practice, raises his kids, and has even given us a reference letter to fill in for a creative writing program he plans to enter. He's one of the compassionate, thoughtful people who live life so fully and who make someone else their pole star. Where is my pole star? William, of course, but I think of Nick every day and can't seem to get out from under the fantasy that all will be well when we return to Florida, that he won't be married to Ginger, that he will love me for the new svelte, laid back, lovely man I have become. I remember running with him in the fall, his favorite red tree, the orange hat I bought him at the hardware store as we ran on Block Island in the bitter cold. Perhaps I'll send him a picture of me lying naked under the red tree - that would be a real turn on, no doubt. "Why would he want to spend his life with some old guy." Ginger's words continue to haunt.

Well, the fall is working out as I had hoped to some extent. The embassy has agreed to pay for our tickets to Bosnia, and the poetry festival organizers have finally confirmed the program and that we will be met at the airport. They have us traveling all over the country, and I wonder just how safe we will be. Two American poets would be fairly desirable hostages I should think. There is only a veneer of nation building it seems and people generally feel war will break out when the US leaves. If the US leaves, the other Europeans will also leave. This is the political mantra in Paris and Berlin.

And classes are going well finally. The students who hung in there in spite of the killer syllabus are making progress. Office hours last night were sweet. One beautiful student brought her little black daughter who sat on her lap while I corrected her essay. A table had collapsed the little girl's thighs while she colored pictures, nothing serious, but it scared her. She even drew a picture for me, a red house with her name, Nicole, scrawled below. The ex- marine who walked out of class when I told him he had to do the reading assignments has not returned. I feel badly about that, but I did talk with him and tried to get to the bottom of how he was feeling and where he stood in the class. Many of them have such Rush Limbaugh opinions about race, America, the myth of money and success. After class last week, I visited Jim and Helen Coleman, retired teachers who offer William dinner on occasion when I am teaching. Jim talked about premature cognitive commitments that Susan Langer describes. A brother calls his sister an air head, and she decides she really is an air head- a self fulfilling prophesy. A student who hasn't done his homework is forced to stand at the blackboard and do equations for an hour decides he hates math and is no good at it. How hard it is to step back from inherited ideas or such skewered thinking. How hard for me to step back from the emotional corner I've painted myself into with Nick.

But I will free myself of it eventually. Time separates us. Each day takes us a step further apart. And I take steps too to some new future. The beautiful Natalie will be replaced by the beautiful Francoise this fall for a visit if all goes well. The gorgeous photographer from Germany I met at Jim Coleman's wedding has written me back and is willing to get together in New York sometime. Other fish in the Black Sea, Nick and I so often joked to each other. I will be able to love him, and let him go, I am sure of it. Off we go to Bosnia and two magazines have agreed to run articles on the festival. I am continuing to run. And I do feel a great sweetness to William in these beautiful fall days of this year, of his life. And now he is up and needs his breakfast and off I go to the kitchen.

October 17

In the Pliska Hotel after dinner in the Chinese restaurant with Krassin. A very long day, but all is well. The lost bag has come in the middle of our sleep, William is not blocked, the Milk of Magnesia has done the trick, I've had my long hot shower after a day of travel, and now to sleep. But a great dinner. Krassin such a hero. He's living with a troubled son, a violent boy. What to do. Do I know anything about psycho therapy? He's taken the boy to Bosnia and he has done well, but the boy will be with him to the day he dies. But before bed, like a good spy, like a good businessman, like a poet, I must make notes, no matter how tired I am:

Abdulla Cidran - the Muslim poet who is promoting Islamic poets this festival.

The Organization for Security and Co-operation in Europe (OSCE) is like the UN for Europe. There are still

US 20,000 troops in SFOR and they have named their streets like Texas, Arizona, Mc Govern, etc. Half of these 20 K are from the US and the others German, Italian, etc.

The war criminal Radovan Karadzic is probably hiding in a monastery in Montenegro and this is why he is still not captured

Krassin's poems have warned children not to step on the grass.

Mostar is unique. 50% Bojniacks (Muslims from Bosnia) and 50% Croats.

The King of Bulgaria got rid of "mini skirts," i.e. the corruption in the foreign ministry where young ladies sleeping their way to the top were taking over all the positions and sending the old diplomats into their golden parachutes (as they are in Bulgaria. Shall we say lead parachutes?)

Under the previous administration, Kostov (Chief of Corruption as Foreign Minister) sold Balkan Airlines to Gad Zeervi for $150K. He was to have paid off $80 million in debt, but the Prime Minister arranged that this debt be forgiven, and for this the Prime Minister received $20,000. Gad in Bulgaria means beast. He did some minor repairs at the airport. The Beastly airport. Now he is suing the Government for $250 million dollars. So it will become bankrupt again, and corruption will begin again.

The previous foreign minister Nadalia Miholaviala bought the Communist party garage, or her husband did for the cheap sum of $500,000

So, your Majesty, what do you plan for Balkan Airlines. We're at the mid-point of the 800 days, 300 left.

150 Bulgarians guard the airport from their international base. Colornel Lliev is the commander of the Bulgarians. He will be organizing a reading for us at the airport at Sarajevo.

30,000 people were saved in the tunnel under the airport during the siege. The heresy of dualism began in Bulgaria. Essentially it said, why believe in Christ when the devil made earth and man. God made the soul. These heretics spent three centuries in Bosnia, fled all over the place. So Bulgaria and Bosnia have a great shared tradition.

Alexander Bashkov is the former member of government known as "Mr. 10%," i.e. he took %10 on everything he did

October 27 ,2002

Day of our departure from Sarajevo and insomniac

once again with gut pain and over stimulation from all the things we've seen and done.

Today I woke early too after last night's final banquet and the drunken Patrick Woodcook and his girl Beth. They pooped out on us today at the Butmir camp reading where we read the troops. What a joy. The beautiful Gerome, a French peace keeper was our escort. A lovely guy. He explained during the war they buried their dead anywhere there was a spare piece of ground - so at the corner intersection as we drive to the base there are beautiful graves lit by candles - always an anniversary. We would bury our dead in a more quiet place he tells me, but they remain as a testament.

We read at the Halloween-decorated rec hall. A small audience but avid. The Colonel in charge of the Bulgarian unit guarding the base introduced us. Great to have a countryman introduce us. And Candi Guzman, what a sweetheart. So open, and carefree, a real American woman at her best. And dinner with Janet Miller and husband Steven. And the new AID Director, Howard and Michelle (Shantos) at a Fancy restaurant, the Capri. But, now possibly I will sleep?

November 1st

Today, we go to Pamela Bond's funeral. She got pancreatic cancer out of the blue and in a month or so was dead. In a way, she never knew what hit her - the drugs confused her- she had an imaginary friend, a buccaneer, who seemed to come to her in her hallucinations. She never had the time for Kubler-Ross's stages of dying, I suppose. What a feisty, classy lady she was. So generous. She like me, as a man. And I her, as a woman. Lovely to flirt with her. Her death makes me realize again, how short life is. "The days don't come back," Helen reminded me once. And so, I must enjoy this fall and my life with William. Travel to Bosnia and Bulgaria was really wonderful for me. A successful trip. And getting the equity line on this house will enable me to breath easier as far as our finances go. Mother's coming to Florida for Christmas. Wonderful. This weekend I must finish the articles on the festivals and my interview with the Prime Minister, prepare my classes, Monday. Then diet again, and seriously. Go to Pittsburgh? I think yes. An investment in the future for the Bulgarian artists. Much to do, but my bladder cancer was not back this time with Dr. Quinn. What a beauty this man is. How lucky I am to have him. Even when the time does come, when I will not have escaped my worst fears, having someone like him will be essential to help me into death. Dying alone must be the worst think one can contemplate. Though, of course, we all die alone. We each must accomplish that solitary act, like birth. This insight: One of two things is true about Nick:

A: he is unhappy, in which case I have a chance of making him happy and being happy with him.

B: He is happy, in which case I am glad for him because I love him and want him to be happy.

I think I believe this now. And today's piece on Bosnia to wrap it up:

Poetry and Politics in Bosnia Herzegovina

By Richard Harteis

As you make your way from the airport into downtown Sarajevo, a spectacular fountain of concrete shoots up to the sky against the mountains surrounding the city. The optical illusion is actually a cascade of destruction, what remains of the tower housing Oslobodjenje, the country's leading newspaper before the war devastated Bosnia. Remarkably, Oslobodjenje still occupies the lower floors spreading out at the base of the building, and the newspaper comes out every day, rain or shine, a tribute to the gut and gumption of a people who survived years of siege and bombardment by Serb artillery in the hills. Many buildings are pockmarked by machine gun fire; impromptu cemeteries fill the median strip or odd corners along the highway, graves that are neatly tended and lit at night with ruby candles as a testament to the spirit that would not die, would not give. It is that same spirit that kept poetry alive in the Sarajevo Poetry Festival, a festival that has continued for 41 years, without interruption even during the darkest days of the war. Thousands of foreigners and diplomats were smuggled out in a secret tunnel under the airport, while poetry was being smuggled in. But this time, William Meredith and I were flying into a free Bosnia, coming through the front door to represent the United States, and sing a little for our supper.

It's wonderful to come to a European country these days where America and Americans are actually loved. Sarajevans, are deeply grateful that Bill Clinton stopped the war, perhaps his single greatest achievement as President. And the mantra among diplomats runs: if we go, the

Europeans go, and the carnage will surely begin all over again. Our old friend, Krassin Himmirski had arranged for this invitation when he worked for OSCE, the European version of the UN trying to rebuild the nation's institutions. Like Beirut, Sarajevo had been a model of ethnic harmony before the war, a harmony now shattered by Serbian aggression. Sarajevans are proud to point out that ancient places of worship for four different religions - Catholic, Orthodox, Muslim and Jewish lie in close vicinity in the center of town. It was a beautiful capitol, elegant host of the '84 winter Olympics, rich in history with mosques, markets and the picturesque old Turkish bazaar called Bašččaršija. And happily, lively cafes have mushroomed once again along what used to be sniper's alley, traffic is busy, and the streets are safe. The UN troops are doing a good job.

The invitation read "It is our honor to invite you to participate in the traditional literary manifestation SARAJEVO POETRY DAYS, international poetry meeting which will for the fortyfirst time be held in the last week of October.... The best Bosnian-Herzegovinian poets will meet their colleagues from other countries, witnessing together that Sarajevo has always been devoted to the mission of peace by bringing different cultures and civilizations closer in order to get to know and understand others better. And so for a week we were carted all over town to cultural centers, theaters, high schools, and even grade schools to read poems and get to know each other. Canadian, German, and Polish poets joined other poets from countries in the region, and with the help of student translators and lots of the local version of plum brandy, managed to form fast friendships. Somehow, even the Serbian poets were welcomed gently for the sake of their common Slavic heritage and for the sake of the art. People made a real effort to be kind to each other, and enjoy each other's company. It was a festival, after all, like one of the many found across Eastern and Middle Europe.

We had just come from a similar festival in Bulgaria called Melnik Nights in the Rhodope Mountains near the Greek Border, where the poet Orpheus is said to have been born. Another famous festival is found at Struga, in Macedonia. All are filled with music, dance, and plenty of wine. A competition is usually held for the best poem dealing with wine. One poet is usually chosen for a special honor, a gold medal or in this case the Bogomil Stone awarded to the Polish poet Tadeusz Rőœewicz. Bagpipes accompany choral music and dancers in folk costume. On long trips on the bus, you get to know people well in a very short time, like any road show. They are interesting people who have suffered a lot perhaps, and are bent on having a good time.

This festival made a particular effort to get us out into the country side as well, and so we were farmed out to various corners of the country: names made famous or infamous from the war - Tuzla, Zenica, Tesanj, and Mostar, named for the exquisite 16th century bridge over the aqua green Neretva River which was destroyed in a gratuitous act of cruelty during the war. Beforc our reading at the cultural center, I took a taxi out to Medjugorje. Like Lourdes in France, and Fatima in Portugal, the town has become a pilgrimage site since the Virgin Mary appeared to six teenagers in 1981. Three still claim to see the vision daily, and the town is awash with pilgrims and souvenir shops. My devotee sister who made the pilgrimage just after the war would never have spoken to me again if I had gotten this close and not visited. It's thought the war didn't come to this town due to the intercession of the Virgin, and miracles are in the air. I said a prayer for my lost wallet which I had looked everywhere for, and sure enough, found it when I got back to the hotel. I don't plan to report this fact to Rome, but I sure was glad to get my wallet back. Latest messages from the Virgin can be found on the internet at Http:www.medjugorje.org.

If you want to participate in such festivals and don't know who to contact, you might simply look up the country's home page of the country you'd like to visit and look for poetry festivals. Other Americans who have participated in such programs would, I'm sure, give you necessary information, as would I. You might simply send a resume and offer your services. Usually, accommodations are provided and meals, along with a small honorarium for reading. But the big ticket item, your transportation, will need to be sponsored by someone else. In this case, the American Embassy generously provided a grant to cover our travel. But there are many funding sources such as PEN, the NEA and others that you might research in books such as Grants Given to American Writers, if you cannot afford the travel.

Much has been made of poetry's central place in the lives of people in Eastern Europe. Poets and writers have led revolutions right up to the present day. Poetry has helped rally nations to throw off the Turkish yoke as well as the Communist. And it has sustained grievances that have fueled ethnic wars for generations as well. This social use of poetry is somewhat foreign to us in America. We do have poets such as Robert Bly and Adrienne Rich and others who make political calls to action, but in the west, critics and college English professors generally hold that poetry fails to the extent it tries to preach. One thinks of James Merrill who rarely reads a newspaper, and lets the avocado seed on the window sill die, yes die. A poetry reading may not fill a football stadium, but it remains a popular art form and people expect a poem to take a position.

Among the five poems I sent to be translated for the festival was a poem entitled "The Dolphins," which deals with homophobia and the AIDS crisis. I read it at the closing ceremony - a little risky perhaps, since homosexuality is still a rather closeted subject in Eastern Europe. But politics is how people live with each other, and I wanted to take this small step. At one point during our visit, we were invited to read to the SFOR troops based at the airport, and I tried to think of poems that might give heart to the difficult work these men and women were doing in the Balkans. The Colonel heading up the Bulgarian contingent responsible for guarding the perimeter of the airport camp gave us a warm and informed introduction as we sat on a stage decorated for the Halloween party to follow our reading. I am sure they would have preferred someone like Marilyn Monroe dropping into Japan, but they were very friendly and glad for our effort in coming to them. William read "Parents" and a couple from the wars he had been in. I read some to amuse them and also read a poem by one of the participants in the festival, Admiral Mahic, whose girlfriend had been killed during the war. I wanted to give a sense of why their work was so important, but I almost couldn't finish the poem hearing the burley poet read it in my head, as I read the poem to soldiers in front of me:

> My girlfriend was
> killed by the conquerors!
> They got her when she went to get water,
> like hunters shooting a doe come to drink from a
> stream even though she never uttered a cross word
> to anyone in Sarajevo
> not even to me.
> Her voice murmured like the birch tree planted by

my mother in front of our wooden house.
What we really cared about
were the kisses!
We kissed until her kisses flowed into death's water can... And then I drowned the sound of the artillery with my voice:
I love you!
I love you!
I love you!

After the reading, we were given many gifts including a tee shirt with bold white letters in black proclaiming: BE MINE AWARE. Sadly, over one million mines still lie buried in the fields of Bosnia, a terrible garden of death awaiting the stray child or lovers in the grass. And there are other dangers. The mad shrink, Radovan Karadjic is holed up in a monastery in Montenegro, waiting for the west to leave to start up his ethnic cleansing machine again once the peace keepers are gone. One prays for the Virgin's intercession, or that our humanity at least will not fail us - a hope which seemed justified at the end of the festival and which William echoed in the small poem that he read for the UN troops before we left:

A Major Work

Poems are hard to read
Pictures are hard to see
Music is hard to hear
And people are hard to love

But whether from brute need
Or divine energy
At last mind eye and ear
And the great sloth heart will move.

And this, earlier in the year, an article for the local paper:

A Walk in a Poet's Garden

For a teacher, New Year's Eve comes on August 31st. Once Labor Day is over, it is time to put off the lovely, lazy indolence of summer and think of new beginnings: new classes, new students, new challenges. The air sharpens and the geese begin to honk their way south. The morning jog is bracing as you run through gusts of leaves raining down from the trees like fire. The hornets fly around in a drunken cloud over the grapes, heavy on the arbor, that you were too busy to turn into jam this year, grapes so purple they look black, their fragrance so pungent it's almost visible.

But there is a sweet nostalgia in the season as well, as nature begins to shut down, and the luxuriance of summer begins to fall into decay. The light begins to fail, the rains begin. Soon, the first snow will come, "hanging in the hollow air, making space tangible, showing him how things are," as William says in a poem. There won't be many more walks in the garden before winter sets in.

For forty years William tended these acres, high on a bluff overlooking the Thames River, playing, like Jefferson, at how many varieties of trees he could get to grow this far north. Visitors could walk the path along river and if they were lucky, might be presented with a weeping dogwood or Chinese beech - all for love, none for money. Trees, students and poetry were the three co-ordinates that fixed his life, a life I joined more than thirty years ago now.

There is a little 18th century graveyard in the far corner of the property with six tombstones marking the lives of the family that once owned this farm. Mikey, our old yellow lab lies buried under the tall pine on the point where he used swim out after swans. Another dear pet sleeps under the weeping hemlock where she took shade on the hottest days of summer. Like India, the land is rich with ghosts. I think of lines in another poem about William's imaginary painter friend, Hazard as he walks this land:

> And what swirling was in residence
> here before the ice-sleds unloaded?
> What is held in perpetuity? The town hall
> with all the records will move off
> one day, without legal notice.
> The air that's passed through his lungs
> or the love through his head and loins
> are more his to keep than this boulder-camp,
> ready to move off whenever the hunt
> resumes.

And yet, despite it's disrepair, looking a bit like Miss Havisham's garden these days, we tend to it still with love. Beech and pine and elm have all grown too large to ball and transplant. Natural selection now, a bit like living in the rain forest, pruning from beneath, the trees too tall to take from the top, too much work to turn to firewood. No Belgian blocks lining the terrace. Gardening has become a kind of holding action against the jungle's encroachment. Far less ambitious than the old days when we set up a secret, English garden in the far corner of the land that a guest might come across miraculously if they walked far enough along the river path. No time now for grafting trees, or laying out a plot of eggplant, tomatoes, peppers. But we prune away as best we can, to maintain a kind of run down charm on the place still.

It is almost twenty years ago now since a stroke left William without speech or movement all those months. But like his garden, he has held on and even thrives. There is a new chocolate spaniel to walk with us these days, bobbing through the fields, tethered by voice and affection. It's still a lovely walk, if only for the memories it provokes.

What is the name of that rare beech as you walk to the river, variegated pink and green, that takes a lacy, paper thin edge to leaf as autumn drains its color? Would this make a good best man someday in the ceremony William once envisioned:

Tree Marriage

In Chota Nagpur and Bengal
the betrothed are tied with threads to
mango trees, they marry the trees
as well as one another, and
the two trees marry each other.
Could we do that some time with oaks
or beeches? This gossamer we
hold each other with, this web
of love and habit is not enough.
In mistrust of heavier ties,
I would like tree-siblings for us,
standing together somewhere, two
trees married with us, lightly, their
fingers barely touching in sleep,
our threads invisible but holding.

How many "green thoughts" have sprung up from walks on this land, poems like children or trees growing from the rich soil? One of my favorites answers the question quite ably of why a person takes on a garden anyway:

Dalhousie Farm

Will you live long enough to sit in the shade
Of that tree, old man? the children asked,
And the old Chinaman planting the sapling replied,
This world was not a desert when I came into it.
Now, I myself have raised some thrifty trees
And children, entirely from words,
But it is friends with real trees and children who will
become,
Probably, my testimony, my best tongue.

Between trees and children there is a resemblance
And men and women nurture
It by their daily commerce. I want to speak for this
And for all such resemblances, having seen
At this farm, in the act of sunrise
And in certain other acts, incontrovertible evidence
Of something too few people speak of: a benign nature,
Ours, mirrored wherever you look, in past, in future.

Sometimes I think trees are best, sometimes children.
But there is no need to choose, they speak of the same
thing:
A continuing kindness in our sap and blood.
What we admire in the green world is a benign selfhood,
And in one another, the ability to speak of this,
Or better, to act it out. What is
The perverse impulse in some men and women
To speak otherwise about themselves or their green lives?
Well, speech is a planting, but not everything thrives.
It would be redundant to bless trees
Or children or anything else on a farm,
But once I fell asleep here listening to the dawn
Wind blessing the trees, and it came into my mind
(Maybe no language can relinquish this pun—
First the trees, then animals were saying it to the sun)
To be of our own nature is what it means to be kind

What lessons a garden can teach if we listen carefully. The seasons passing, the cycle of life and death, yes. But how to live, what to make of friendship, dealing with adversity, stopping time to save the past or bring it back to life.

Two weeks ago we entered the secret garden as though it were a tomb, the arch become a magician's sarcophagus. "William, it will never balance out," I protested years ago when he took eight of the trees out of the east wall, and replaced them with smaller trees. But, of course, the trees all rose to uniform height and grew back into formal discipline. With the great Chinese beech towering over, and no sun to feed them, the dead branches at the entrance reached out for us like knives. Within, we seemed, finally, to have lost the battle to the Wooly Aldegid, the nasty little cobweb killer that threatens genocide for the entire species. One whole wall of the garden facing the river had become a dead grey thicket. Dismal, and sad to see what this green living room had become, where visitors used to set up tents, where once two friends had married, where the moss carpet waited to accommodate lovers, or just some traveler looking for a quiet place to lie and sort things out.

"Cut them down," William said pointing to the dead trees.

"But it will ruin the symmetry," I objected.

"Just here," he said, marking the trunk at about waist high level.

So, with a little Druid tipping of the hat to the

hemlocks, and after an hour with the chain saw, we had a new bay window on the river. The Thames Boat Yard didn't even charge me for the line I used to cap the tree trunks making a ship's rail in place of the dead wall. Breezes now come off the river and blow away the mosquitos with their dark Nile aspirations. Light and air. A little victory. And William and I head back up to the barn under the twin oaks that have held the bank rooted like us to this land all these years now.

A Couple of Trees

The two oaks lean apart for light.
They aren't as strong as lone oaks
but in a wind they give each other lee.

Daily since I cleared them I can see
them, tempting to chain saw and ax—
two hardwoods, leaning like that for light.

A hurricane tore through the state one night,
picking up roof and hen-house, boat and
dock. Those two stood: leafless, twigless,
giving lee.

Last summer ugly slugs unleafed the trees.
Environmental kids wrote Gypsy Moths
Suck.The V of naked oaks leaned to the
Light for a few weeks, then put out slight
second leaves, scar tissue pale as bracts,
bandaged comrades, lending each other lee.

How perilous in one another's V
our lives are, yoked in this yoke:
two men, leaning apart for light,
but in a wind who give each other lee.

November 8,

Brilliant fall day. Little chocolate Daisy squeals a little at my side. She wants to play, it is wonderful outside, but I must sit here and watch the leaves fall in the sunshine and listen to the train chug away at William's bedside. Seems he has a cold, something I always dread since it may lead to pneumonia as often happens in the elderly. Trail elderly? Terrible medical term for those who are at the end of the line. I will prepare some of the honey and pine nut syrup that Pancho gave me as a gift when we were in Bulgaria this summer. Honey and yogurt, that's what the

Bulgarian mystic Vanga told William he must eat every day.

Walking to the mailbox, I thought how much I love this little dog that has come into our life, how sad I will be when she dies. Have I gotten too deep into this anticipatory grief syndrome. What I must do is enjoy the little beauty today, of course and stop thinking of the long run and the future, where, as Keynes points our, we are all dead.

My triumph this week was that I managed to do the gruesome bowel prep for a colonoscopy and taught my class the night before without exploding in the classroom. Found our housekeeper to bring me back from the procedure. Two polyps. Cancer? We shall see. But the class was the best I ever had, amazingly, despite my dehydration, or perhaps because of it. I was totally unselfconscious and able to really critique their work and listen carefully. They each had a collaborative project to work out involving a problem in the community. They had to do a proposal and bring all sorts of evidence in. Flyers., minutes, photos, interviews, etc. The purple group chose to look at the need for sidewalks along route 32 since a woman pedestrian was killed there. Aquamarine, took on the need for a student lounge. And Pink Associates looked into the new co-location proposed for the two branches of the college. They came dressed like business women, had computer slides, photos, interviews with the President. Amazing. I was so proud of them. This project really worked.

So, today I will pick up my new, "trendy" glasses at Dr. Mann's. And continue the diet. We will have a wonderful winter. Nancy Frankel will come for New Year's. I guess Nancy loves me. I'm lucky in that. She is remarkable. Who could imagine what a great partner she is. Beautiful figure. Willing. Adult. I guess I really am a lucky in love finally. And I thank God that I have been given these challenges, these loves, this bright world.

December 22, 2002 Nick Marries Ginger

In the photo, Nick looks so handsome in his yellow shirt. He and Ginger are setting up their Christmas tree. My house is a total disaster, but William and I will survive Christmas. Perhaps I failed as a lover, as a friend, but I did my best. I just couldn't hand him citizenship on a platter, the way this marriage will make possible. But I helped him a lot, consider that, and my love was more than obsession. There were wonderful times along the way, moments of joy for him and me and William. Those can't be denied.

I can't fault him his desire to get out of that dead-end village in the middle of Bulgaria and follow his star to

America. You do what you have to do in life. Loretta Cobb, my sister confident, says, “I guess I am going to have to forgive that floozie because it is so understandable,” when I give her news that wedding bells have rung for Nick and Ginger, how the melodrama has ended. And once again, I will let poetry show me the way.

How to Love

By January Gill O’Neil

After stepping into the world again,
there is that question of how to love,
how to bundle yourself against the frosted morning—
the crunch of icy grass underfoot, the scrape
of cold wipers along the windshield—
and convert time into distance.

What song to sing down an empty road
as you begin your morning commute?
And is there enough in you to see, really see,
the three wild turkeys crossing the street
with their featherless heads and stilt-like legs
in search of a morning meal? Nothing to do
but hunker down, wait for them to safely cross.

As they amble away, you wonder if they want
to be startled back into this world. Maybe you do, too,
waiting for all this to give way to love itself,
to look into the eyes of another and feel something—
the pleasure of a new lover in the unbroken night,
your wings folded around him, on the other side
of this ragged January, as if a long sleep has ended.

www.ingramcontent.com/pod-product-compliance
Lightning Source LLC
Chambersburg PA
CBHW030644120726
47905CB00001B/51

9780990925750